Marilyn W. Rattray

Muffin & Crumpet Bistro

1990.

Antony & Araminta Hippisley Coxe's

BOOK OF SAUSAGES

Antony & Araminta Hippisley Coxe's

BOOK OF SAUSAGES

LONDON
VICTOR GOLLANCZ LTD
in association with Peter Crawley
1987

For
Tacina Rae Smith
and
John Peel

This revised and enlarged edition first published 1987
by Victor Gollancz Ltd,
14 Henrietta Street, London WC2E 8QJ

Originally published by Pan Books 1978
under the title *The Book of the Sausage*.

© Antony & Araminta Hippisley Coxe 1987

British Library Cataloguing in Publication Data
Hippisley Coxe, Antony D.
    Antony & Araminta Hippisley Coxe's book of
sausages.—Rev. and enl. ed.
    1. Cookery—(Sausages)
    I. Title   II. Hippisley Coxe, Araminta
    641.6'6   TX749

    ISBN 0-575-04004-1

Typeset by Centracet
and printed in Great Britain by
St Edmundsbury Press Ltd, Bury St Edmunds, Suffolk

M. W. Rattray

Contents

Preface and Acknowledgements

Although this is primarily a cookery book, we hope it may also serve both geographically and gastronomically as a guide. Apart from the recipes for cooking and serving sausage dishes and making various kinds of sausage at home, it provides information on what the sausages you buy contain, the way they are made, where they come from and when some of them first appeared. We would have liked to say, here are all the sausages in the world, but there are still a few gaps. One or two countries in Eastern Europe appear to think that sausage recipes would make an excellent code for military intelligence, or maybe they are worried about economic penetration. While some countries are most forthcoming, others consider their sausages a matter for the highest security. Apart from these bare patches, there are anomalies which we would have liked to reconcile and mysteries which still remain unsolved. However, as this is the first attempt—as far as we know—to produce a book about sausages on an international scale, let us explain how the material we have managed to collect is set out.

First, there is a section on sausages in general, written from a personal viewpoint, but including an outline history. Here, it might perhaps be pointed out that, although there are two authors, we do not always use the first person plural. Sometimes the royal or editorial 'we' seems pompous, sometimes merely absurd. So 'I' may refer to either of us—but we take joint responsibility for all the opinions expressed.

The next section contains recipes for dishes in which sausages of various kinds are the main feature. By way of an introduction there is a section of general information on cooking and serving sausages, together with a few suggestions on what drinks should accompany them. When it comes to weights and measures in cooking, the actual amount is never as important as the ratio between one ingredient and another. In translating ounces into grammes, and vice-versa, the figures have been rounded off to simplify weighing, while maintaining the correct proportions. For instance, in one recipe you will find 3 lb kale, 1 lb sausages and 6 oz bacon, which we have converted into 1.35 kg kale, 450g sausages and 175g bacon, because this is much simpler than 1.365 kg, 455g and 171g. You may get a little more—or a little less—on your plate, but a 'portion' is arbitrary anyway.

We hope that the dishes will have given readers enough pleasure for them to be tempted to try their hand at making their own sausages. So the next chapter is devoted to the basic principles of sausage-making, and closes with a list of simple and more elaborate recipes to achieve this end. The recipes themselves will be found in the last section—An International Glossary of Sausages—which is as complete a list as we can produce, up to now, of the sausages of the world.

In writing a book about sausages, as indeed in actually making them, the raw materials have to be gathered from many sources. To carry the simile further, our task has been to assemble the ingredients, chop, blend, and season them, and to put the mixture into a casing. We do, therefore, owe a great number of people in many countries our warmest thanks for supplying a vast amount of information.

At home and abroad, friends have entertained us and told us of their discoveries; sausage manufacturers have shown us their processes and even put their equipment at our disposal; spice merchants have lent us handbooks; and the Trade Press provided many facts and figures.

So, first, for their generous hospitality and enthusiastic help, we offer our warmest thanks and appreciation to Luciana Agnoli, Inger Bassingthwaighte, Philip W. Bishop, Harry Bradshaw, Kemmis Buckley, Carlo Cavalieri, *La Confrérie des Chevaliers du Goûte Andouille de Jargeau*, May Cullen, T. L. A. Daintith, L-R Dauven, David Emmet, Jack, Jean and Sian Evans, Dan Farson, The Federation of Women's Institutes,

Gordon Fergusson of the Tarporley Hunt Club, Nichola Fletcher, Jacques Garnier, Richard Garrett of Scot Bowyers, Leni Miller, Cecil Gysin, the late Dr K. G. Hadija, Christianne Hammond, R. D. Harborne of Catermasters, Frank L. Hill of W. J. Hill and Sons Ltd, Sheelagh Hippisley Coxe, Pat Kerr, Barbara Kerr, Dr K. Kuncar, the Austrian Commercial Delegate in Great Britain, P. Lenain of *L'Institut Belge d'Information et de Documentation*, Jean Mackarel, Paul Mackarel senior, Jane Maskell, Cav. Gino Mazzacurati, M. Michaliszn of Anglo-Dal Ltd, Robin Oldland of Swiss Fair, Norman Parkinson, John Peel, Elfreda Powell, Peter F. Price of T. C. Price and Son, Dr Robin Pulvertaft, Tacina Rae Smith, Dr Fausto Razetti, Monica Renevey, Arthur Saxon, Daria and Alexander Schouvaloff, Vernon and Mary Schiller, Dr K. Smolka of the Austrian Association of Food Manufacturers, G. Tamburini, Messrs Terimpex of Budapest, Pauline Viola of Danish Agricultural Producers, P. A. Weber of Bell S. A. Geneva, Sam Weller, Peter West of *Meat*, Konrad Werner Wille of Alois Dallmayr, and lastly the late Guido and Mimina Zucchini-Solimei, who should really head the list.

We also found a lot of information in various cookery books, both those published and those which remain in manuscript. Although traditional recipes cannot be copyright, it would be extremely churlish not to acknowledge how much we owe those who have researched various aspects of the subject before us. First comes Jane Grigson, whose *Charcuterie and French Pork Cookery* has not only inspired, but sustained us over the years. H. Babet-Charton's *La Charcuterie à la Campagne*, revised by Henriette Lasnet de Lanty, and *Porc et Cochonailles* by Françoise Burgaud have also proved invaluable. The works of Elizabeth David have become classics in her lifetime. Her description of French *saucissons*, and particularly Italian *salami*, sent us off to remote villages in search of sausages. *Larousse Gastronomique* remains the cook's bible, and J. Audrey Ellison's translation of *The Great Scandinavian Cook Book* must earn universal respect for the way in which it shows so meticulously how dishes are prepared. Then there are *The Complete Asian Cookbook* by Charmaine Solomon and *The Complete Middle East Cookbook* by

Tess Mallos. Books such as these cover much more than the subject in hand, but there are a number of specialized works, which those professionally interested will find indispensable: amongst these are Frank Gerrard's *Sausage and Small Goods Production*, Douglas' *Encyclopaedia*, *The Packers' Encyclopaedia* edited by Paul I. Aldrich, Law's *Grocer's Manual*, revised by W. G. Copsey, *Butchering, Processing and Preservation of Meat* by Frank G. Ashbrook, and Thomas B. Finney's *Handy Guide for Pork Butchers*. Some of these are difficult to find; even the British Library does not appear to have a copy of Finney. Just as we were correcting proofs for the first version of this book we found, in our own library, *The Breakfast Book*, published by Richard Bentley in London in 1865; but who wrote it remains a mystery. The title page gives no author's name; and the preface ends with an address, but not even an initial above it. So to the anonymous inhabitant of Browning Hill, we must also extend our gratitude, not only for the recipes, a number of which we quote in the pages that follow, but also for enlightening us on Victorian breakfasts in general. 'Generally speaking', he (or she) writes, 'breakfasts may be classed under four heads: the family breakfast, the *déjeuner à la fourchette*, the cold collation and the *ambigu*. In the *déjeuner à la fourchette* things are introduced in courses, similar to a dinner. Cold collations need scarcely be defined ... The *ambigu* is an entertainment of a very heterogeneous character, having resemblance to a dinner, only that every thing is placed upon the table at once; and *relevés*, soups, vegetables and hot *entremets* are held to be ineligible. Our everyday breakfasts are in a small way served *en ambigu*, in as much as broiled fish, cold pasties, devilled bones, boiled eggs, cold ham, etc., all appear together.'

How very different from today when breakfast may consist of a plate of what Peter Ustinov once described as pencil sharpenings covered with milk.

To return to sources which have enabled us to write this book, we must on no account omit the magazine *Meat*.

One must also include *Gourmet, Cuisine et Vins de France* and *Gastronomie Magazine*.

There are also those cookery books which may contain only

some passing reference to sausages, but which nevertheless have helped enormously by giving us a line to be followed. It was, for instance, a reference in *English Recipes* by an erstwhile Fleet Street colleague, Sheila Hutchins, which led us to find out more about the Tarporley Hunt Black Pudding.

Where does one stop? We think it best to give a bibliography of the books which we have found helpful to a greater or lesser degree. And we hope that the authors, wherever they may be (some are long since dead), will nod acceptance of our gratitude, even if they smile at the inadequacy of such a general acknowledgement.

A. & A. H. C.

Sausages in General

Sausage . . . even the word has a sizzling, succulent sound, and what memories it evokes. It could form the framework for an autobiography, starting with sausages for breakfast on Sunday, which is one of the first things I can remember. Then, during World War I, when I was about four years old and living in Hampshire, my grandparents provided refuge for a displaced Belgian family. Monsieur Schoof was a *charcutier* and he soon found a job with a butcher in the nearest town. On his first free day he bicycled eight miles simply to tell us that on no account were we to consider buying sausages from the shop in which he worked. They were a travesty . . . the ingredients utterly deplorable . . . the abysmal ignorance of his master beyond comprehension . . . etc. etc. At that age I was amazed that sausages could arouse such vehement passion in a man.

I am just old enough to remember the days when no pantomime was complete without the Harlequinade. That joyous mixture of slapstick and ballet was much more magical and entrancing than the spells of the Demon King, or the wishes-come-true of the Fairy Queen, in the pantomime itself. Harlequin and Columbine were as ethereal as angels, but Clown and Pantaloon always brought one back to reality with a red-hot poker and a string of sausages.

At Dartmouth in the 1920s, the Royal Naval College provided some revolting beef sausages in the Mess, but after we had 'shifted into games rig' we rushed up to the Canteen on the playing fields where we could buy delicious pork sausages, accompanied by a fried egg and bread, for what is today less than three pence.

As a student in London, dwindling funds at the end of every

month forced me to patronize S.P.O.s, which—as some readers may remember—stood for Sausage, Potato and Onion, and was the name given to cheap eating houses where, if one peered through the steamy window, one could see three big enamelled pans sizzling away behind the glass. Then, in the 1930s, a theatrical company, led by Lionel Birch and Alistair Cooke, went from Cambridge University to Munich, and I was asked to design the sets. Here, I first sampled *Münchener Weisswurst*, washed down with *steins* of Löwenbrau. My German was so bad that when I asked for sausages and beer in the Tyrol, they brought me wild strawberries and milk.

In 1937, I started a column on food and wine in *Harper's Bazaar* called 'Let's Eat Out', and in my very first article I drew attention to the sausages imported from Germany by Horcher, who had just opened a branch of his famous Berlin restaurant in London.

In those days one could buy kipper sausages at Harrods; but sausages seem to evoke stronger memories of being abroad . . . a picnic on Tahiti Plage just outside St Tropez, of *saucissons d'Arles*, goat's milk cheese and a bottle of wine whose name I don't remember, or never bothered to find out.

The less said about most products in wartime the better, but there were some American tinned sausages which were very good. Or did they just taste delicious because everything else was so dreary? After the liberation of France in 1945, I spent six months in Paris and often ate *choucroute garnie* at the Brasserie Lipp in the Boulevard St Germain. More recently, I recall frankfurters on Coney Island, and sharing *chorizos* with my wife in the Calle Vittoria in Madrid . . . and so it goes on, right up to travelling round Europe in search of sausages to include in this book. That tour taught us a lot. We were staggered by the variety of ingredients and the different proportions used for each type of sausage. We were also amazed by the complacent insularity of the Italian sausage-maker. I know that the unification of Italy took place more than a century ago historically, but among the sausage-makers of one town, let alone one province, there remains an intensely individual attitude which dismisses everyone else's product out of hand.

Not with disdain, mind you, for disdain implies a positive reaction, but a complete disinterest. What we were told in one street, for instance, about *mortadelle*, would be flatly contradicted in the next. Both sausage-makers would consider themselves right because, in their eyes, that is how *mortadelle* should be made. Whether there is a standard recipe could only be determined by a survey of all producers, and that was not for us to undertake. In any case, we think it is better to give a genuine individual recipe than try to find a norm; which brings us to the subject of using the recipes in this book to make sausages at home. We make our own because we find that most of the ordinary run-of-the-mill sausages are neither as meaty nor as savoury as we would like. I once asked the director of a large firm of sausage manufacturers if the meat content was so low because that was what the British really wanted, or if it was the least that the company thought it could get away with. 'A bit of both,' was his reply. 'We had to give up making our high-meat-content sausages in the factory nearest you, because the public simply would not pay the price.' Historically, it seems possible that the increase of cereal 'binder' in sausages in England, Scotland, Ireland and Wales, but *not* in France, may have been due, at least in part, to a shortage of meat. After all, a mealie pudding contains no meat at all, but it makes a good accompaniment to ham and bacon. Yet, if one traces its genealogy, it must be descended from the *boudin blanc*, which has always contained a very high proportion of meat, and may include chicken, veal and pork, to say nothing of truffles. So perhaps a lack of meat influenced the contents of some sausages, as well as the taste buds or disinterest of the consumer and the profit motive of the producer.

Most people, unfortunately, still look upon the sausage as the cheapest form of meat. They do not realize that much more care and hard work goes into making a sausage than into the preparation of, say, a fillet steak. There is chopping, blending and seasoning, and preparing the casing which is in itself a complicated and delicate operation. (It involves attaching the gut to a tap and running water through it like a hose; then turning the whole thing inside out and scraping the inner surface.) Then there may be salting and smoking. And all this happens before it gets anywhere near the kitchen stove. Such human effort should be devoted to the finest ingredients, but if the public will not pay the money, they are not going to get more than 65% meat, which is what the law stipulates as the minimum for pork sausages in this country. (It is even lower for beef sausages; in these only half the content need be meat.) And of that meat 80% must be pork. This sounds fine if you think that pork means good white lean meat and the kind of fat you find on a roast. It doesn't; it includes 'Skin, rind, gristle and sinew'. In an article which appeared in *The Sunday Times Magazine* in 1984, Rosemary Atkins wrote:

> The waste that is left on animal carcases after trimming can now be retrieved by subjecting the bones to heavy pressure and heat, causing the meat to flow off in a slurry. This is called Mechanically Recovered Meat (MRM), and is now widely used in sausages. A Food Standing Committee report in 1980 had serious doubts about MRM and recommended that if it was used in amounts over 5% it should be declared on the packaging. . . . The trouble is that it is very difficult for a food analyst to tell MRM from any other emulsified meat.
>
> Another recent technological breakthrough has been the incorporation of gristle into sausages, a feat which has been achieved by chopping it into a glutinous material and mixing it with the 'meat'. Rind has always been added to sausages, but it had the drawback of involving an expensive process of boiling. The answer to the problem was provided by a go-ahead company called Protein Foods Ltd., which found a way of dehydrating the rind and converting it into easy-to-handle granules called Drinde. Sausage-makers bought it by the thousands of ton, and dried rind now legally accounts for about 10% of a pork sausage's meat content.

But apparently this also poses a problem for the analysts, because it is apt to give a high reading which of course benefits the sausage-maker. Legislation on the Continent ensures a much better product, though a more expensive one. And even here one occasionally finds meat which some English may find distasteful. We were recently sent the wrapping of a *Saucisson D'Arles* which stated that its composition included '*viandes bovine, porcine et asine*' Our informant says that others 'have more bluntly listed "*âne*".'

There is a lot to be said for making one's own sausages at home; but most people must rely on buying from shops, as the figures reveal. Over £200,000,000 a year is spent on sausages in Great Britain, and this refers to fresh sausages made in this country, and does not include any imported varieties, which according to the German Food Centre are now worth more than another £12,000,000.

As far as our own products go, let us hope that local tastes and traditions will not become swamped by a national mean. At present, the inhabitants of Cumbria and Lincoln like their filling coarsely chopped, while those living in the south prefer a finer consistency. The Scots prefer beef sausages; northerners like long, thin links, so pale they look almost white; southerners choose pork sausages known as 'eights', because eight weigh a pound; here in the West Country, we like them to be a reddish colour. Obviously, mass-production demands the maximum standardization. When a machine fills sausages at the rate of one-and-a-half miles per hour, all the previous processes—chopping, blending, seasoning etc.—have to be highly stream-lined. In *The Frank Muir Book* you will find a splendid lament for the passing of the old-fashioned sausage. The author writes, 'Even the sausage, the fine old British banger, knobbly and individual, is being displaced by a product of automation, a computerized, portion-controlled, geometrically accurate disc. As T. S. Eliot might have written, "this is the way the World ends, not with a banger but a Wimpy".'

From an article in a supplement to the trade magazine *Meat*, one is led to suppose that a growing number of people are becoming dissatisfied. It stated, 'Sausage manufacturers cannot help being aware of the general disenchantment with the Great British Banger. They are concerned with their falling sales, but seem content to let the sausage trade pass slowly but surely into the hands of the butchers. . . .'

People who like a little more sage in their sausages can hardly expect it from national manufacturers, unless it turns out to be a commercial proposition. An example of this was given to me by a director of C. & T. Harris Ltd. Many Midlanders retire to the West Country, and a number asked if Harris's local factory would make their favourite sausage, a Midland speciality strongly flavoured with tomato. The factory gave the recipe a trial run, but demand did not justify production. One cannot blame the factory; in fact one must give it all credit for trying. A local butcher might be able to cope better, though he is more likely to prefer his own variety. The only way to get exactly what you want is to make your own.

One must presume that standardization will include different, supposedly regional varieties, but on a national scale. Even now, Cambridge sausages are not limited to Cambridge, and there are reports from all over the country of the growing popularity of the Cumberland sausage. What is a Cumberland sausage? Traditional recipes give the ingredients as coarsely chopped pork spiced with black pepper and sage, and it is *not* divided into links. The big firms will sell them in links, and, of course, add a proportion of rusk or cereal, while even the Cumberland farmer's wife may add a little breadcrumb. But apart from the additives such as emulsifying salts, sodium caseinate, colouring etc., which all big manufacturers seem to use, one popular brand includes mutton, which we have not come across in any recipe. Perhaps it is a local variation.

Writing this book has taught us that no recipe is definitive. Had there been no taboo against pork, one might be tempted to think that the sausage was invented by a Moslem. I believe somewhere in the Koran there is a passage, particularly applicable to sausage making, which points out that nothing is absolute except in the eyes of Allah . . . and his ways are inscrutable.

If one looks at a trade recipe one is staggered, not only by the vast quantities of the ingredients but by some of the ingredients themselves. Who would believe that sausages require ice? Yet there it is in the list of ingredients: 15 kg of ice, along with 18 kg of back fat, 20 kg of belly of pork, 10 kg of 'head meat', 6 kg of flank, 2.5 kg of seasoning and 1.5 kg of soya among other things. The meat content of that sausage— all 60 kg of it—is 66% of the total, if one does not count the ice. And what is the ice for? Before we could ask the experts, the answer was found in Murray Handwerker's description of how Nathan's Famous Coney Island Frankfurters are made. 'Salt, spices and sodium nitrate', he writes, 'are added to the basic meat and then the mixture is chopped in a bowl-shaped machine. The blades revolve so fast that crushed ice must be added to keep the meat from overheating.' Bacteria breed at a temperature of between 28°–38°C (80°–100°F), and one must also remember that as the ice melts the water can be absorbed by the cereal and binder which is nowadays added dry to the mixture in the chopping bowl.

In many old recipes no binder was used at all. Then bread came to be used, and this had quite a long history. But for the last thirty years the methods of baking have not completely destroyed the action of the yeast, and rusk has taken the place of bread as a binder. Rusk also absorbs water very easily and so increases weight without adding to manufacturing costs.

Looking at the list of ingredients on a packet of pork sausages gives one no idea of the quantities involved, but it does sometimes make one wonder what purpose some of the additives serve. One popular pork sausage, described as 'Country Style' contains, according to the label, 'pork, cereal binder, other meats, dried skimmed milk, salt, dextrose, emulsifying salts, spice extracts, flavourings, preservative and colour.' We were a little surprised not to find monosodium glutamate, without which any 'convenience food'—ghastly phrase—is incomplete. Another imported tinned sausage contains isolated soya protein, carboxymethylcellulose, sodium phosphates, guar, locust beans, sodium ascorbate and sodium nitrite. We thought it might be interesting to see exactly why some of the additives used in Britain are considered necessary. Here is the result:

Dried skimmed milk helps the sausage to keep its colour and good looks.

Dextrose, apart from providing a sweet taste, helps to preserve colours because it inhibits oxidization. It also facilitates browning when the sausage is fried.

Emulsifying salt is straightforward. There is a large proportion of fat in a sausage, and if one is going to add all that ice, something is needed to help them to blend.

Sodium caseinate is a milk protein which helps to maintain colour and good looks.

Sodium phosphate is a salt which helps emulsion.

Sodium ascorbate helps to maintain colour.

Monosodium glutamate enhances some pleasant natural flavours and stimulates the taste buds. It is very diluted, 0.15–0.19% being the amount used.

Egg white improves 'binding'.

Vegetable protein, usually soya, is added to many sausages, but particularly the 'catering' varieties which often contain very little meat, since they are not covered by the law governing pork and beef sausages offered for sale to the public.

Carboxymethylcellulose—Cellulose is used as a binder and emulsifier, but this variety, listed on a Danish can, had an English expert foxed.

Preservative is usually sulphur dioxide, which the British law allows up to a strength of 450 parts in a million. It can be metabisulphide. This is not allowed on the Continent; but the people there rely more on local *charcuteries*. If they depended more on national distribution they might well have to include some form of preservative.

Colouring is used all over Europe for some types of sausages. One type, Red 2G, is banned by the EEC but still used in Great Britain.

Of course you will find very different kinds of fresh sausages on the Continent, and an extremely wide range of keeping sausages, such as *salami*. Manufacturers in Britain say, 'The European taste is different.' Certainly, on the other side of the Channel sausages are not regarded simply as a cheap form of meat. But although British sausages have become stodgier, I do not think that they have always been so different from those found on the Continent. You will find plenty of fresh sausages to grill and fry all over Europe and in Britain we have the saveloys, which, like many continental sausages, are boiled. The black pudding can be traced back through France to Rome; and in the *crépinette* you will find the forerunner of our faggots. The biggest difference between British and foreign sausages is the complete absence in the U.K. of traditional dried and smoked varieties to be eaten raw. We have often wondered why this should be; in the same way we cannot understand why for centuries in Britain, few, if any, soft cheeses were made. Normandy and Brittany are very similar to Dorset, Devon and Cornwall—after all, England and France were once joined together. Perhaps one reason why we never made our own versions of Camembert, Boursin and Pont l'Evêque is because we had to preserve our cheeses to provide protein in the winter, so we hard-pressed them. The rich lands stretching away to the south from the Channel coast made this unnecessary for the French. But then surely it would be the English who made sausages that keep, and not the French? Maybe we were better content to produce good bacon and ham. British bacon is certainly cured better than French.

On the other hand it may well be that different laws which existed in the two countries forced things to develop in their own way. In France, until 17 January 1475, *charcutiers* could only sell cooked meat. The origin of their name is *chair cuitier* and they were brethren of the *rôtisseurs* rather than the butchers. However, on that memorable day, they were not only granted a monopoly of selling cooked meats, but also allowed to sell lean or fat raw pork, and they became *saucissiers* and *boudiniers* as well as *charcutiers*. An interesting point is that *saucissiers* at that time were forbidden by law to reheat their wares. The following year they obtained the monopoly of selling pork, but were still forbidden to slaughter. They were forced to buy their meat from the butchers. Obviously stocks had to be maintained; and it strikes me that to avoid being at the butchers' mercy, the keeping quality of the produce became extremely important. The ban on slaughtering was not lifted until the sixteenth century. The fact that we have no equivalent of *charcutier* here shows that the trade developed along different lines.

'Peers fight to save our sausages,' ran a recent headline in *The Times*. Apparently the EEC proposed legislation which would have prevented sausages in England being made by small local butchers because 18 different rooms would be necessary under the new health regulations! What nonsense!

Sausages, of course, have a very much longer history than 500 years. In fact it has been said that they go back 5,000 years; that they formed a part of Sumerian diet and that the Assyrians living in Tyre were expert sausage-makers. Homer mentions a type of sausage in a throwaway line in the *Odyssey*; a rough translation runs '. . . in the same way as a man, having filled the stomach with fat and blood, stands in front of a great fire and turns it this way and that in his eagerness to get it roasted . . .' This sounds exactly like a black pudding.

There is a legend that *salame* came originally from Salamis in Cyprus, a city founded in the Bronze Age. And, to forestall the Italians from taking umbrage at the mere suggestion that *salame* is not Italian in origin, we would point out that it was under the Romans that Salamis enjoyed great prosperity as the principal town of Cyprus.

The Romans produced a wide variety of sausages. Even the word sausage is derived from the Latin *salsisium*, something salted; and in a sausage known as *farcima* we can see the origin of our word 'farce', or forcemeat. Strict laws were passed controlling the manufacture of these and two other types, *tobelli* and *tomacula*. During the reign of Nero, sausages became very popular and were associated with the Lupercalian and Floralian festivals. Maybe the phallic shape and spicy ingredients helped to turn these feasts into orgies. Anyhow, the early Christian church condemned sausages. Constantine was actually persuaded to prohibit the eating of them during festivals.

Emperor Leo V disapproved strongly of black puddings. 'We

have been informed,' he is said to have stated, 'that blood is packed into intestines, as into a coat, and set before man as an ordinary dish. Our Imperial Majesty can no longer permit the honour of our State to be tarnished by these abominable devices of the gluttonous. Whoever henceforth converts blood into food shall be severely scourged, smoothly shaved and banished from our realm forever.'

But the black pudding survived, and together with other sausages was brought to England by the Romans. Their recipes were rather more highly spiced than our modern ones. Apicius, a gourmet of the 1st century AD lists cumin, pepper, savory, rue, parsley, mixed herbs, bay berries, *liquamen*, peppercorns and pine kernels in one recipe. *Liquamen* was rather like soy, taking the place of salt in some dishes. Even in those days breadcrumbs were added, and goat intestines were used for casings as well as those of pigs and sheep. Sir Mortimer Wheeler, the prominent archaeologist, suggested that there was a Roman sausage factory at St Albans, where the anonymity of the product was abused by the use of horsemeat, which, even in those days, was frowned upon.

After the Romans left Britain, remnants of the Saturnalia remained disguised in Christian festivals. Monks dressed up as women, bawdy songs replaced the litany and the Abbot of Misrule ordered mock masses to be celebrated in which cakes and sausages replaced the host.

Although from time to time seasonings changed, and sometimes the method of serving, basically sausages have remained the same for at least 2,000 years. At the end of the fourteenth century they were served in a sauce made of butter, eggs, sage and spices. In her fascinating survey *Food and Drink in Britain*, C. Anne Wilson gives a recipe from the middle of the fifteenth century for a black pudding made from porpoise (see page 192).

A cookery book of King Richard II contains these instructions:

Take hens and pork and boil them together. Take the flesh and hew it small and grind it all to dust. Take grated bread and mix it well with the broth, and add to it yolks of eggs. Boil it, and put therein powder of ginger, sugar, saffron and salt—and look that it be stiff.

This sounds very like sausage meat to us, perhaps for a white pudding.

An Elizabethan white pudding contained raisins, dates, cloves, mace, sugar, saffron and salt as well as pigs' liver, eggs and breadcrumbs.

A Grace, attributed to Joshua Cooke in 1602, mentions another sausage ingredient—chitterling:

> *Gloria Deo*, sirs, proface,
> Attend me now while I say grace,
> For bread and salt, and grapes and malt,
> For flesh and fish and every dish,
> Mutton and beefe of all meates cheefe,
> for cow-heels, chitterlings, tripes and sowse
> And other meats that's in this house . . .
>
> For all these and many moe
> *Benedicamus, Domino.*

Twisting sausages into links probably began in the middle of the seventeenth century, and at that time rabbit and capon were used to fill the casings. During the next hundred years you could buy mutton or pork sausages that contained oysters. Then, in the middle of the eighteenth century, beef became a popular ingredient.

Sausages, were sold in large quantities on the fairgrounds. In 1778, a reporter visiting Bartholomew Fair in London found it advisable to stand half a point to windward of the sausage stalls. By the turn of the century these had become more than stalls.

The ground of Smithfield was entirely parcelled out in booths and ftandings. In the centre among the fheep-pens, were thofe who fold in booths or at ftalls oyfters and faufages.

Tables were fet for company in a moft fafcinating ftyle, and in 1808 women invited paffers by into the faufage rooms with an appeal to their patriotifm—for the popular political feeling ftill had its reprefentation in the Fair. 'Walk into Wilkes's parlour,' was their cry; the faufage-rooms being in thofe days called Wilkes's parlours.

(from *Memoirs of Bartholemew Fair*, Henry Morley)

In the last century, sausages maintained their popularity and not only with fair-goers. Queen Victoria had very strict rules regarding her sausages. The meat had to be chopped, not minced, because mincing squeezed the juices out of it. The casings had to be filled by hand, the mixture pressed down through a funnel with the thumbs, and the recipe included eggs.

The great chefs, such as Charles Elmé Francatelli, made black puddings for princes, and sausages of all kinds were treated with respect. At the other end of the scale, sausages appear to have been frequently used as prison-fodder. I have been told that Oscar Wilde, while serving his sentence, had sausages thrust upon him 'like buns at a bear through the bars of a cage'.

When factories took over from the individual, some of the respect for the craftsman was inevitably lost. Expansion in business is usually based on three fundamental assets: a good product, reliable distribution and well-organized publicity. The rise of the sausage kings in Britain was apparently largely due to two aspects of Victorian industrial enterprise: a growing, remarkably efficient and cheap railway service and the increasing power of press advertising. This interesting discovery was made by Philip W. Bishop, who has most generously passed on to us the results of his research.

The first reference he came across was in *The Grocer*. On 15 September 1868, an advertisement of a type not previously seen announced that Messrs Hillier of Stroud, Gloucestershire, had been enabled to improve the distribution of their sausages by the opening of the Great Western Railway station at Nailsworth. Whether Hillier had taken this advertisement off their

own bat, or whether some far-sighted space-seller had suggested it, is not known. I am inclined to think that Hillier
originated the idea, but *The Grocer* was not slow to develop this
new source of advertising revenue. In the very next issue
Hillier's company got editorial support in the shape of an article
on the factory, where 'women of exceptional cleanliness' and
men, 'clothed in blouses of spotless white', with the aid of
steam-powered machines, turned out 215,000lb of sausages
and 7,000lb of saveloys in 1865. The bulk of their production
has been distributed by rail in 20lb packages at ninepence per
pound, carriage paid. *The Grocer* urged its readers to 'interest
themselves in the new trade for the personal advantage they
will no doubt ultimately derive from it ... *and so assist in
breaking up the butchers' monopoly.'* (The italics are ours) *The
Grocer* then searched for other sausage manufacturers who
could increase their turnover by distributing their products to
grocers over a wide area by using the railways. The next firm to
appear in *The Grocer's* columns—both advertising and editorial,
for the pernicious policy of giving editorial support to advertisers
even then seems to have been rife—was David Hedges of
Birmingham. His advertisement for pork sausages, 'made at
the noted London House on Bull Ring, as supplied to Her
Majesty the Queen', appeared in December 1866, though he
had to wait a year for the editorial article on his firm. Other
manufacturers followed this lead. In 1869, the September issue,
which traditionally marked the opening of the sausage season,
drew the attention of its readers to the reputable firms on
whom grocers could always rely for a regular supply of good
pork sausages. These, not unnaturally, turned out to be those
who advertised.

As far as Philip Bishop could tell, out of all the products that
were advertised in *The Grocer*, the sausage alone was treated in
this way; and the practice continued until the end of World
War I.

A number of advertisers were old-established firms who had
started out as small pork-butchers or pie shops in country
towns. Hilliers had been established in 1819, while C. Shippam
had been trading for more than fifty years when he took space

in 1866. Not all those of long standing rushed into print. Bowyer, Philpott and Payne for instance, who could trace their history back to 1808, did not advertise until 1904, while Harris of Calne, started by Sarah Harris in 1769, held out until 1909. But before the end of the 19th century, firms such as T. Wall, Palethorpe, Aplin & Barrett and many others had all taken space in *The Grocer*, simply because the railways in those days provided a fast, reliable and economical distribution service for perishable goods. And this enabled the manufacturers to keep the price stable at ninepence per pound for half a century.

Inevitably smaller firms were bought up, rivals taken over and empires built. Raymond Harris from Calne bought the original Bowyer company in 1924, but kept the name. Bowyer bought the Beechwood company of Plymouth in 1960, then Hughes Brothers of Aintree in 1964 and the Brazil company in 1970. Yet the small pork butcher survives, and a few still make good sausages. Some people believe that the discriminating will always want to patronize the individual craftsman, and the ranks of the discriminating are growing. Richard Garrett of Scot Bowyer believes the 'little man' who is a craftsman will continue in business, and has no wish to see him go because he is supplying a section of the market which the big manufacturers would find uneconomic, but at the same time is stimulating an interest in sausages.

In compiling this book we have collected information on some 600 sausages, tasted at least 300 of them, and have ourselves made almost a score. The following pages are the result. We hope that those tempted to make their own sausages will find the book useful; but, even if making them fails to appeal, perhaps they will try cooking the bought ones in a different way. We also hope that those who neither make nor cook sausages will at least try some of those they find on menus at home and on the Continent with more curiosity and understanding.

Cooking and Serving Sausages

Before we come to the chapters dealing with sausage recipes and how to make your own sausages we would like to give some ideas about cooking and serving sausages and what to drink with them. For a start you do not *have* to fry, grill or bake sausages.

We do not for a moment suggest that there is anything wrong with traditional ways of cooking English sausages, although we would not go so far as the gourmet who is convinced that the only way to serve them is grilled in pairs, lying on hot buttered toast. While we both prefer grilled sausages to fried, we like them to be accompanied by fried bread rather than toast, which seems to get soggy, or by what some people call 'oven toast', which is bread lightly buttered on both sides and put in the oven till golden. But if they are to be treated in such a simple way, then they have to be excellent sausages, cooked so that they are brown and crisp all round, sealing in the succulence. And that raises the question of pricking. . . .

Controversy still rages about whether to prick the English sausage or not. The only reason for pricking is to prevent them bursting. Home-made ones may well need it because the filling will probably be more coarsely chopped and either too loosely packed, which creates pockets of air, or packed too tightly. Bursting occurs when the air or the solid contents expand by being heated. Factory-made sausages are usually made of finely chopped ingredients and filled by machine so that no air-pockets are left in the casing. It has been pointed out to us that in a factory, casings are meticulously examined to see that no holes exist in them. It therefore seems rather absurd to prick them when you get them home. Whatever the case, sausages must be fried or grilled slowly and evenly. Baked sausages do not burst because the heat is evenly applied. But they must be well-cooked. As *The Breakfast Book* said in 1865: 'Observe that underdone sausages are execrable.' Sausages such as black puddings, hog puddings and *boudins* of all kinds which require boiling, must be pricked. It is the one sure way of seeing that they are cooked. Although one can argue that the heat is applied evenly in water, the latter must soften the casing and make it more vulnerable.

You will find more variety in the USA simply because the immigrants introduced the national sausages of their homelands to the New World. But although you may find a greater variety of sausages in America than in any one European country the ways of cooking and serving them are essentially European. The one outstanding exception is *Jambalaya aux Chaurices* whose very name reveals the Creole as well as its French and Spanish origins.

But no matter how sausages are cooked, or even if they are eaten raw, once they have been set before you, most people will look around for the mustard pot.

When we were young there was not much choice, and neither of us particularly liked mustard anyway. We can only remember the still familiar rectangular tin of Colman's powder which was mixed with milk or water in the pantry; and at school one belonged to the Mustard Club. Savora, we think, came later. Today things are very different; you can buy innumerable kinds of mustard all over the country. Recently one of our Christmas stockings contained a jar of Elsenham Whole Grain Mustard and four different kinds of Urchfont. We now have ten different kinds of mustard on the kitchen shelf. The latest addition is *Moutarde au Poivre Vert*, made from Dijon mustard and green peppercorns; we find it excellent.

Mustard as an accompaniment to sausages has a long and fascinating history. The Greeks used it, so did the Romans. In those days it was sprinkled over food like pepper. It was not until the Middle Ages that the ground powder was mixed with vinegar or verjuice to form a paste. Today in France the black and white varieties of seed are still mixed with verjuice, which is what the French call the juice of unripe grapes, but in England originally referred to crab-apple juice. Mustard then became extremely popular. In 1336, at a banquet given by the King of France, 300 litres of it were served. Louis XI would never dine away from his palace unless he had his own special pot of mustard with him, and it was he who ordered nine kilogrammes of mustard to be delivered to an apothecary in Dijon. And so, in the middle of the fifteenth century, Dijon became famous for mustard; not that the plant was ever grown there. Apart from a quantity coming from Northern France, the grains used in Dijon have always been imported from Italy, Alsace, and Holland.

Mustard manufacturers seem to make good publicists, and Alexandre Bornibus could see no point in staying in Dijon when he could use his advertising to much greater effect in Paris. He was one of the first Frenchmen to use sandwich men. His delivery vans were the smartest turn-outs on the road. He was the first to use stoneware mustard pots, and his 'ladies' mustard—which we now know as tarragon—was sold in pots of Sèvres china. 'The contents are worthy of the container,' was his slogan. It was probably his friend Alexandre Dumas who suggested the formation of gastronomical clubs which have become so popular, such as La Confrérie des Chevaliers de Goûte-Andouille and the Black Pudding Tasters. You will find Bornibus mustard is stipulated for certain recipes; *andouillettes à la moutarde* is one, though it is not so well-known in England as some of the other makes from Dijon and Meaux. David James is, we believe, the only sausage-maker to blend a special mustard to go with his product, and Tewkesbury mustard does indeed provide an excellent accompaniment to his Gloucester sausage. Shakespearean scholars will remember that Falstaff told Doll Tearsheet that Poins' wit was 'as thick as Tewkesbury mustard'. It is a pale smooth blend of mustard seed, wine vinegar, horseradish and salt.

The Germans, too, produce a wide range of mustards. The sweet Bavarian kind is specially good with *Münchener weisswurst,* the delicate flavour of which would be killed by a stronger variety. Then there is the pale, sharp Düsseldorf mustard, and

many others containing various herbs as well as those flavoured
with paprika and horseradish. The ordinary table mustard is
tafelsenf.

Next come ketchups and sauces. Although using a cold relish
or sauce with a hot dish, particularly with a grill, is a very
English habit, we have heard that Worcestershire Sauce is now
made by a German firm, and what is more, given its proper
name, not, as we recently read in an English cookery book—
whose author should surely have known better—*Worcester*
Sauce.

As alternatives, we can recommend Scott's Sherry Sauce,
and, if you like making your own ketchups, Pontac Sauce. This
was invented by a Monsieur Pontac who owned an eating house
in Lombard Street, London. It is made of elderberries and the
sharp taste cuts fat very well. As David and Rose Maybey point
out in *Jams, Pickles, and Chutneys*, it goes well with pig liver, so
is an excellent accompaniment to sausages containing this
ingredient. It is easy to make and the recipe will be found in a
number of books, including Mrs Beeton.

A hot, as distinct from cold, sauce which is not found in
many books is Gubbins' sauce. It is made on a plate over hot
water. A soup plate on top of a saucepan of boiling water is
ideal. Melt a piece of butter the size of a walnut on a plate, stir
in two teaspoons of made English mustard, two teaspoons of
wine vinegar, one teaspoon tarragon vinegar, and one tablespoon Devonshire cream. Mix very well and season to taste
with salt, pepper and cayenne 'according to the requirements
of the breakfasters'.

For cold sliced sausages, pickles and chutneys make excellent
relishes, and there is such a wide variety that most people will
find more than one to suit their taste. Finally, do not forget the
gherkin. Some are preserved in too strong a solution of vinegar,
but if you can get the baby ones in a sweet vinegary brine, they
are delicious.

Having chosen what sausages you would like to eat and the
way you would like them served, and having cooked them with
all the skill they deserve and decided what mustard, sauce or
relish should accompany them, now comes the final question:

'What shall we have to drink?' Beer or wine? Tea or coffee? It must depend to a large extent on where you are and the time of day.

At breakfast, only a sausage can lure me away from coffee. I find that tea brings out the peppery flavour much better. For other meals, the first drink that comes to mind is beer. Our breweries seem to realize that there is an affinity, but what awful sausages are usually served in pubs. However, Buckley's Brewery now produces paper beer mats with Country Recipes printed on them, including the one for faggots which you, will find on page 144.

German beers naturally go extremely well with German sausages, and there is an even greater choice of the former than the latter. Like the sausage, beer has a long history, going back to the first century AD. There are some 2,000 breweries in Germany, and if each of these were to limit itself to producing no more than three types, one would have a choice of 6,000 beers. These breweries produce 1,760,000,000 litres (391,111,110 gallons) of beer a year, but it is not all consumed in Germany. German consumption seems to be rather modest; an average of 135 litres (236 pints) per person per year. Munich and Dortmund are famous for both their light (*helles*) and dark (*dunkel*) beer. Hamburg, Bremen and Frankfurt are better known for the light variety. But some small-town breweries produce splendid beers, and you won't go far wrong if you select a local beer to go with a local sausage. Eighty-five years ago, George Ellwanger suggested in *The Pleasures of the Table*, that *bockwurst*, a subtle mixture of veal and pork, should be accompanied by *bock* beer, but a juicy *knackwurst* required something heavier. (The chief difference between German and English beers is that traditionally we brew by infusion and top fermentation, the Germans by decoction and bottom fermentation.)

The same principle applies to wine; there is an affinity between various types of produce which come from the same soil and grow in the same climate. Many Germans consider that the wines of the Palatinate are an excellent accompaniment to sausages.

Alsace can also offer very good beers and delicious wines which go particularly well with Alsatian sausages. These include some delectable *boudin blancs*, truffled and creamy. The dry Alsatian wines are robust enough to stand up to this richness. *Andouilles* and *andouillettes* demand wines such as Beaujolais, Brouilly, Mâcon, Julienas and Chiroubles. Of course one must also take into account the way in which the sausages are cooked. *Andouillettes à la Tourangelle*, for instance, are better accompanied by a wine from the Coteaux du Layon, which lies south of the Loire and the towns of Bourgeuil and Chinon, possibly because the wines there have an apple flavour which goes well with pork. For *crépinettes de porc truffées*, at least one French authority suggests a Mercurey from Côte Chalonnaise. In Vouvray, Jane Grigson tells us, they serve tiny *boudins noirs aux raisins*, and miniature *andouillettes* and *boudins blancs*, grilled and accompanied by bread and mustard, to eat as an hors d'oeuvre with the famous wine of the district. With Toulouse sausages, which are amongst our favourites, try the black wine of Cahors, or, if you are cooking them *à la paysanne*, Françoise Burgaud suggests a rosé de Béarn or Saint Pourçain. For *fegatelli*, choose an Italian wine. Although Chianti and Valpolicella can be excellent, try the Piedmont wines from Barolo and Barbaresco as well. And we certainly did not despise the Barbera with our picnics of salami in the olive groves. Lambrusco, that slightly sparkling, fruity red wine from just north of Modena, was recommended to us as an ideal accompaniment to *zampone*—once again the produce of the same region complementing each other. This wine is also excellent with black pudding. But, as Hugh Johnson found, you must be careful to get the real thing. There are, Signor Bruno Roncarati wrote in *The Times*, in November 1976, four basic types of this wine, each coming from a different district, three of which are near Modena. Incidentally, this wine also goes very well with *cotechino*.

A really dry sherry, or better still a manzanilla, goes well with a slice of *chorizo* eaten as a snack; for a more substantial meal you need a Rioja.

What else is there? Certainly one can drink cider with most

sausages; and, for those which have been cooked in cider, it is much better than beer or wine, which seem to produce conflicting flavours. Sausages from Brittany and West Country Hog's Pudding go particularly well with cider. Nor can one omit *apfelwein*, that strong older cider beloved by the Hessians, who drink the new pressing every autumn in much the same way as the Viennese drink *heurige*. For haggis, of course, there is nothing like pure malt whisky. Gin seemed to be the one thing that didn't go well with sausages, but suddenly we remembered a steaming hot Dutch sausage with an ice-cold tot of Geneva, which was a marvellous snack. We finally decided that the only drink we would never recommend is cocoa.

Of course nobody would suggest drinking an exquisite château-bottled claret of outstanding vintage with even the most elaborately prepared dish of sausages. Most are, after all, homely things, rugged and rustic, and they need a simple honest companion, strong enough to cut the fat and stand up to the herbs and spices they so often contain.

Now for the dishes. The recipes have been arranged country by country in alphabetical order.

Regional Sausage Dishes

American Dishes

Frankfurter and Rice Casserole

> *Ingredients* (*serves 4*)
> 2 onions, sliced
> 2 tablespoons oil
> 225g (8oz) rice
> 1 large can tomatoes
> 1 dessertspoon sugar
> salt and pepper
> 25g (1oz) chopped green pepper
> 3 whole cloves
> bay leaf
> 8 frankfurters, sliced, or cut in half

Method Wash and cook the rice and drain well. Gently cook the onions in oil until they are transparent. Add all the remaining ingredients except the rice and frankfurters. Simmer for 15 minutes, then remove the cloves and bay leaf. Add the rice and mix well. Grease a casserole and fill it with alternate layers of rice mixture and frankfurters, finishing with frankfurters. Cover the casserole and cook in a moderate oven for one hour. Remove the lid for the last 15 minutes.

Frankfurter, Apple and Cheese Pie

Ingredients (serves 4)
8 frankfurters
English mustard
3 sharp apples, peeled and cored
50g (2oz) Demerara sugar
25g (1oz) grated cheese, or more if wanted

Method Put the frankfurters into a greased baking dish and spread them with the made mustard. Cover with the sliced apples and sprinkle with sugar. Bake in a moderate oven for 20 minutes. Take out the dish, cover with grated cheese and put under the grill until the cheese is bubbling and browned.

Frankfurters with Hot Potato Salad

Ingredients (serves 2/3)
675g (1½lb) cooked, thinly sliced potatoes
4 tablespoons oil
1 tablespoon of vinegar
salt, pepper
350g (12oz) cooked green beans, well drained
½ medium onion, thinly sliced
225g (8oz) frankfurters (preferably large ones) thinly sliced

Method Gently mix the oil, vinegar, salt and pepper with the potatoes. Grease a casserole and put in alternate layers of beans, potato salad, onions and frankfurters. Cover the dish and cook in a hot oven for 30 minutes.

A description of different types of Frankfurter sausages and how to make your own will be found on page 148.

Austrian Dishes

Würstelbraten
Not a sausage, but a way of using them to 'lard' a lean joint of beef. Sausages are inserted into incisions made through the meat before it is slowly braised in the oven with a little stock.

Cream is added before serving, and the joint is carved so that a section of sausage appears in every slice.

Chinese Dishes

Lap Cheong

In Hong Kong we found that these Chinese sausages are often served with a sort of rice porridge called congee. Ken Hom, whose programmes on the BBC have made Chinese cookery so popular, says that the way to make this is first to boil the rice and then let it simmer for a good 30 minutes, stirring occasionally. In this way 'the starch is released gradually, without the grains disintegrating'. It is better to use unwashed, short-grain rice. He uses 700 ml (1¼ pints of water) for 150 ml or 5 fluid ounces of rice. After 35 minutes, add the sausages diced fairly small, and simmer for a further 5 minutes. Add finely chopped spring onions and coriander just before serving. In his book, *Chinese Cookery*, he also gives a recipe for a chicken, sausage and rice casserole.

Lap cheong (and sometimes other kinds of Chinese sausage, see index) can be bought at most Chinese grocers.

English Dishes

Chipolatas with Tomatoes

> *Ingredients (serves 4)*
> 8 chipolatas
> 2 tablespoons oil
> 1 small can tomatoes
> 1 onion
> 1 clove garlic
> bouquet garni
> ½ glass white wine
> 200g (7oz) noodles
> 50g (2oz) butter
> 100g (4oz) grated cheese
> salt and pepper

Method Prick the chipolatas (if you think it really necessary) with a fork and let them brown all over in a frying pan with the oil. Peel and chop the onion and garlic. Take the tomatoes out of the can, chopping them and reserving the juice. When the sausages are well cooked, remove to a fireproof dish and keep warm. Then fry the onion, and when it has softened add the garlic and tomatoes, mixing well. Add a little more oil if necessary. Leave to simmer gently for 5 minutes. Now add the reserved juice, the white wine and bouquet garni. Season, and allow to simmer for another 15 minutes with the lid on. Meanwhile cook the noodles according to the instructions on the packet. When they are done, drain them and place in a warmed serving dish. Mix in all the butter and half the cheese and season with salt and pepper. Arrange the chipolatas on a fireproof dish and pour the sauce over them, having first removed the bouquet garni. Sprinkle with the remainder of the cheese and put under the grill or in the oven to brown.

Cumberland Sausage with Red Cabbage

Ingredients (serves 4)
450g (1lb) Cumberland sausage
1 small red cabbage
1 medium onion
2 red-skinned apples
2–3 teaspoons ground coriander
1–2 teaspoons crushed juniper berries
⅓ litre (½ pint) red wine
1 tablespoon red wine vinegar
2 tablespoons red currant jelly
salt and pepper

Method Finely slice the cabbage, peel and slice the onion, peel, core and slice the apples and place in layers in a casserole, seasoning between the layers with salt and pepper and the coriander and juniper berries. Place the sausage on top and push well down. Melt the red currant jelly in the wine and pour over the sausage and cabbage with the vinegar. Cover with a well-fitting lid and cook in a slow oven for 2–3 hours.

Devilled Sausages

Slash the sausages and spread them with the following Devil Mixture which was given by Francatelli in 1845: 'Mix on a plate the following articles; viz. a spoonful of mustard, either French or English, the same quantity of chutney and of anchovy, twice as much salad oil and a little cayenne pepper.' Then place the sausages on a dish in a hot oven for about 20 minutes, turning once or twice and basting with the mixture. Serve with mashed potatoes.

Sausage Fritters

Remove the skins from sausages and split them lengthways. Cover the cut side with mustard then dip each half in batter and deep fry.

Sausage Surprises

Ingredients
225g (8oz) plain flour
3 teaspoons baking powder
1 teaspoon salt
50g (2oz) butter or lard
milk to mix
10 chipolata or cocktail sausages

Method First make a scone dough by sifting the dry ingredients and rubbing in the butter until the mixture resembles fine breadcrumbs. Add enough milk, mixing with a fork, to form a soft ball which comes away from the sides of the bowl. Turn on to a floured board and knead gently for half a minute. Roll out very thinly and using a biscuit cutter make twenty circles of dough. Place each cooked sausage on a circle and cover with the remaining ones. Seal the edges with a fork and make a slit in the top. Place on an ungreased dish in a hot oven for 15–20 minutes. These can be served as a cocktail snack, or with hot apple sauce.

Tudor Sausages

Ingredients (serves 4)
2 tablespoons butter
1 finely sliced onion
450g (1lb) pork sausages
1 glass warmed beer
1 glass white wine
2 tablespoons tomato purée
1 tablespoon plain flour
1 lemon
dash of made mustard (preferably Dijon)
salt, pepper
4 slices fried bread

Method Melt half the butter in a frying pan and add the onion and sausages. Let them brown lightly, then pour in the warmed beer, the white wine and the tomato purée, stirring well. Cover the pan and simmer for 15 minutes. Lift out the sausages and put them in a serving dish on top of the fried bread, and keep them warm while you make the sauce. Make a *beurre manié* with the remainder of the butter and the flour (that is, knead them together in a small bowl with a wooden spoon). Add this mixture to the juices in the pan in little bits and stir until smooth. When the sauce has thickened, add the salt, pepper, mustard and a squeeze of lemon. Pour over the sausages and serve.

French Dishes

Andouille Vigneronne

Don't worry if you cannot get andouille or andouillettes locally; though with the growing number of French charcutiers opening in the provinces, they will be increasingly easier to find. Sausage recipes are very accommodating and you can see how you like the dish with Toulouse sausages. And I doubt whether the pig's tail will make all that much difference.

Ingredients *(serves 2/3)*
300g (10oz) dried haricot beans
1 *andouille*
100g (4oz) fat bacon
1 pig's tail
rind of pork
3 carrots
2–3 onions
bouquet garni, pepper, salt
100ml (3 floz) red wine
parsley, butter

Method Soak the beans overnight, and at the same time simmer a pork *andouille* for 2 hours and leave in the water overnight. Next day, strain the beans and put them in a casserole with the pig's tail, the bacon rind cut into dice, the carrots and onions, sliced, the bouquet garni and the seasoning. Cover with cold water and bring to the boil. Add the wine and continue to simmer. After 1 hour, add the *andouille* and continue to cook gently for about 2 hours more. Serve the meat on one dish and the beans, topped with butter and chopped parsley, separately.

Andouillettes à la Moutarde
Madame Yvonne, proprietress of *Le Bassano* restaurant in Paris gives this recipe.

Ingredients *(serves 4)*
6 *andouillettes* (any sort)
mustard Bornibus
tarragon mustard
2–3 chopped shallots
½ glass white wine
1 ladle jellied veal stock
knob of butter
fresh breadcrumbs

Method Put the *andouillettes* in a hot oven to heat through for 10 minutes. Remove them, smear with mustard Bornibus and grill on all sides. Poach the shallots in the white wine until they are tender and the wine reduced. Take them off the fire and add 1 tablespoon of mustard Bornibus and 1 of tarragon mustard, then add the ladle of veal stock. Arrange the *andouil-lettes* in a fireproof dish, add a knob of butter to the sauce and pour over the *andouillettes*. Sprinkle with breadcrumbs and brown in the oven.

Andouillettes à la Strasbourgeoise
These are also grilled or fried, but they are served on a bed of *choucroute* (pickled cabbage), and accompanied by boiled or steamed potatoes.

Andouillettes à la Tourangelle
This recipe comes from M. Barrier of Tours, and is published in *Porc et Cochonailles*.

> **Ingredients** (*serves 4*)
> 4 andouillettes
> 1 lemon
> 450g (1lb) mushrooms
> 1 glass armagnac
> 1 glass white wine
> 25g (1oz) butter
> salt and pepper

Method Make three or four light incisions in the *andouillettes* and place them in a dish. Sprinkle them with the armagnac and leave to marinate for 24 hours, turning them occasionally, then drain them. Finely slice the mushrooms and sprinkle them with the lemon juice. Butter a fireproof dish well, and spread the mushrooms on the bottom. Season, then sprinkle with the white wine. Place the *andouillettes* on top and cook in a hot oven for 40 minutes. Meanwhile, heat a serving dish and when the andouillettes are cooked, remove them from the fireproof dish and keep them warm. Pour the other ingredients into a saucepan and boil over a hot flame until the liquid has disappeared, then tip the mushrooms over the *andouillettes* and serve.

(A description of *andouillettes* and how to make them will be found on pages 97–102, but I would not advise trying your hand at making them as your first attempt at sausage-making. Try something simpler to start with.)

Boudins Blancs d'Epernay

Ingredients (serves 6)
12 *boudins blancs truffées* (these have to be bought)
125g (5oz) butter
salt, pepper, nutmeg

Method Gently remove the skins from the *boudins*. Butter a fireproof dish and arrange the *boudins* on the bottom. Cover with little pieces of butter, grated nutmeg and ground black pepper and salt. Put this dish in a moderate oven for 15–20 minutes, basting with the juices from time to time. This is a very delicate dish, and must be treated with the utmost respect as the skinless *boudins* are very fragile. The dish can be served with a purée of spinach or with a compôte of apples, and fried potatoes.

(Recipes for making your own *boudins blancs* will be found on pages 116–119 and they are well worth the effort.)

Boudins entre Ciel et Terre
(Black Puddings between Heaven and Earth)
This is also a speciality of Brabant. Potatoes are cooked and mashed with butter, two egg yolks, pepper, nutmeg, salt and a little milk.

Apples are peeled, cored and sliced and cooked with a sprinkling of sugar in a very little water, then made into a purée. They are both put into a serving dish and kept warm while the *boudins* are slit and rubbed with oil, then well grilled on all sides. When they are brown, place them on the potatoes and apples and pour melted butter over them.

Boudins Noirs à la Normande
In this recipe the *boudin noir* is cut into chunks and sautéed in butter. To this is added half as much cooking apple as sausage, peeled, sliced and cooked in butter. When the *boudin* is lightly browned the two are served together.

(You can make your own *boudins noirs*, see pages 119–122, but, as in making black puddings, it can become a bit messy.)

Cervelas aux Oeufs Brouillés et Epinards
(Cervelas with Scrambled Eggs and Spinach)

Ingredients (serves 6)
900g (2lb) spinach
6 *cervelas*
6 eggs
3 tablespoons cream
100g (4oz) butter
1 tablespoon oil
salt, pepper

Method Wash and cook the spinach, then drain well and squeeze out all the water. Slit the *cervelas* along three-quarters of their length and let them heat gently in the oil, over a low flame. Break the eggs into a bowl with the seasoning and beat lightly with a fork. Melt half the butter in a saucepan, add the spinach and keep it warm over a gentle heat. Melt the rest of the butter in a pan, add the beaten eggs and the cream and let them cook, gently stirring all the time. Put the spinach in the middle of a heated serving dish and surround it with sausages. Gently spoon the scrambled egg into the slit in each *cervelas*. Serve at once.

Cervelas Sauce Rouge
(Cervelas with Red Sauce)

Ingredients (serves 6)
6 *cervelas*
6 thick slices or 'sticks' of Gruyère cheese
tomato sauce
cream, salt, pepper
6 thin slices of smoked bacon

Method Skin the *cervelas* and split them three-quarters along their length. Insert a length of Gruyère into each sausage and wrap it in a slice of bacon, securing it with a cocktail stick. Place them on a grill pan in a very hot oven for 15 minutes. Serve with piping hot home-made tomato sauce, with plenty of cream in it and lots of pepper.

Caillettes, Crépinettes

Although making and serving most sausages can be treated separately, when it comes to those enveloped in a pig's caul, such as *caillettes*, *crépinettes* and their poor British cousin the faggot, no such distinction can be made, so for these dishes the reader is referred to the last section of the book.

Potée

Ingredients
1 large cabbage
1.35kg (3lb) potatoes
1 onion
50g (2oz) lard
nutmeg, bay leaf, salt and pepper
600g (1¼lb) fresh pork sausages
800g (1¾lb) green streaky bacon, in one piece

Method Separate the leaves of the cabbage and wash them, removing any hard stalks. Peel and cut the potatoes into quarters, peel the onion and slice thinly. Melt the lard in a large, heavy pan and add the onion to soften over a gentle heat until it is golden. Then put in alternate layers of cabbage and potatoes, season with pepper, a little salt, grated nutmeg and a bay leaf. Slip the sausage and bacon into the middle of the vegetables and barely cover with water. Bring to the boil and let it simmer gently for 2½ hours. Just before serving, remove the sausage and bacon and keep them warm. Mash the vegetables with a fork and place them in a heated deep serving dish. Finally chop up the sausages and bacon into little bits and cover the vegetables with the pieces. Serve very hot.

Saucisse à la Catalane

This recipe is for a sausage in a coil, like the Cumberland.

Ingredients (serves 4)
1kg (2lb) coil of sausage
50g (2oz) fat
2 tablespoons flour

300ml (½ pint) white wine with a little
   meat stock added
1 tablespoon tomato purée
24 blanched cloves garlic
bouquet garni
twist of bitter orange peel

Method First fry the sausage whole and when nicely brown
remove it from the pan. Add flour to the remaining fat to form
a *roux*. Gradually add white wine and stock until you have a
good thick sauce. Stir in a little concentrated tomato purée and
let it blend well, then strain the sauce into a jug. Put the
sausage back into the pan with plenty of garlic. *Larousse* says 24
cloves. This may seem a lot, but those who have cooked *tranche
de gigot* on a bed of garlic will know that this amount is far
from overpowering, particularly if the cloves are blanched
beforehand. A bouquet garni and a twist of bitter orange peel
are also added. The sauce is poured over the sausage and
simmered for 30 minutes.

Saucisse de Morteau au Vin Blanc

Ingredients (serves 2)
1 Morteau sausage
1 tablespoon butter
300 ml approx (½ pint) white wine and stock in equal
   quantities
bouquet garni
1 clove garlic
1 large onion
1 tablespoon tomato purée
450g (1lb) potatoes, all the same size
salt, pepper and parsley

Method Cook the sausage gently in butter until it is golden,
then add the white wine and stock in equal quantities so that it
is just covered. Now put in the bouquet garni, tomato purée,
garlic and the chopped onion. Bring this to the boil and add
the potatoes. Cook for 30 minutes or until the potatoes are

tender, and then remove the sausage and put it into a serving dish with the potatoes all round. Sprinkle with parsley and keep warm while you reduce the juices in the pan by fast boiling. Pour over the sausage and potatoes.

We heard somewhere that *saucisse de Morteau* could be eaten raw, but Madame Pernollet of the Hotel Pernollet at Belley was adamant that this was not so. It doesn't really matter as they are quite delicious cooked.

Chou à la Saucisse de Morteau

Ingredients (serves 2/3)
1 cabbage, approximately 675g (1½lb)
750g (1½lb) potatoes
350g (12oz) Morteau sausage
200g (7oz) sliced smoked bacon
50g (2oz) lard
1 onion, minced
pepper, salt, 2–3 juniper berries

Method Peel the potatoes, cut into large cubes and dry them with a cloth. Detach the cabbage leaves and blanch them for 10–15 minutes. Drain and chop coarsely before putting them into a casserole in which you have melted the lard. Add the potatoes, minced onion and juniper berries, and seasoning. Cook this in a moderate oven for about 1½ hours. After ¾ hour add the sausage. When all is cooked, pile the vegetables into a dome in the centre of a serving dish and put the sliced sausage and fried bacon slices on top.

Saucisse de Toulouse Soubise

Ingredients (serves 2)
450g (1lb) Toulouse sausage
4 very large onions
50–75g (2–3oz) butter
250ml (⅓ pint) stock
1 dessertspoon plain flour
pepper, salt

Method Fry the sausage in butter, then drain and keep warm. Fry the finely sliced onions in the same butter until they are soft, then sprinkle in the flour and slowly add the stock, stirring all the time. When it is well blended, add the seasoning and simmer until the flour is cooked. Now replace the sausage in the sauce and simmer together for 10–20 minutes.

Saucisse de Toulouse à la Languedocienne

Ingredients (serves 4)
900g (2lb) Toulouse sausage
3 tablespoons goose fat or lard
300 ml (½ pint) demi-glace sauce
2 tablespoons tomato purée
2 tablespoons wine vinegar
4 cloves garlic, bouquet garni
3 tablespoons capers
1 tablespoon chopped parsley, pepper, salt

Method Twist the sausage into a coil and secure it with two skewers. Heat the fat in a frying pan and put in the sausage together with the chopped garlic and bouquet garni. Cover the pan and cook gently for 18 minutes. Remove the sausage from the pan and keep warm. Add the vinegar to the juice in the pan and the demi-glace, then the tomato purée, and bring to the boil. Finally add the capers, parsley and seasoning to the sauce before pouring it over the sausage.

Saucisses à la Bretonne

Ingredients (serves 4/6)
800g (1¾lb) haricot beans, soaked overnight
1 onion, studded with a clove
1 head of garlic
bouquet garni
salt and pepper
4 Breton sausages (or any pure pork sausages)
peppercorns
150ml (¼ pint) light stock
1 wineglass of white wine
100ml (4 floz) fresh cream

Method Put the beans in a large pan and cover them with cold water. Add the onion and one crushed clove of garlic. Bring the water to the boil and let it simmer gently for 1½ hours, adding salt and pepper half way through the cooking time. Twenty minutes before the beans are ready, crush a few peppercorns, prick the sausages and put them both into a small saucepan. Cover them with stock and white wine and let them simmer gently for 10 minutes. Meanwhile, separate the other cloves of garlic but do not peel them, and put them in a pan with cold water. Bring to the boil and let them cook until the garlic is soft enough to squeeze between your fingers. Drain, peel and crush them to a fine paste which you then mix with the cream. Now heat the grill and, having drained the sausages, let them brown under it on all sides. Drain the haricots, and, after removing the onion and bouquet garni, put them through a mouli-sieve. Mix this purée with the garlic and cream. Put the mixture into a heated serving dish and arrange the sausages on top. Serve very hot.

Saucisses au Muscadet

> *Ingredients (serves 4)*
> 2 large wine glasses of Muscadet
> 6 fresh *saucisses de campagne*
> 1 egg yolk
> juice of 1 lemon
> a little consommé or the jelly found at the bottom of a
>   bowl of dripping
> 6 fried croûtons of bread to fit the sausages
> purée of chestnuts (Tinned unsweetened chestnut purée
>   is quite acceptable when fresh chestnuts are
>   unavailable.)
> butter or lard
> salt and pepper

Method Cook the sausages gently and keep them warm on the croûtons. Pour away excess fat leaving enough for the sauce. Scrape up the residue in the pan and add the Muscadet. Reduce the liquid by fast boiling then add the lemon juice and a very little consommé. Thicken with the egg yolk, heating very gently so that it will not curdle, then add a knob of butter. Warm the chestnut purée, place the croûtons and sausages on top and pour over the sauce.

Saucisses grillées

Ingredients (serves 4)
4 Frankfurt sausages
3 tablespoons tarragon mustard
4 slices Gruyère cheese (fairly thick, and the same length and width as the sausages)
4 thin slices smoked bacon
4 cocktail sticks

Method Heat the grill. Cut the sausages lengthways, but not right through. Spread the cut sides lavishly with mustard and insert a slice of cheese. Wrap a slice of bacon round each sausage and secure with a cocktail stick, then grill them on all sides.

Some years ago we found ourselves attending a Congress of fakirs in Lyons. They had challenged the prestigitators; *magie blanche* against *magie noire*. It seemed to be a good story for a journalist; but that is by the way. We took the opportunity of eating at Nandron's Restaurant. Here is his recipe for:

Saucisson Chaud Lyonnais

Ingredients
1 Lyonnais pork sausage
1 kg (2lb 2oz) potatoes
1 small onion
olive oil
wine vinegar
Dijon mustard
black pepper
chopped parsley
salt
dry white wine

Method Put the sausage in cold water and boil for 20–25 minutes. At the same time cook the potatoes in their skins in water brought to the boil from cold. Peel and slice while still hot and season with oil, mustard, a little white wine, salt and a drop of vinegar and two squeezes of onion juice (squeezed in a garlic press). Sprinkle the hot potato salad with chopped parsley. Simply slice the sausage when cooked, and serve with the salad.

Saucisson en Brioche
A Franche-Comté recipe. Make a brioche dough and leave it to cool overnight. One hour before using, break down, knead and roll the dough to a size which will envelop the sausage. Meanwhile boil the sausage in a *court-bouillon* for 15–20 minutes, according to size. Place the sausage on the pastry, fold over and seal by moistening the edges with water or beaten egg. Use the remainder of the egg to brush over the pastry and bake in a moderate oven for 25 minutes.

This can be equally well made with a *Cervelas truffé*.

German Dishes

Bratwurst in Bier nach Berliner Art
(Sausages Cooked in Beer, Berlin Style)

> *Ingredients*
> 450g (1lb) *bratwurst*
> 1 large sliced onion
> 300 ml (½ pint) beer
> butter
> potato flour (farina)
> salt, peppercorns, bay leaves

Method Scald the sausages in boiling water then drain and dry. Fry the onions in butter and, when they are softened, add the sausage and fry together. Throw in one or two bay leaves and a few peppercorns with salt to taste. Add half the beer, bring quickly to the boil and allow the mixture to reduce for a few minutes. Then add the other half of the beer, bring to the boil again and let it simmer gently for 15 minutes. Thicken the liquid with the potato flour and serve.

Another delicious way of serving *Bratwurst*:

Bratwurst mit Saurer Sahnensosse
(Bratwurst with Sour Cream Sauce)
The *bratwurst* is first scalded and fried, then cut into slices 5mm (¼ in) thick and poached in a thickened, sour cream sauce.

Brunswick Salad
Strips of *jagdwurst* are mixed with finely chopped pickled cucumber, sliced tomato, grated apple and cooked French beans. This is sprinkled with chopped parsley and dressed with olive oil mixed with the juice of the pickled cucumber, pepper and salt.

Cervelat Sausage Casserole

> *Ingredients (serves 2)*
> 300ml (½ pint) white sauce (not too thick)
> 75g (3oz) grated cheese
> 1 grated onion
> Worcestershire sauce, celery salt, garlic salt
> 225g (8oz) mixed cooked vegetables (peas, beans, sweet corn etc.)
> 225g (8oz) *cervelat* sausage, cubed
> 75g (3oz) fresh fried breadcrumbs

Method Add 50g (2oz) of the cheese to the white sauce, along with the onion, and stir together over a gentle heat until the cheese has melted. Arrange the vegetables, sausage and sauce in layers in a well-buttered fireproof dish, finish with the breadcrumbs mixed with the remainder of the cheese sprinkled on top. Place in a hot oven for 20 minutes, or until the top is brown.

Grilled Knackwurst with Potato Salad

Ingredients (serves 4)
1kg (2lb) potatoes
4 fat knackwurst
100g (4oz) Bergkäse or Emmental cheese
100g (4oz) streaky bacon
mayonnaise
1 small carton yoghurt
parsley, vinegar, salt, pepper, sugar, made mustard, olive
oil

Method Boil the potatoes in their skins and then peel and slice
or dice them. Pour over them a mixture of vinegar, mustard,
sugar, salt and pepper. Mix the yoghurt with the mayonnaise
and add the chopped parsley. Stir this into the potatoes and
leave to get cold. Cut slits in the *knackwurst* along one side, and
insert alternate slices of bacon and cheese. Brush with olive oil
and cook under a pre-heated grill for about 4 to 5 minutes on
each side. Serve with the potato salad and mixed pickles.

Kartoffeln mit Apfeln und Geräucherter Blutwurst
(Potatoes with Apples and Smoked Blood Sausage)

Ingredients (serves 2/3)
450g (1lb) apples, peeled, cored and sliced
900g (2lb) potatoes
450g (1lb) blood sausage
butter, pepper, salt, sugar
white wine
fried breadcrumbs

Method Boil the potatoes in their skins until just cooked, then
peel, slice and keep them warm. Place the sliced apples in a
saucepan and simmer with just enough water to prevent them
sticking. By the time the apples are cooked the water should
have evaporated. In the meantime, slice the sausage and fry in
butter. Place the potatoes in the middle of a serving dish with a
lump of butter and cover with the fried breadcrumbs. Then
arrange the sliced and fried sausages on top. Surround them

with the apples sprinkled with a little sugar and white wine. Serve hot.

Potted Brunswick Sausage

Brunswick sausage can be potted and used like a pâté. The skin is removed and the contents blended with sour cream, mushrooms fried in butter, parsley, thyme and a little brandy. When the pots are filled the tops should be covered with a layer of clarified butter.

Hungarian Dishes

Kolábszos Rántolla
(Sausages with Eggs)

Ingredients (serves 2/3)
100g (4oz) *Gyulai* or other smoked sausage
50g (2oz) green bacon
1–2 green peppers, de-seeded
6 eggs
butter, salt, pepper

Method Dice the sausage, bacon and pepper roughly into small cubes and fry them in butter. Break the eggs into a basin, season and whisk well. Stir in the other ingredients. Melt a little butter in a frying pan and add the mixture. Stir constantly and serve just before the mixture sets. It should have the consistency of thick cream, or underdone scrambled eggs.

Italian Dishes

Cotechino with Lentils

> *Ingredients* *(serves 4)*
> 1 cotechino
> 325g (12oz) brown lentils
> 1 medium onion
> 2 stalks celery
> 50g (2oz) fat salt pork, diced
> olive oil and butter
> salt and freshly ground black pepper

Method Prick the *cotechino* and place in a small pan. Just cover it with water, bring to the boil and let it simmer for 2 hours. Then remove the skin, allow to cool and cut into thick slices. Cook the lentils, with the onions and celery, until they are soft, then drain. Sauté the diced pork in a mixture of butter and olive oil until golden brown, then add the lentils and a little of the liquid in which they were cooked. Let the lentils absorb this, cover the top with the sliced *cotechino* and place in a moderate oven for 1 hour.

Salsiccie alla Romagna

Prick the sausages with a needle, then poach in water for a few minutes before drying them and sauté-ing them in a mixture of butter and oil, adding perhaps a leaf or two of sage. When they are well browned, cover them in the pan with half their weight in really ripe, peeled and chopped tomatoes. (Tinned ones are very good for this purpose.) Simmer for 15 minutes.

Salsiccia cotta sotto la cenere

(Sausages cooked in ashes)
This is the Sardinian method. The sausages are wrapped in brown paper and baked in the ashes of an open fire.

Zampone au Chou
(Zampone with Cabbage)

Ingredients (serves 4)
1 zampone
8 chipolatas
2 tablespoons lard
1 large white cabbage
2 carrots
2 turnips
1 stick of celery
3 leeks
1 can tomato purée
bouquet garni, salt, pepper

Method Soak the zampone for 12 hours. Prepare the vegetables, excepting the cabbage, and boil them in water with the *zampone* and the bouquet garni for 2½ hours. Meanwhile, wash the cabbage and remove the outside leaves and hard stalks. Cut it into four and blanch for 10 minutes, then drain and cook in fresh, salted water for 10 minutes. Fry the chipolatas in the lard until they are brown on all sides, then remove them from the pan and keep warm. Drain the cabbage, squeezing it hard to remove all the water. Chop it coarsely and put it in the pan with the fat in which the chipolatas were cooked. Mix the can of tomato purée with a ladle of the *zampone* and vegetable liquid (the remainder can either be kept as stock or thrown away) and add it to the cabbage, stirring well. Let it cook gently for about 10 minutes. Drain the *zampone* and cut it into slices. Put the cabbage into a heated serving dish and arrange the chipolatas and the sliced *zampone* on top. Serve at once.

Netherlands Dishes

Stampot van Boerkool met Worst
(Hotpot of Kale and Sausage)

> *Ingredients (serves 4)*
> 1.35kg (3lb) kale
> 1.35kg (3lb) potatoes
> 450g (1lb) smoked sausage
> 175g (6oz) unsliced bacon, without rind
> salt, pepper

Method Chop the kale leaves, put in a saucepan and barely cover with boiling water. Simmer for 20 minutes, then add the peeled and halved potatoes, the slab of bacon and the sausages. Simmer for 45 minutes. Remove bacon, dice it and brown in the frying pan. Mince the kale and potatoes and mix with enough of the stock in which they were boiled to moisten the mixture, and add the fat which has come from frying the bacon. Cut the sausage in 5mm (¼in) slices and place in a fireproof dish with the vegetables. Strew the diced bacon on top and brown in the oven.

Uien met Aardappelen, Rijst en Verscheworst
(Onions, Potatoes, Rice and Fresh Sausages)

> *Ingredients (serves 2/3)*
> 900g (2lb) onions
> 550g (1¼lb) potatoes
> 125g (5oz) rice
> 225g (½lb) fresh sausages
> pepper, salt, vinegar

Method Peel and boil the potatoes. Peel and chop the onions and add them to the potatoes. Wash the rice and put it in the pan with the potatoes and onions. Add more water, if necessary, and bring to the boil for half an hour. Now throw in the sausages and boil for half an hour. Remove the sausages and keep warm while you drain and season the vegetables. Place these in a dish with the sausages on top and sprinkle with vinegar.

Zuurkool met Verscheworst
(Sausages with Sauerkraut)

> *Ingredients (serves 4)*
> 900g (2lb) zuurkool (a Dutch form of sauerkraut)
> 900g (2lb) potatoes
> 350g (12oz) sausages
> salt and pepper

Method Wash the *zuurkool* and boil it in slightly salted water for 30 minutes. Add the peeled and sliced potatoes and the sausages. Cook for a further 30–40 minutes.

Polish Dishes

Kabanos with Lentils

> *Ingredients (serves 4)*
> 350g (12oz) brown or green lentils
> 1 onion
> salt, pepper
> bouquet garni, powdered cloves
> 225g (8oz) diced ham
> 2 kabanos sausages
> 5–6 tablespoons olive oil
> 4–5 cloves garlic
> 1 tin anchovies
> fried croûtons to garnish

Method Wash the lentils and soak them in plenty of cold water for 12 hours. Put them in a pan with the water they were soaked in, adding more if necessary. Slice the onions finely and add to the lentils along with the pepper, bouquet garni and a pinch of powdered cloves. The lentils should cook slowly. Times vary with the age of the lentils, and the heat of the fire, but between 30 and 40 minutes should be enough. About 10 minutes before they are cooked, add the chopped ham and the sausages, cut into 5 cm (2in) lengths. Meanwhile heat the oil in a frying pan and, using the garlic press, squeeze the garlic into it. Fry gently until this is golden brown. When the lentils are

done, drain them well and then put them into the frying pan,
stirring gently so that they are quite covered with the garlicky
oil. Now add the anchovies chopped very finely, and their oil,
and season to taste. Mix well and put the lid on the pan. Let
the mixture heat through slowly before serving very hot with a
sprinkling of croûtons on each helping.

A salad of witloof chicory goes very well with this dish, which
can itself be served cold as a salad. The procedure is the same
as before, except that you allow it to get quite cold and add the
sausages cut into chunks just before serving, with a little
additional olive oil.

Kielbasa and Potatoes

Ingredients (serves 3–4)
350g (12oz) finely chopped onion
100g (4oz) chopped green pepper
175g (6oz) peeled and chopped tomatoes
900g (2lb) new potatoes
350g (12oz) kielbasa
2 teaspoons Hungarian paprika
pepper, salt
bacon fat for frying

Method Lightly fry the onions in the bacon fat. After 5 minutes
add the green pepper and fry for a further 5 minutes. Then
add the tomatoes, cover the pan and cook for another 5
minutes, or until the vegetables are tender. Grease a fireproof
casserole and put half the contents of the frying pan on the
bottom. Cut the potatoes and the sausage into thin slices. Put
half the slices on top, cover with the remainder of the vegetables
and finish with a layer of potato and sausage. Sprinkle with salt
and pepper and a little bacon fat. Pour in 150ml (¼ pint) of
water or chicken stock, cover the casserole, and place in a hot
oven for 20 minutes. Reduce the oven to a medium heat and
continue the cooking for another 15 minutes, after which time
the lid is removed so that the potatoes can be browned. This
could also be done under a hot grill.

Kielbasa Salad

The diced sausage is mixed with cold cooked kidney beans, spring onions, diced beetroot, a few capers and a French dressing. Another version uses brown or green lentils, shredded green pepper and hard-boiled egg.

Scandinavian Dishes

Korv Stroganov

For this dish they use Medister sausage in Denmark and Falukorv in Sweden; but Vienna sausage of any similar type can be used equally well. Although in Scandinavia they often skin the sausages first, this should not be necessary with English sausages in natural casings. They are sliced (or cut into strips) and fried in butter with chopped onions till brown. Then for every 450g or 1lb of sausages, 2 tablespoons of tomato purée, about 150 ml (¼ pint) of cream and a teaspoon of lemon juice are added. This is simmered gently in a closed pan for ten minutes, and served with rice or mashed potatoes.

Hot Liver Sausage

Skin the sausage, cut it into thick slices and place them in a fireproof dish. Cover them with fried mushrooms in a thick cream sauce and brown in the oven. *Leverkorv* also makes an excellent spread for sandwiches or toast.

Spanish Dishes

Cazuela à la Catalane

This is a famous dish using *butifarra*, a sausage from Catalonia.

Minced meat is first fried in olive oil in an earthenware dish. When it has browned, it is removed, and carrots, onions and tomatoes are fried in the same oil. As the onions turn golden, a little flour is sprinkled over them and the meat put back in the dish. Stock is added, and the whole is simmered for 45 minutes. Finally slices of *butifarra* are placed on top and the dish is heated through in the oven or under the grill.

Chorizos with eggs

Ingredients (serves 4)
8 eggs
2 *chorizos* cut into thin slices
a small amount of butter or lard
salt and pepper
fried breadcrumbs

Method Melt a knob of butter or lard in each of four small ovenproof dishes and break two eggs into each dish. Season with salt and pepper, then add the sliced *chorizos* evenly divided. Cover with fried breadcrumbs and bake in a hot oven (Gas 8, 450°F, 230°C) for about 10 minutes.

Chuletas de Cordero à la Navarre
(Navarre Lamb Cutlets)
The lamb cutlets are lightly fried in olive oil to seal them, then arranged on the bottom of a casserole and covered with fried, diced ham, and then a mixture of onion and tomatoes, peeled, chopped and fried to form a thick sauce. The dish is covered and cooked in a moderate oven. Just before serving, the lid is removed and slices of Pamplona *chorizo* are spread over the contents of the casserole. It is returned to the oven or put under the grill for the sausages to heat through. When the fat of the sausages starts to run, the dish is ready.

Lentejas Guisadas con Chorizo
(Lentils and *Chorizo*)
Lentils are first boiled until nearly done and then drained and put into a large frying or *paella* pan with olive oil, sliced onion, tomatoes, pimentos, garlic, parsley, salt, pepper and the sausages which are all fried together. This is sometimes served with *aïoli*, a garlic mayonnaise.

Paella de Montaña les Panolles
(Rice with Chicken and *Chorizo*)

> *Ingredients (serves 4)*
> 675g (1½lb) chicken, cut into pieces
> 225g (8oz) chorizo, sliced
> 100g (4oz) lean pork, diced
> 100g (4oz) fat ham, diced
> 50g (2oz) each of parboiled green beans and green peas
> 50g (2oz) peeled, de-seeded and chopped tomatoes
> 1 red pepper
> 350g (12oz) rice
> garlic to taste
> olive oil and saffron
> salt and pepper

Method Lightly fry the chicken pieces, *chorizo*, ham and pork in olive oil. When they are golden, remove them and in the same oil fry the onions and garlic, then add the diced pepper and tomatoes. Cook for three minutes, stirring well and adding more oil if necessary. Now add the rice, mix thoroughly and then pour in 450 ml (¾ pint) of boiling water. Add enough saffron, steeped in a little hot water, to colour and flavour the rice. Stir in the other vegetables and put the chicken and other meats on top. Season with salt and pepper. Cook gently until all the liquid is absorbed.

Salchichas con Judías
(*Salchichas* with beans)
This dish is both simple and delicious. You boil the required amount of soaked haricot beans and set them aside. This could be done the day before. Fry the *salchichas* gently in butter and when they are done place them in a fireproof dish in the oven to keep warm. Then fry the beans in the butter in which the *salchichas* were cooked, adding more butter if necessary. Stir them and shake the pan to prevent sticking. When they are golden brown, mix them with the *salchichas* and serve very hot, sprinkled with parsley and chives.

Swiss Dish

Kräuterwurst à la Montreux
Leeks are cut into short lengths and boiled in water for five
minutes. They are drained and laid on the bottom of a pan
with the sausage on top. Some rich brown gravy is poured over
and the pan is then simmered for about half an hour. This dish
can be served with a few boiled potatoes.

Making Your Own Sausages

Making your own sausages is quite hard work, but, if you enjoy pottering about the kitchen, it is also most satisfying. Cooking dishes in which sausages feature as a main ingredient, from toad-in-the-hole to *cassoulet*, can be extremely interesting, but this is not sausage-making. The real fascination comes from chopping, blending and flavouring the ingredients and then filling the farce into the right casing. The enormous variety of meats, herbs and spices, the wide range of textures, from diced chunks to smooth paste, the many different sorts and sizes of casings, alternative methods of preserving . . . all these things— let alone personal taste—prevent any sausage recipe from being definitive. The sausage-maker must experiment. The recipes for making sausages in this book should be regarded as basic instructions for making individual products; but we think that with such a diffuse subject some general guidelines are essential.

Hygiene

Sausages are no more and no less a hazard to health than any other meat product. Botulism, tapeworms and *trichiniasis* are not solely attributable to sausages. The only recorded death which resulted from a perfectly pure sausage was due to asphyxia caused by swallowing it whole. However, if raw meat has been subjected to chopping or mincing, blending with other ingredients and being pushed down into a length of gut, it runs rather more risk of contamination than, say, a joint of beef which is taken straight from the fridge to the oven. So first see that everything you use, from your own hands to the nut on the spindle of the mincer, is scrupulously clean; scald all implements and scrub before and after use.

With fresh sausages there is one other danger: under-cooking. Dr Robin Pulvertaft, the eminent pathologist, told us that there have been two explosive epidemics of *trichiniasis* in the last thirty years. Infestation by *trichina spiralis*, a parasite living in muscular and other tissues, is usually spread by rats and occurs in isolated cases. However, the two epidemics, one in Wolverhampton and one in Liverpool, each involved about 100 cases, and *they were all women*. 'This puzzling fact', said Dr Pulvertaft, 'was eventually explained. Instead of meat paste, women, it appears, sometimes use raw sausage meat. In both epidemics, women in factories had eaten sandwiches made in this way.' Dr Pulvertaft used to tell his students that 'this selective infestation is nowadays one of the few reliable ways of distinguishing women from men'. *Trichina spiralis* is killed by heat, so to be on the safe side, make sure all fresh sausages are well cooked. Walls advise 30 minutes for unpricked sausages.

We would suggest that you first try your hand at making fresh sausages. Not only can you taste the result soon after they are made, but we have found they are much easier. Also, as some fresh sausages are lightly salted and air-dried or smoked, you can practise on a small scale using the techniques required for the larger sausages for long-term keeping.

Ingredients

Sausages can be made out of almost any part of any animal, although pork is the best known. Some sausages require obscure pieces of offal, such as mesentery. Chitterling, tripe, lights and cow's udders are also found in some recipes. There is nothing wrong with this. If you like tripe, use tripe, but see that it is well dressed. If you want to incorporate some of the lesser known organs of an animal in your sausage, you may have to go to the local abattoir, or order them specially from your butcher. Personally, we find it is rarely worth the trouble.

Scraps and trimmings *can* be used, but they have usually been removed from a good piece of meat because they contain gristle, sinew, or—that horror of every child—'pipes'. It is, therefore, worth bearing in mind that the better the meat, the better the sausage.

Fat is an essential ingredient of all sausages, but until one comes to make sausages one does not fully appreciate the different kinds of fat: the hard back fat and soft belly fat of the pig for instance, and how this differs from beef suet. While you need not always stick meticulously to the quantities set out, it is not advisable to change the kind of fat that is specified. Leaf and flare fat are soft: flead is mesenteric fat from veal or beef. Hard back fat from a pig is most often used. Everybody in England will tell you that some form of binder is necessary. Most people on the Continent of Europe will disagree. In *Dainty Dishes* which was published in 1866, Lady Harriett St Clair's recipes for pork, beef and veal sausages contain no binder whatsoever. This may be partly due to the fact that the fresher the meat the better it binds: its powers of absorbing moisture decline steadily from the time of slaughter. And one must not forget that, apart from helping to bind, water and cereal are the basic ways of increasing commercial yield. We have found that a little breadcrumb actually does improve the taste of some sausages. Kipper sausage is an example. One seems to need something to hold the fat. We have, however, only met one good pork pie and sausage-maker who says that the 65% meat laid down by law for pork sausages is too high, although a number of English pork butchers say they find French sausages too rich.

Eggs may be used instead of bread to bind, although they won't absorb water, but most professionals have had to abandon bread anyhow. Although the original 100-year-old recipe for Tunbridge Wells sausages included bread, our friend Vernon Schiller wondered if this could still be the case. Modern methods of baking bread make it difficult to eradicate the effects of the yeast. We checked with Mr Hill and found that he had indeed been forced to substitute rusk since the end of World War II. If you are a home baker and want to use breadcrumbs, why not do so? You should soak and squeeze them to get rid of anything that might impair the sausage. One would have thought that yeast would be killed in the cooking, but apparently badly baked bread can still ruin a good sausage, and not only in the obvious way of making it stodgy, but by the yeast spoiling its keeping quality. Rusk is the most popular binder in commercial production today, not only because it is yeast-free, but because it can absorb up to its own weight in water.

The Swedes use potatoes, and farina, which is another name for potato flour, is found in a number of recipes, but it does not absorb water as readily as rusk and therefore is not so popular with manufacturers.

All we can say is *experiment*, but start with a little and gradually increase the amount of rusk or bread or potato until you have what best suits you.

Equipment

Having chosen the type of sausage you are going to make and assembled all the ingredients, you must decide whether you are going to chop or mince the meat. Mincing is usually quicker and easier, but it tends to squeeze out the juices. Some high-speed electric mincers have another disadvantage; if the meat, whether it is lean or fat, has any skin or sinew in it, the machine is apt to spin these into a web which clogs the cutting plates. Kenwood, however, do have an excellent sausage-making attachment, and, of course the speed on this machine is variable. On the whole we would advise using a mincer to obtain a fine consistency, and mincing the ingredients more than once when a smooth paste is required, as for liver sausage. For a coarser mixture we suggest that you chop; and when the cubes of fat, tongue or ham are needed, the meat should be diced. For the finest paste, you must use a pestle after the final mincing. Most hand mincers are provided with different-sized cutting plates. The holes in these range from circles 3mm (⅛ in) diameter, to oblongs almost 2.5 cm (1 in) in length. The 3 mm (⅛ in), 5 mm (³/₁₆ in) and 9 mm (⅜ in) are the most useful.

The old English chopper was a square blade with a horizontal handle directly above, joined to it either by a central neck or at each end. It was used on a chopping board which had a raised fillet round three sides to prevent the crumbs falling off. We use a French rocking chopper (*hachoir*) which is crescent-shaped with a vertical handle at each end. One of the good points about sausage-making is the simplicity of the equipment needed. If you don't have a chopper, you can make do with a knife. Chopping, mincing and slicing can be speeded up by using a food processor; in fact, it will be accomplished so quickly that there is a danger of meat being too finely chopped. Furthermore, food processors do not include any means of filling the casing.

If you have not got a sausage-stuffing attachment for your mincer, you, can either use an old-fashioned sausage funnel, thumbing the forcemeat down into the casing, or—which is much easier—you can get a Catermaster 'Syssyl' sausage-making kit. This will probably be cheaper in the long run as funnels are very difficult to find. The kit consists of a cylinder with a nozzle and a plunger—a cross between an icing syringe and a grease gun. You fit a pointed plastic cover over the nozzle and slide the empty skin or casing over it so that it lies, wrinkled like a concertina, along the neck of the nozzle. The cylinder is filled with the sausage meat, and the plastic nozzle cap removed. Push the plunger down into the cylinder and the meat will begin to appear. It is better to wait until this moment before tying a knot at the end of the casing. If you tie it too soon you will get a balloon of air at the end of the sausage. Sausages can be made in links of any length by twisting the casing or tying it with thread. We found this gadget invaluable; but the person who has put this apparatus through the most comprehensive test must be Sheila Black who has used it to make sausages containing eggs and bacon, curry and rice and even fruit—as described on page 150. So successful was this gadget that Mark II is now available, more elegant, easier to clean and with a beechwood plunger.

Catermasters, whose address is West Street, Dunster, Somerset, TA24 5N, also sell sausage seasoning, two sizes of natural casing and a black-pudding mix. This firm was started by a man whose experience includes twenty-one years with the Fatstock Marketing Corporation as By-Products Manager. He is assisted by his son, who studied at the Birmingham College of Food and Domestic Arts. 'Syssyl', believe it or not, stands for 'Stuff Yourself Some Sausages You'll Love'! It struck us as highly improbable that someone coined that catch-phrase and then found the initials spelt Syssyl, so we asked Catermasters for the origin. After World War II an American business school organized a course on Salesmanship. The slogan on the brochure was: 'Don't sell the sausage—sell the sizzle.'

Seasonings

Having prepared the meat, one comes to the seasoning. If one is surprised by the range of meat that can be used, one is astounded by the variety of spices, condiments, herbs and liquids which are used to add flavour. One firm which supplies pork butchers, boasts that it can provide 4,000 different seasonings: This probably refers to blends, as spice merchants mix blends to their customers' own specifications. Malory might well have had sausage making in mind when, in *Morte d'Arthur*, he wrote '. . . and therewithal there was such a savour as all the spicery of the world had been there'. The home sausage-maker has to be very selective. You can, if you like, rely on Catermasters' blend, but if you want to experiment, we would suggest considering the matter under the following headings.

Spices, Herbs and Condiments

No one, as far as we know, can be categorical about these; all three overlap.

We must begin with salt; it is after all, the origin of the word sausage. Salt has been used as a preserving agent for thousands

of years, but this function will be covered elsewhere. Salt which
is used to add flavour can be bought in several forms. We like
sea salt or bay salt best. The difference between the two is that
sea salt is the result of artificially evaporated sea water, while
bay salt comes from evaporation by the sun. Both have more
tang than table salt, which is usually adulterated by magnesium
carbonate to prevent it clogging in damp weather. It is very
damp near the coast in North Devon and even keeping the
salt-box right above the Rayburn does not always keep the sea
or bay salt in good condition. However, a few grains of rice
added to the salt ensures perfect dryness. These salts are ideal
for flavouring sausages, though they are more expensive than
block or kitchen salt. Kitchen salt is refined pure salt and
usually comes from Cheshire. As a child it was a joy to be
allowed to break down the block, as big as a sandwich loaf, and
make it ready for the salt-box; for although it had eventually to
be reduced to powder, one could carve the block with a kitchen
knife into all sorts of fascinating shapes during the process.

Saltpetre—potassium nitrate—is used simply to give the
meat a pleasant pink appearance. Sal Prunella is sometimes
used for the same purpose. Either should be used very sparingly,
as they tend to make the meat hard, although this is not so
noticeable in minced meat as it is in large pieces.

Seasoning really begins to diversify when it comes to pepper.
First there are the black and white, and more recently, people
in this country have discovered the green variety. All three are
the berry of *piper negrum*, used at different stages of ripeness.
Green peppercorns are the youngest. Black are the most
aromatic and are ground with the husk still clinging to the
berry. White peppercorns are the oldest and strongest and are
stripped to their essentials. At St Chamond, which is about
50km south-west of Lyon, they make a delicious *saucisson pur
porc garanti, spécialité du poivre vert*, which contains whole green
peppercorns. Black and white corns are used unground in a
number of *salami* and similar sausages. For fresh sausages it is
better to grind your pepper as you want it. You can buy ready-
ground white pepper when a very fine powder is required, but
with black pepper the aroma disappears too quickly if it is

pre-ground. The French grind black and white peppercorns together—perhaps someone is already adding green peppercorns to the combination.

Both sweet and hot peppers belong to the *capsicum* family, of which there are fifty varieties. Hungarian paprika and Spanish pimento are examples. *Capsicum annuum* is never very hot and can be mild or sweet. *Capsicum acuminatum*, from which cayenne is made, is particularly hot, even more so than *capsicum frutescens*. Chili pepper usually comes from *capsicum baccatum*, although some varieties are made from *capsicum acuminatum*.

Allspice may sound like a mixture, but in fact is is *pimenta officinalis*, or Jamaica pepper, which combines the characteristic flavours of nutmeg, cinnamon and cloves. Mace is used extensively in sausage-making. It comes from the outer covering of the nutmeg, and the latter can be substituted when mace is not available. Ginger, cloves, coriander, cardamom, cumin and aniseed are also used. The most common blend of spices used in France is called *quatre épices*, but even here the formula varies. *Larousse* gives one recipe which is 62% white pepper, 18% nutmeg, 15% ginger and 5% powdered cloves. Jane Grigson gives 70% pepper or allspice, 10% cloves, 10% cinnamon and 10% nutmeg; and we are told that the current formula contains not four, but five spices; 62% white pepper, 13% ginger, 13% nutmeg, 7% cinnamon and 5% cloves. In this book we refer to *quatre épices* as French spice.

Saffron seems to provide the link between herbs and spices; it is a remarkable product. Over 5,000 flowers of the autumn crocus, *crocus sativus*, are needed to provide 30g of saffron. Only the pistils and stamens can be used and they have to be dried. Jane Grigson says that it used to be grown at Saffron Walden in Essex and at Stratton, which is just over the Cornish border, a few miles from where we live. But for many years the Cornish have considered that the best saffron comes from Valencia. As it is so expensive, it is much imitated; so, unless you know your supplier, never buy it in powdered form, as this may well contain turmeric or arnica, or both.

The most important herb to the sausage-maker is garlic. If you hate the taste you might as well give up all idea of making

those sausages which are eaten raw, for there are very few
which are not improved by a little garlic, and we like a lot. The
other members of the same family—onions, shallots, and even
chives—all find their place in *boudins* and *crépinettes*, black and
white puddings and faggots; but you will see from some of the
recipes that onions are not to be recommended for 'keeping'
sausages as they are liable to go sour.

Sage is the most traditional herb to be found in British
sausages. It not only enhances the flavour of pork, but blends
well with both onion and breadcrumb; so, when making pork
sausages, if you feel you must add bread, you could do worse
than add a little sage and onion stuffing.

Rosemary and thyme give a pleasant bite to some sausages,
while basil—apart from its individual flavour—is supposed to
keep flies away. Sorrel is rarely used, but when you come
across it, you should remember that like tarragon, there are
two varieties. Russian tarragon is much milder than the French
variety and not nearly so tangy, but with sorrel you can use
either the French or the common variety. The French is less
acid. A sausage-maker in San Francisco uses tarragon, chives,
basil and parsley in his pork sausages, and orange and green
peppers in a *boudin* made of duck breasts.

In Britain one usually finds the curly-leaved variety of parsley,
but some people prefer the flat-leaved kind, amongst whom are
the Turkish community in England who buy parsley specially
flown in from Cyprus. A friend of ours who lives in London
says that you will find it fresh in Cypriot shops on Thursdays,
ready for the Muslim day of rest. She also tells us that the
reason this variety is not grown in England is because it
resembles a very poisonous plant.

Fennel is sometimes used. Indeed it is essential for that
tuscan speciality, *finocchiona*, and we never realized how subtle
a flavour fennel can provide until we tasted this delicious
salame.

Tansy is the traditional herb used in *drisheen*, and also keeps
flies away. Pennyroyal is found in old recipes. In fact, its country
name, 'pudding grass' is testimony of its culinary use. Juniper
berries, pistachio nuts and sesame seed are all to be found in one

recipe or another. Truffles are a luxury. There are five varieties, but we are concerned with only two, the black and the white. The French consider the black fungus, *tuber melanosporum*, from Perigord and the Lot, to be the finest, but those who have been to the Truffle Fair at Albi will know that the Italian white truffle, *tuber magnalum*, is also delicate and delicious. When we were there, they were fetching over £130 per kilogramme. During the Fair, which lasts for two weeks and takes place at the beginning of October, the local restaurants each in turn put on a special dinner featuring the truffle, for under £5 a head. This included an aperitif, wine, and often a *grappa* as well. Several of the menus included *cotechino, salsiccia* and *cacciatorino*; so the sausage can still hold its place in a gourmet's feast.

Listing the seasonings, as we have done, will give you little idea of proportions. As we have said, the amounts you use is entirely a matter of taste, but the ratio of salt and pepper to other spices and herbs is very marked. It would be impossible to scale down trade seasoning recipes for domestic use, because we would be using minute amounts. So we will give you a butcher's recipe, and after the salt and pepper, it must become a pinch of this or a sprinkling of that, according to your own taste.

In the following recipes 15g (½oz) of the seasoning should be added to each 450g (1lb) of sausage meat. The proportions are approximate:

Yorkshire Sausage Seasoning
30% ground white pepper, 1.75% ground mace, 1.75% ground nutmeg, 0.50% ground cayenne, 66% fine salt.

Epping Sausage Seasoning
15% ground white pepper, 2% ground sage, 2% ground ginger, 1% ground cayenne, 80% fine salt.

Manchester Sausage Seasoning
16% ground white pepper, 2% ground mace, 2% ground nutmeg, 4% ground ginger, 3% ground sage, 3% ground cloves, 70% fine salt.

Cumberland Sausage Seasoning
24% ground white pepper, 1% ground cayenne, 1% ground nutmeg, 74% fine salt.

Beer, Wine and Spirits

Finally we come to liquid flavouring. Fresh sausages require more liquid than one would expect. In fact, our first attempts, with both fresh and 'keeping' sausages, were much too dry. We have experimented with cider but have not yet found the exact proportion to give a well-balanced flavour. Perhaps cider is not a good flavouring agent, yet apples and pork go so well together that one feels it should be. Calvados, too, is worth trying. The French use cognac in some sausages, and Alexandre Dumas used anis to flavour *andouillettes*. Whisky can go into haggis, and although we have not included beer in any sausages we have made—the question of yeast again—one of our favourite ways of cooking them is called Tudor Sausages (see page 41) which includes beer. Wine, of course, is found amongst the ingredients of many different types of *salame*, and some fresh sausages, such as the Cypriot sausage from Paphos. The Chinese always include wine in their product. While wine can be used in both fresh and dried sausages, it would seem that hard liquor is best used in hard sausages.

Casings

Most people talk about sausage 'skins', but professionals refer to them as 'casings'. What is more, purist prefer the terms 'hog' and 'ox' to 'pig' and 'beef'. There is literally no part of the alimentary canal which is not used as an envelope for sausages, from weasand, the lining of the gullet, to bung (the last section of the intestine); stomach, caul and pig's bladder, all are used for one mixture or another. But today weasands are rarely used, because they are difficult to get.

These are natural casings. There is no need to know in any

detail how they are prepared. It is a highly skilled and complicated craft, often found in the hands of descendants of German
families who came to England after the Franco-Prussian War.
If you have or want to do the whole thing yourself, you will find
Self-Sufficiency, by John and Sally Seymour, most helpful. It is
interesting to know which casings are traditionally used for
each type of sausage. As N. V. Wheeler wrote in the *Meat
Trade Journal*, the intestine 'is not just a waste disposal unit,
but more essentially a protein recoverer . . .' and he went on to
point out that gut is a remarkable substance, invaluable to
guitarists, tennis players and ophthalmic surgeons.

Gysin & Hanson (96 Trundleys Road, Deptford, London,
SE8 5JG) supply natural casings for home sausage-making,
and their mail order price lists contain some useful information
on calibres and what lengths are needed for a given weight of
finished product. A summary is given opposite.

Instructions and recipes are included with the order and
seasoning is included with the hog and sheep casings. Actually
this firm supplies seasonings for 24 different sausages to the
trade, including those for *chorizos*, *cabanos*, saveloys and venison
sausages.

As anyone who has been given a tough, wrinkled sausage to
eat must know, not all casings are made of natural gut. Artificial
casings go back to the 1930s when cellulose was first used.
Many of the slicing sausages today have plastic casings. The
collagen casing, which is made of reconstituted hide and is
edible, gives the manufacturer the advantage of a constant
diameter and thickness, which is well suited to mass production.
Natural casings vary in strength, porosity, and diameter. In a
supplement to the magazine *Meat*, W. C. Anstis wrote, 'A
Devon long-wool, off good pasture in a soft water area, which
has had plenty of sun on its back, will produce a wider,
stronger, clearer, fleshier casing than a Welsh lamb off the hills
. . . after a long rainy spell.'

Messrs Walls have experimented with a co-extrusion process,
that is, extruding a sausage through a nozzle and at the same
time extruding a substance which forms the casing through an
annular aperture situated round the nozzle. The sausage is

Type	Diameter approx. mms	ins	Usual use	Weight of finished product kgs	lbs	Length needed metres	yards
HOG CASINGS			Pork, beef and Cumberland, bratwurst, boerewors, kielbasa, kishka, savaloys, bierschinken, etc.				
Narrow	32	1¼					
Medium	32–38	1¼–1½					
Wide	38–42	1½–1¾					
Extra Wide	42+	1¾+		9	20	23	25
HOG FAT ENDS (or HOG BUNGS IN USA)	50 approx	2 approx	Liver sausage, hard cervelat, braunschweiger			Sold in full lengths in GB but 24″ (60cm) lengths in USA)	
CHITTERLING used as ingredient	N/A	N/A	Andouilles, andouillettes		N/A	N/A	
BEEF or OX CASINGS							
Runners	35–48	1⅜–1⅞	Black pudding, White pudding, Bologna etc.	14	30	17½	20
Middles	45–55	1¾–2⅛	Cornish hog's pudding, salami, Knackwurst, cervelat	18½	30 40	17½	20
Bungs	75–150	3–6	Haggis, copocolla, large Bologna etc.	5½	12	Cut to size Full length 1–2 m	
SHEEP CASINGS			Chipolatas, bockwurst, frankfurters, Bavarian bratwurst etc.			Number of links	
Narrow	16–18	⅝				32	
Medium	18–20	¾				16	
Wide	20–22	⅞				14	
Extra Wide	22–24	1				12	

then passed through a solution which makes the substance cling to the forcemeat.

We consider excessive uniformity a bore, and this includes artificial casings for sausages. But our preference is not merely based on such a frivolous reason. Natural casings are stronger, more permeable and taste better than the artificial ones we have come across. Maybe we have been unlucky, but when we have grilled these sausages the casing sometimes becomes almost inedible, and when fried they have stuck to the pan. Even when cooked in a sauce, the artificial skin seems to become tough and the flavours do not blend well. Perhaps the skins are waterproof? Certainly one can sometimes see the fat bubbling inside the casing.

For smoked or salted slicing sausages, natural casings are best as they absorb salt and phenols much more readily than artificial ones, and they are also much more elastic, which is important when so much shrinkage occurs.

There is also the question of shape. Natural casings give a pleasing curve, best appreciated in fresh sausages, and the tighter the packing, the more pronounced the curve becomes. The artificial casing is always straight and sometimes the links are not even twisted. It is as if a blunt guillotine came down and pressed the ends together so that they are wedged-shape. We do not like this. However, the makers of most of the dry sausages such as *salami*, string these so that the curve will be straightened out for easier slicing. The sausages can be twisted to form links, or tied tightly with twine. The Chinese use straw. In the slicing sausages the twine is used to form links as well as to straighten the natural curve. The twine runs longitudinally down the outside of the sausage, the strings on the outside of the curve being the tightest; and also latitudinally, round and round the sausage. Sometimes tapes are used, binding the sausage diagonally along its length and then returning in the opposite direction so that it is 'cross-gartered'. There is also a ready-made net which can be used; but only by stringing each sausage individually can you get the pressure right to straighten the curve and maintain a rugged individuality. The more rugged and rustic *salami* and *saucissons secs* are, the more appetizing they look. You feel that you are going to get an individual product, not a mass-produced stereotype.

Synthetic casings may well dominate the popular undiscriminating convenience-food market, but we doubt if they will ever be adopted by the craftsmen. In the USA, natural casings are always used for the highest quality sausages—and they are, therefore, an expensive luxury—which is all to the good.

Salting

With the sausage safely encased, we come to the question of preservation. Fresh Sausages, as I have already said, are, in England—but not in many other countries—allowed a certain amount of preservative. This does nothing to enhance the flavour so is of little use to the home sausage-maker, who, if the product is not to be eaten straight away, can usually put it in the deep freeze. We are more concerned here with the slicing sausages, usually eaten raw, and their preserving methods include salting, air-drying, smoking, and, in some cases, cooking.

Cooking by itself does slightly prolong the life of a sausage. Usually this amounts to parboiling, and it is sometimes necessary to consolidate the ingredients before embarking on further methods of preservation. It is most frequently used in German sausages.

Salting, which is the basic method of preserving, goes back to well before the time of Christ. It can be wet or dry, the former involving a solution of brine. Sometimes, one or more of the ingredients of the forcemeat is salted before chopping and mixing. There are many different mixtures used in both dry salting and in brines. One American recipe lists ten different ingredients which may be excellent for ham and sides of bacon, but are quite unnecessary for sausages. In sausage-making you get the flavour you want by blending the actual ingredients. This is impossible with a ham which cannot be reconstituted, so the joint has to absorb flavour and thereafter the cure becomes all-important.

The most complicated cure you are ever likely to need for sausage is *Italian brine*. This consists of 1kg (2lb) sea salt to 1.5 litres (2½ pints) each of water and white wine, 50g (2oz) saltpetre and 25g (1oz) bicarbonate of soda, with spices added to taste.

In Scotland and the West Country beer is sometimes used to take the place of the wine and water. Sal Prunella is an alternative to saltpetre, but does not contribute to the preserving; it merely gives a pinkish colour to the meat. If you do not want to use wine or beer, you can make a brine with 1.75 litres (3 pints) of water, boiled with 225g (8oz) sea salt, the same amount of sugar and 25g (1oz) of saltpetre. For the technically minded, what is needed is a brine between 80% and saturation point. The amount of salt needed to reach saturation varies slightly with the temperature, but at 20°C (68°F), 100 parts of water will absorb up to 35.8 parts of salt by weight. In an 80% solution an egg or a raw, peeled potato will just float.

An important point to remember when using brine is that the solution tends to be stronger at the bottom than at the top, so it needs 'overhauling' or stirring up, every three or four days.

Dry-salting is simpler. It consists of rubbing the sausage with salt, saltpetre and spices; but this does draw the moisture out of the meat, and, since we have found that sausages tend to be too dry, we prefer to use a brine. The time a sausage is left in the brine depends on its type, whether it is to be smoked and how you intend to keep it. A Swedish dried sausage, such as *linköping*, may be dry-salted for two weeks or left in brine for one.

But *medvurst* and *fläskkorv* are dry-salted for as little as two days, in a mixture of 4 tablespoons of salt, 2 tablespoons of sugar and ½ tablespoon of saltpetre. A commercial dry cure may consist of up to 75% salt, with 24% sugar and 1% saltpetre.

Värmslandskorv is rubbed with a curing mixture, and left until the next day. Sometimes it is kept in brine for several days if it is not to be cooked and eaten right away. Light has a bad effect on the fat in curing, so the salter should always be well covered. Nowadays, plastic bowls have supplanted the great old earthenware receptacles; but you can still find the latter at farm sales, and also smaller crocks, which are useful if you are not salting a lot of meat.

Smoking and Drying

Air-drying alone takes considerably longer than smoking. Some Italian *salami* may be left in the Mediterranean air for as long as eight months. Smoking is in the English tradition, but one must remember that farmhouse recipes for curing and smoking are basically designed to preserve, so they are much stronger in flavour than those to which we are accustomed. The turnover in bacon and ham, for instance, is so enormous now that there is no need to ensure that it will keep for a long period, so curing and smoking are much milder than they used to be. Actually, some commercial products are not smoked at all. When a smoke-oven can cost £10,000, one can see why a firm may be tempted to give a product a smoky flavour by synthetic means which have no preserving qualities whatsoever. We have found one or two recipes in which a smoke-powder called 'Reekie' is added to the ingredients. You will not find them in this book.

Before smoking, sausages are usually left to dry for a day or so in an airy place with a temperature of about 15°C (60°F). Remember that a sausage can lose as much as half its weight in drying and smoking.

The smoke from all hardwoods is good, but on no account should any kind of fir or pine be used because the resin produces a pronounced flavour of turpentine. Wood smoke contains formaldehyde, alcohols, and phenols (or tar). Apple-wood has a sweet smoke and may be better than oak or beech, but we cannot honestly say that it makes much difference. Our smoking is done up the chimney of an open hearth. It is impossible to give specific times, because obviously a smaller chimney would give a more concentrated volume of smoke, thereby allowing the sausage to absorb the phenols more quickly. How steadily, and at what rate, the smoke rises will also affect the length of time a sausage should remain up the chimney. The figures given in this book should only be regarded as a guide, and you must experiment with your own chimney or smoke-house until you get the best results.

Ideally, sausages should be 3.5 metres (10ft) above the flame, as there is a danger of the fat going rancid if it gets too hot. It is for this reason that most home-smoking should be confined to the cool-smoked method, with a temperature not higher than 20–30°C (68–86°F). A hot smoke (95°–105°C or 200°–250°F) will produce a smoky flavour in three to four hours, while it will take two to three days with a cool smoke. We have found that hardwood sawdust lessens the heat. Humidity, weather, temperature and the size of the sausage will also affect the duration of the smoking process. In Pennsylvania, Weaver's Lebanon Bolognas hang in the smoke of specially cured timber from four to six days. Other recipes give four to six weeks.

If you have not got a convenient chimney then you will have to construct your own smoke-house. Some people make one out of a barrel with both ends knocked out, raised on bricks and the top covered with damp sacking. There are several ingenious ideas on home-made smoke-ovens in *The Home Book of Smoke Cooking* by Jack Sleight and Raymond Hull, including the conversion of an old refrigerator.

Should you simply want to give your sausages a smoky flavour, without any keeping qualities, then there is a Scandinavian smoke-box, which burns different aromatic sawdusts with methylated spirits, and has proved very satisfactory. This costs only a few pounds.

When hanging in the air, even after smoking, sausages sometimes become covered with a greenish mould. It is quite harmless and should be brushed off, or wiped with a cloth dipped in vinegar. Do not confuse this mould with 'white flowers', which are yeasts, and since they play an important part in the maturing process, these should on no account be wiped off. In air-dried sausages, these should appear in four to six weeks.

Storage

The deep freeze is not a good place for storing salted and smoked meat for long periods. The traditional method of hanging hams, bacon and dry sausages in the fresh air of a larder works well as long as the air is cool, dry and moving. It does not work at all in stagnant air, and if this is damp as well the situation becomes hopeless. On the other hand, one can store such produce by burying it. According to the Ministry of Agriculture, kiln-dried salt, slaked lime, charcoal, wood ash, malt culms, oat hulls or meal must be free from mice and mites. We have not tried burying sausages, but in Valloire they keep sausages in ashes for about a year.

We have two final tips. First, an old saying which runs: 'In love and sausages only one thing is required—perfect confidence.' And if the results are so successful that your friends ask how you make them, reply by quoting Mark Twain: 'If you like sausages and love the law, never ask how either is made.'

The pages which follow contain a number of recipes for making different sorts of sausage, both simple and elaborate. The index to them can be found on p. 248.

Introducing the Sausages
of the World

Sausages, like everything else, reflect national characteristics. Some of these are shared by a number of different sausages, yet it would be tiresome in the extreme to mention them each time they occur under a different product in the alphabetical list. So here we will set out geographical differences and define regional terms, starting with Europe.

Sausages fall into three main categories in Europe. Great Britain could be added as a fourth, but such a high proportion of its many varieties originated on the Continent that we consider it best to limit the main categories to France, Germany and Italy. If one lumped England, Scotland and Wales together, one would be equally justified in introducing a fifth category for Denmark, Norway and Sweden. More important than classifying sausages, however, is the need to appreciate the number of different countries which make the same sausage. *Kabanos*, which is Polish in origin, is now made in Belgium; *kolbasa*, another East European product, is manufactured in the United States; and frankfurters are made all over the world. This is not always plagiarism: frequently the towns in which a certain sausage was first made have, in the course of history, belonged to several different countries. The country to which each sausage is ascribed is defined by contemporary boundaries, not those which prevailed when the product was developed, nor under all the places where it is now manufactured.

Historically, Germany and Italy have followed a similar pattern. Before 1871, there was no German nation, merely a handful of independent kingdoms, and the dominating influence was the Hapsburg dynasty, whose empire stretched far beyond the Austrian border, from Belgrade in the south almost as far as Dresden to the north, and from Brasov in the Carpathians, westward to the Swiss border, and, in isolated pockets even further, to the shores of the North Sea. In 1795, Cracow was on the Austrian frontier, so it is really quite natural to find *Krakauer* in Viennese shops, and also *kolbasa* for that matter. It is, however, extremely hard to say which today should be called Austrian and which German; let alone Italian, Hungarian, Polish, Czechoslovakian and so on. We may have attributed some German sausages to Austria, and some Austrian ones to other countries. If this is so, we can only hope to be forgiven.

Although names such as *Regensburger, Braunschweiger, Frankfurter* and so on denote their birthplace, the fact that they are now made in many other places as well—like Cambridge sausages in England—means that original recipes have been adapted to suit conditions in other localities. If the nationalities of some sausages seem doubtful, at least the types can be easily categorized. German and Austrian sausages fall into three main groups; the *brühwurst*, the *rohwurst* and the *kochwurst*.

Brühwurst are scalded by the manufacturer. They are usually lightly smoked before scalding, but they are not meant for keeping. They should be stored in a refrigerator in the same way as fresh English sausages. *Frankfurters, bockwurst* and *bierschinken* are some of the varieties which are classified as *brühwurst*. Boiling or steaming is the most usual way of cooking them, or heating them up in their cans; *bratwurst*, however, is an exception, it should be fried or grilled, and for this reason is sometimes put into a category of its own.

Rohwurst is a keeping sausage. It is made of raw meat which is cured, air-dried and/or smoked. German *salame* is an obvious example, and *mettwurst, landjäger, plockwurst* and *teewurst* are others. Although most *rohwurst* are sliced before eating, some are soft enough to be spread on bread or toast.

Kochwurst is literally a cooked sausage. It is not merely scalded but boiled or steamed for quite a long time, but this does not mean that it is more suitable for keeping. The many different liver sausages come under this heading and so do the

German versions of black, and white, puddings. In the farce of many *kochwurst* you will find large chunks of meat—tongue in *zungenwurst*, bacon in *Berliner rotwurst* for instance. Some are suitable for spreading, some for slicing, and they are usually eaten cold.

Most types of German sausage are forbidden by law to contain any form of cereal binder. When tradition demands the inclusion of any ingredients other than meat or seasoning, these have to be listed on the labels. The majority are 100% meat, seasoned with herbs and spices. One important point to remember is that in Germany, beef is more expensive than pork, and a beef sausage is usually considered superior to one made of pork.

The Germans claim that the sausage was invented in their country. Whether this pre-dates the Romans is difficult to establish. The Roman Empire included quite a lot of what is now Germany in any case. Certainly they were eaten extensively there in the Middle Ages, and since then German sausages, in all their amazing variety, have enjoyed a wide and well-deserved popularity. There is no better place to see and sample this magnificent array than at Alois Dallmayr's store in Diener-strasse, between Maximilianstrasse and Marienplatz, in Munich. This shop, a sort of Fortnum-cum-Jackson but with a character very much its own, has a history which goes back 300 years, although it was not until 1870 that it came into the hands of Alois Dallmayr. Twenty-five years later he sold the business to Anton Randlkofer, and his grandson is still a partner in the enterprise today. In the first decade of this century it carried the royal warrants of sixteen ruling houses in Europe. In this magnificent emporium you will find between 120 and 130 varieties of sausage.

The Germans say that they produce 1,458 different sausages, but this does not refer to types. It must, we think, cover the personal variations introduced by individual manufacturers. However many types there may be, at one time Germany certainly produced the biggest sausage in Europe, weighing 555kg (1,230lb). It contained four pigs, one-and-a-half cows and 50kg (100lb) of spice, so reported the *Sunday Express* on

27 March 1977. What type of sausage this was remains unrecorded.

The Austrian way of making sausage is on the basis of a *brät* (which is a mixture of finely minced beef, ice and additives) and blending this, in varying proportions, with pork, veal etc. This *brät* may form as little as 15% of the whole, as in the Austrian version of *schinkenwurst*, or as much as 75% in *Salzburgerwurst*. Anyone who wants to make Austrian sausages professionally should read *Osterreichisches Lebensmittelbuch: Fleisch und Fleischwaren*. There are two booklets, which between them list more than thirty main categories, and some of these categories contain as many as a score of recipes. One of the things that struck us about Austrian sausages is the variety of local *salami*. We should have remembered the extent of the Hapsburg dominions. Austrian *salami* are manufactured in very much the same way as Italian, Hungarian or Danish.

Although the Germans claims to have invented the sausage, the other day we were told quite seriously that it originated in China. But no matter where it came from, the Romans were responsible for introducing it to the furthermost corners of their empire. However, Latium is not now as famous for its sausages as Emilia-Romagna. Most, if not all Italian provinces, have their specialities, from Trentino—Alto Adige to Calabria; but the capital of Emilia-Romagna is Bologna, which for the sausage-hunter is the city of the blessed. *Salami, cacciatori, cotechini, salsiccie* and, of course, *mortadelle* confront one at every turn. Many of the citizens are only too pleased to provide information about their products. The difficulty comes in reconciling conflicting reports. The Italians are so self-confident that they are not interested in what the man in the next street says, let alone a man in a neighbouring province. In Tuscany we were told categorically that nowadays *salame* is never made purely of pork, but in Bologna and other cities we frequently found nothing *but* pork being used.

In Bologna, as in Genoa and elsewhere, the Regional Tourist Information office was most helpful. We were given introductions to the President of the Restaurateurs' Association in Bologna, the Publicity Department of the Trade Association and to a couple of manufacturers. The President of the Restaurateurs' Association was then Cavaliere Gino Mazzacurati (at whose restaurant, incidentally, you can eat the best *zampone* in Bologna, amongst other delicious food), but in spite of his backing, the Alcisa company refused to let us visit their factory. Two visits to the Association Salsamentari proved fruitless; the door was locked. An old woman who happened to be passing told us—if we understood her correctly—that 'they had gone away to the country, perhaps to a conference—who knows?' Our frustration was ameliorated by finding that bus rides were free during the day, and melted completely away when we visited the Salumerie Tamburini where we were welcomed with enthusiasm by Giovanni Tamburini the younger, and provided with a mass of information on how they made their *salami* and *mortadelle*.

Emilia-Romagna prides itself on the classical simplicity of its gastronomy. Pure ingredients of the highest quality with the minimum of added flavouring are the basis. The further south you go in Italy, the more highly spiced the sausages become. 'If you have the best meat in perfect condition,' said Signor Tamburini, 'you should not try to disguise the flavour; and the basic meat for *insaccata* is pork. The sequence, since before the Dark Ages, has been the same. Cows produce milk; buttermilk goes to the pigs; pigs are turned into sausages and other products'. He became almost poetic as he described the sea-breezes from the Mediterranean passing gently over the conifer-covered hills, and how this salty, resinous air is funnelled up the valleys to transform joints of pork into Parma hams, *capocolla* or *coppa* . . . *salami* . . . . But the balmy air is not the only requisite, the good earth of these parts produces particularly delicious meat, and the warmth of the sun is needed too. Here, in Emilia-Romagna, nature seems to have devoted all her artistry to producing the perfect pig, to whose flesh nothing should be added but salt, pepper and garlic. This makes the perfect *salame*.

A pure pork *salame* is indeed superb but, after eating it every day for a month or more, we found that we liked highly spiced sausages for a change. Unless one is an expert, with the palate of a wine-taster, one cannot possibly tell, as we were assured *cognoscenti* could, whether a pig had been reared on the northern or southern slope of a valley. However, we came to appreciate not only the pure classic product, but the wide variety of flavours from *finocchiona* to the more peppery *salami* of southern Italy.

Another enthusiast implored us to use the correct terminology. *Salami*, the word most frequently used in England, is plural. One should talk about a *salame*, which is singular. *Salamini* are small *salami*. *Salumerie* are places where you buy *salami*. *Salumifici* are manufacturers. All sausages—*salami, cacciatori, salsiccie, budini, zamponi* and so on—are *insaccata*, which quite simply means 'encased'.

The Italian influence can be traced, first, historically, when the Romans introduced the sausage in so many different ways. No sausage other than *salame* has been produced in such a wide variety of flavours and textures. In contrast to this, France has developed a great number of completely different types of sausage. With such profusion crowding the market, it is not difficult to appreciate why supporter clubs have sprung up. Examples are La Confrérie des Chevaliers du Goûte-Andouille de Jargeau, and La Confrérie des Chevaliers de Saint Antoine which is concerned with *charcuterie* as a whole, its interests including all kinds of sausage. In *Le Grand Livre des Sociétés et Confréries Gastronomiques de France*, Fernand Woutaz explains how St Antoine came to be associated with pigs. Until the twelfth century these animals were allowed to roam the streets of Paris and other towns, snuffling in the gutters for food. In 1131, one such hog caused the eldest son of Louis VI to be thrown from this horse and killed. From that day, pigs were banished from towns, except the twelve kept by the *Prieuré du Petit St Antoine*. They were allowed to continue scavenging so long as each wore a bell round its neck, engraved with the cross of St Antoine. The *Chevaliers* today wear round their necks an enamelled badge depicting the saint and a pig. Other more specialized societies include La Confrérie des Chevaliers du Goûte-Boudin de Montagne-au-Perche, and even a Club des Haggicheurs Maltés. The French have enjoyed a strong affinity with Scotland for centuries. The women seem particularly fond of wearing tartan, and the men of drinking whisky. In fact, one of the most comprehensive books on the subject— *Le Livre du Whisky*, winner of the Glenfiddich Award in 1976, is written by our old friend L. R. Dauven, in collaboration with Jacques Morlaine. The idea of Frenchmen solemnly dressing up in kilts and glengarries on 13 May to eat haggis astounds one. But if one detects a spirit of levity among the haggis eaters, one must remember that there are ninety or so other gastronomic societies, many of whose members take the role of gourmet very seriously indeed. Amongst the most distinguished are L'Académie Rabelais, whose members include such eminent gastronomes as Henry Clos-Jouve and Georges Prade, and L'Association Française de la Presse Gastronomique et Touristique.

Although the French make such delicious *charcuterie* of their own, they still buy English produce at Marks and Spencer's Paris shop. Whether this is because it is still fairly new, one does not know. We, in England, are eating an increasing amount of French sausages—and not only French. There has never before been such a variety of foreign sausages on sale in this country.

Although the main influences in Europe are Italian, French and German, we feel that at least passing reference should be made to the present position in Great Britain. The historical development has been sketched in the first section of this book. Today we have two distinct groups of professional sausage-makers, and a growing number of do-it-yourself enthusiasts. The main group consist of (a) large companies with a number of factories spread all over the country, and sometimes abroad, and, (b) the butchers and proprietors of pie shops. If the sausage-maker in this latter category is a craftsman, he has a good chance of remaining in business. If he is content to make sausages that simply conform to general standards, his prospects are not so bright. The big manufacturers are quite prepared to leave the craftsman alone. His share of the market is not very large and it would not pay them to compete. The more enlightened also realize that the craftsman stimulates interest in sausages in general. But the butcher who makes a run-of-the-mill product, or worse still, buys sausages made elsewhere and pretends they are his own, is fair game. The manufacturers would rather see their branded products, which are sometimes better than those produced by the small-town butcher, sold to the same public in a supermarket or cash-and-carry store.

When friends heard we were writing this book, time and time again they said, 'I hope you're going to mention the shops where you can still get a really good sausage . . . the one in Burford . . . that shop in York . . . the place in Portsmouth . . .' Alas! as it is impossible to include anything like a definitive list, we decided that Hill of Tunbridge Wells,* and our local manufacturers, would have to represent the traditional British sausage-maker. After all, if we started listing English shops, we would have to consider French *charcutiers* and so on. We quote a letter from Frank Hill on page 228, but we have not yet visited his shop. Our favourite butchers are on the other side of southern England, near the Cornish border.

In the square at Bradworthy, there is, at the time of writing, a butcher's shop with the name Cory on the fascia. There have been Corys in this part of Devon for many hundreds of years. Like Gifford and Galsworthy, some gave or took their names to or from the place where they lived. Whether John Cory of Cory, who was born in 1505, is an ancestor or not, we do not know, but his grandson started a Cory line in Bradworthy which is only three miles away, so it seems probable that there is some connection. Though the name is still used, Mary Cory married Vernon Schiller and it is they and their daughter Linda who spend every Tuesday making sausages and other products to take to Holsworthy market the following day. Here, in the Arcade, you will find a notice which reads:

* Subsequently sold to Dewhurst's

Yer Tis
Cory of Bradre*
Hog Pudden
Pork Sausages
Gerty Meat Pudden
an' they'm
Bootiful!

And they are. The sausages contain egg, and the casings are natural. You can see them being made any Tuesday. Vernon Schiller is perhaps typical of the craftsman. He is willing to experiment, and will talk sausages for hours. In the old days he might well have gone the way of Sarah Harris and created a business which became nationwide. In those days the railway was only six miles away; now the nearest station is at Barnstaple, which must be twenty-five miles or more, with a future which is far from assured. We are also fortunate in being fairly near Susan Edwards, who started from scratch and now makes up to 1,500lbs of sausages a week. You will find her base on the Highampton to Holsworthy road. Maybe she inherited her interest from her mother who used to cook for Winston Churchill.

Heal Farm, tucked away in an even more remote part of Devon, some six miles south-west of South Molton, specializes in ensuring the survival of rare breeds, such as the Gloucester Old Spot and Tamworth pigs, Red Ruby beef cattle and St Kilda sheep. All are reared naturally, without resorting to hormones. Here Ann Petch makes sausages, amongst other things. She started in 1980 and gradually increased her list of produce so that now she can offer 14 different kinds of sausage alone. Apart from some half-dozen varieties of pork sausages (both with and without rusk and preservative) you will find *salame Milanese, landjäger, chorizo*, venison and bacon, hog's pudding and smoked garlic sausages. Do not expect them to be cheap. Naturally reared animals take longer to mature, and you are getting the best meat without any padding of offal. As Ann

---

* This is roughly how Bradworthy is pronounced. Elision occurs in most place names ending in 'worthy'. Woolfardisworthy is pronounced, and sometimes written, Woolsery. A nearby farm used to be called Bugworthy, but when a new parson was shocked at being directed there, the name was changed.

Petch says, 'Our methods are as old-fashioned as our livestock, and you can taste the virtue of both.'

It looks as if the growing interest in sausages may well produce another type of sausage craftsman; the amateur who turns professional. Norman Parkinson is one example, and at the Devon County Agricultural Show one year we came across David James who has revived the Gloucester sausage.

Obviously, if one is going to write a book about sausages, one should visit a large factory, not that there is much difference in the way that fresh sausages are made on a commercial scale. The meat is generally minced, put in a bowl chopper, then seasoning and ice are added and chopped in. When the mixture is emulsified and sticky, with a uniform colour throughout, dry rusk is poured in, and any special ingredient such as fleck fat is then added. One-fifth of the total amount of water has usually been held back and is also added at this point. Directly all this is mixed in, chopping stops and the casings can be filled. Although we knew all this we still wanted to see it being done in a factory. We pondered long and hard over which firm we should approach. Obviously we wanted to visit one which made traditional English products and we settled on Bowyers. We have already pointed out that English sausages fail to meet the minimum Continental meat requirement. They were banned from the Brussels Exhibition of 1958 until Bowyers made a special high meat content product to overcome the ban. At Bowyers' Trowbridge factory, we met Harry Davis, their Development Supervisor, who was largely responsible for the Britannia sausage, sold in the British Pavilion in the Exhibition, at the 'Britannia', a typical English pub. He told us it was made of 96% pork, half fat and half lean, with 2% seasoning (black and white pepper, salt, freshly chopped sage and rosemary), and 2% rusk, all contained in a natural casing.

The Britannia sausage continued to be made; but market research found that although this sausage might well be up to Continental standards, it was too rich for general home consumption. The meat content has gradually been lowered, first to 85%, then 80% and later to 72%. It also became more finely chopped than originally. Of course there are many people in Britain who like sausages with a coarsely cut, high meat content. These you will find not only at Fortnum's, but at Marks and Spencer, who sell a 90% meat sausage, which is specially made for them by firms such as Bowyers according to the St Michael specification, but the market is not large.

For their own brands, Bowyers set out to give the public what it wants, and to make each product the best in its class. We were interested to find that they never add vegetable protein to their sausages. The pig is the most economical animal we eat. There is the absolute minimum wastage because almost every part of it can be used in some way; Bowyers' production schedule seems equally efficient. Their pigs are turned into hams, bacon, sausages, black puddings, sausage rolls, veal and ham pies, faggots, Scotch eggs and no doubt they plan further development. Furthermore, Bowyers recently bought up a factory in France, L'Huissier, at Le Mans.

The sale of French and other imported sausages is booming throughout Great Britain. We only hope that the EEC won't bring about a situation in which we can only get good Continental sausages here and have to go abroad to find good English ones.

Everyone knows that Asia starts at the Bosphorus, yet it always comes as a slight shock to realize that Israel is Asian; so is Turkey, Iraq and what used to be Armenia. These are the only places in the Levant where we have found sausages. That word 'Levant' refers to a region which is the only subject in the whole book about which the two authors passionately disagree. The distaff side, who was born in Egypt, persists in calling it the Middle East, to which her husband replies, 'You cannot have a middle without two sides. It was always known as the Near East until the British Army, for some quite incomprehensible reason, called it the Middle East in the last war. The French refer to *Proche, Moyen* and *Extrême Orient*. Why should be complicate things by being out of step?' So we compromised by calling it the Levant.

Anyhow, the Levantine sausages are more under the influence of Eastern Europe than Asia. As the pig remains the basic raw material you will not find pork sausages in Moslem countries, or, of course, Israel, but you may find beef. You have to go to the old Chinese Empire—or Chinese communities in the old British Empire, such as Singapore—to find out about oriental sausages.

The Chinese way of making and cooking sausages is very different from ours, but there are certain similarities. Although some manufacturers may use pork trimmings and beef scraps, the most reputable use nothing but prime meat, mostly pure pork. Where fresh pork is not readily available, frozen meat has to be used, but the best cuts still go into sausages.

One manufacturer, Tse Hing Chuen, Executive President of the King of King's Company, is a third-generation sausage-maker. His family started the business in Canton and Macao, but for nearly thirty years now he has been established in Hong Kong. In the boom days before 1970, he employed 450 workers in his factory. He generously provided us with a mass of information on the difference between the oriental and occidental sausage.

The pork, lean and fat, is chopped by hand. The Chinese do not like mincing machines—probably for the same reason that Queen Victoria gave—they squeeze out too much juice from the meat. The chopped meat is mixed with sugar, soy, salt, a little preservative and Chinese wine. This farce is fed, again by hand, down a funnel into the casing which hangs vertically below. You will find exactly the same process being used in the Bavarian alps. The Chinese use hot, dry natural casings, but no machine has yet been found to fill these satisfactorily. Before they are formed into links the sausages are pricked with a pin-studded board. Once again, machinery proved inadequate. The links are divided with straw and long chains of sausages are hung above numerous buckets of glowing charcoal and hot-air-dried for three days. During this process the buckets are re-filled and the tiers of sausages interchanged so that each is equally well dried. If the weather is dry and sunny, the sausages may be hung in the open air.

In Hong Kong they cost about £1.70 per pound and are considered such a luxury, even by middle- and upper-class Chinese, that they are often offered as New Year presents. They are usually eaten in December and January and they are steamed above a pot of boiling rice, never grilled or fried, except by expatriates who like to have them for barbecues. Like some occidental manufacturers, the King of King's Company makes ice-cream in the months when they are not making sausages.

There is no need to go to the Far East for your Chinese sausages, they can be found in London and other large cities, including ones made in Canada. In fact, we found that they were much better known than we imagined. The other day in Holsworthy market, we offered a Chinese sausage to our butcher for him to taste. A Devonshire farmer's wife, standing nearby, said, 'Ah! Chinese! Yes, they do make a nice change, don't they?'

Finally, we come to the United States, Australia and Africa. Most of the sausages in these regions originated in Europe. The South African *boerewors* reveals its Dutch ancestry. We have not heard of Africans making sausages, although Algerian *merguez* does appear to be indigenous. Neither do we think Aborigines made sausages down under, nor the North American Indians on the other side of the Atlantic. But Australia is strategically placed to draw on the best sausages of both the Orient and Europe to meet the ever-increasing demands of an ever-increasing polyglot population. The variety of sausages available shows signs of rivalling that of the USA.

In the United States you will find some 250 different varieties on the shelves of the shops. Most, if not all, originated in Europe or Asia. In the first chapter of the book we suggested that the sausage might well form the basis of an autobiography. It might equally well serve as a basis of a history, from the Roman invasions in Europe, to the waves of colonists and immigrants which swept over the New World, bringing frank-furters and *wienerwursts* from Germany and Austria, *salami* from Italy, *medvurst* from Sweden, *kielbasa* from Poland and *chorizos* from Portugal and Spain. So the method of cooking and eating is much the same.

So here they are, probably not every sausage in the World, but at least most of them—nearly 600 in all—from the Aber-deen sausage to *Zwyczajna*.

An International Glossary
of Sausages

Aberdeen Sausage (Scotland)
Right at the outset we run into a problem, and one that recurs throughout the book. We have found two distinct recipes for this sausage. One Aberdeen recipe uses minced mutton in a casing 30 cm (12 in) long. The other gives two parts of minced beef, one part of fat bacon and one part of oatmeal. Which is the original? Few sausages with the same name differ as much as this.

Alpenklüber/Alpiniste (Switzerland)
A *rohwurst* (see page 85) made of lean pork, beef and pork fat. It is preserved by air-drying and is eaten raw.

Andouilles and Andouillettes (France/Belgium)
These very popular French sausages are made from chitterling, tripe and sometimes calf mesentery. We are sorry to have to confront the reader with such mysterious ingredients so very early on. Most sausages are made of good, plain meat: *andouilles*, and the smaller *andouillettes*, however, are very different. Chitterling is roughly the middle section of pig gut, separated from the stomach by about 18 m (19½ yds) of hog casing (see page 75). Mesentery, also known as mudgeon, frill or crow, is defined in the *Concise Oxford Dictionary* as 'a fold in the peritoneum which attaches part of the intestinal canal to the posterior wall of the abdomen'. The English version of *Larousse Gastronomique* uses practically the same words in one section, but in another says it is a membrane which envelopes the intestines. Jane Grigson's description is much prettier: 'a beautiful frilly object like a creamy ruff. . . .' In her excellent book

Charcuterie and French Pork Cookery, she traces the origin of *andouille* to the Latin *inductibilis*, 'that may be drawn over something'; and quotes John Palsgrove (who was Henry VIII's chaplain, and tutor to his sister Mary in 1513). In his book *L'Esclaircissement de la Langue Francoyse*, the sixteenth-century versions of both French and English words are given: 'endoile' and 'chyterling'.

Few people would associate the majestic valley of the Loire with any form of sausage. Yet, if one travels up river, past the vineyards of Saumur, Bourgeuil, and Vouvray, through the shadows of the châteaux of Amboise, Blois and Chambord, one finds oneself, twenty kilometres east of Orléans, confronted with a sign that reads 'Jargeau, Capitale de L'Andouille'. This is the headquarters of a gastronomical society called La Confrérie des Chevaliers du Goûte-Andouille, which has branches as far afield as Canada and Japan, as well as representatives in Holland, Italy, Switzerland, and the United Kingdom. The authors were made *Grande Dame d'Honneur* and *Grand Bailli* for Great Britain at the 1977 Festival.

I had thought that this might be a courtesy title, but when I found myself on a Grand Jury, confronted by 160 *andouilles* and *andouillettes* I realized that my responsibilities were not to be taken lightly. The Annual International competition is divided into six classes, for each of which there are gold, silver and bronze medals, and certificates for runners-up and highly commended entries. Fortunately an eliminating jury, consisting of two *charcutiers*, two cooks and two consumers, whittled down the entries to 80, before the Grand Jury was called in. I am ashamed to say that after tasting 44 I asked to be excused from further jury service—not, I hasten to add, because of illness, but simply because by then I found it extremely difficult to differentiate between the remaining entries. We greatly enjoyed our annual visit for several years before handing over our titles to others with more time to spend in that lovely part of France.

However, I learnt two important points: (a) there are several different types of *andouilles* and *andouillettes*, and (b) that any of them may range from the quite delicious to the almost inedible.

The classes in the Jargeau competition may serve as a useful list of the main categories:

(a) *andouilles* (made of pure pork) and *andouilles de campagne*, containing chitterling and tripe;   (b) *andouillettes* of pure pork and *andouillettes* containing a proportion of calf mesentery; (c) *andouilles sèches*;   (d) *andouilles fumées*;   and (e) *andouilles façon Vire ou Guéméné*.

There is actually a considerable difference between the two mentioned under (e). They are now made all over France, but originally came from Normandy and Brittany. The former is black-skinned and a cross-section looks like a piece of grey-brown marble with random mottling. The latter consists of concentric rings of gut. In general, *andouillettes* contain nothing but chitterling and tripe, while *andouilles* contain at least 50% pork meat as well, usually from the shoulder. Colour can vary from white to black through various shades of brown, according to whether they have been smoked or boiled with onion skins.

After the competition, the *Confrérie* holds a meeting at which new members are installed, followed by a banquet which is attended by members of other gastronomic and wine societies. It all takes place on the second Saturday in June and there is another meeting on the third Sunday in October. These are occasions which should not be missed.,

The Chevaliers du Goûte-Andouille are not the only Knights of the Dinner Table to extol this food. There is the Docte, Insigne et Gourmande Confrérie des Taste-Andouilles du Val d'Ajol in the Vosges, and the Association Amicale des Amateurs d'Andouille Authentique. President of the A.A.A.A.A. is the distinguished author and gastronomic correspondent of *Le Monde*, Robert J. Courtine.

You do not have to belong to any society to sing the praises of *andouilles*. In Jargeau there is a catchy little tune with words which run:

> Si t'étais venu, t'aurais mangé de l'andouille,
> Comme t'es pas v'nu, elle est restée pendue!

There is also *un petit poème libertin*, by Edward Vicq, which describes how a young girl is so enchanted by the sight of an *andouille* on her plate that she asks if she can have a live one.

In the following recipes, first for *andouilles* and then for *andouillettes*, it is assumed that the ingredients have been bought already dressed or prepared.

If you are starting with your own pig, then *Self-Sufficiency* by John and Sally Seymour will provide valuable information.

Andouilles Bretonnes (France)

Ingredients
the tripe and chitterling of a pig
half the combined weight of these in hard pork fat
salt, finely ground black pepper, spice
beef runners

Method Cut the tripe and chitterling into strips as for *Andouilles de Vire* (see p.101). Lay them in an earthenware dish, sprinkle with salt, pepper and spice; leave for 24 hours. Form into bundles using eight to ten strips around a central core of hard pork fat. Turn the casing back on itself, insert the bundles and put the casing back over. (In some parts of Brittany the ingredients are just jumbled up and stuffed into the casing.) Tie the ends, salt for a week, and smoke for three days over an applewood fire if possible. Hang in a cool, airy larder. Brush off any soot, cover with flour, and boil gently in water for 2 hours before serving.

Andouilles Fumées (France)

A smoked *andouille*, for which Guéméné, in Brittany, is famous.

Andouilles de Nancy (France)

Ingredients
450g (1lb) calf mesentery
450g (1lb) belly of pork
100 ml (3 floz) madeira, or white wine
salt, freshly ground black pepper
beef runners

Method Proceed as for *Andouilles de Vire*. Onions and mushrooms softened in butter over a low fire may be added if desired. When the casings are tied, they should be pricked with a fine needle and thrown into a bouillon of boiling water containing onion, carrot, garlic and a bouquet garni. Simmer for 2 hours and leave to cool in the water.

Andouilles de Vire (France)

Ingredients
the tripe and chitterling of a pig
half of the combined weight of these in fat bacon
chopped onion, shallots and parsley (to taste, but 1 cupful altogether is a good basis)
1 glass white wine
salt, freshly ground black pepper
beef runners

Method Cut the tripe and chitterling into strips about 1 cm (½ in) wide and 20 cm (8 in) long (or just a little shorter than you plan the finished sausage to be). Now you can either leave the strips in salt, freshly ground black pepper and mixed spice, or you can follow Alexandre Dumas' advice and marinate them for 6 hours in white wine, thyme, basil, garlic and a dash of *anis*. The onions and shallots should be softened in butter over a slow fire and mixed with the parsley. Cut the bacon into strips the same size as the chitterling, and form all the strips into bundles. Season with pepper, salt, spice and onions etc. Tie one end of each bundle together and draw it into a large casing. The sausage, tied at both ends, can then be simmered for 3 hours in a bouillon of half milk and half water, with a clove-studded onion, two or three carrots and a bouquet garni; or it can be salted in brine for 48 hours, smoked for 3 days and simmered in equal parts of white wine and water for 3 hours.

Andouillettes Fines de Porc (France)

Ingredients
a calf mesentery
half its weight in lean bacon
thyme, bay leaf, bouquet garni, parsley
1 litre (1¾ pint) stock
clove-studded onion
100g (4oz) mushrooms, chopped
2 or 3 shallots, sliced
6 raw egg yolks
casings

Method Cut the mesentery and bacon into squares and simmer in the stock together with the herbs and onion for 2 hours. Soften the mushrooms and shallots in butter over a gentle heat and add the chopped parsley. Remove the meat and chop coarsely. Reduce the stock by fast boiling and add a little of it to bind the ingredients. Mix. Fill the casings, and tie to form sausages about 13 cm (5 in) long. The *andouillettes* can now be heated in a bouillon before serving, or they can be salted and smoked as described for *andouilles*.

Andouillettes de Savoie (France)
They contain chitterling, mesentery and tripe, seasoned with cumin.

Andouillettes de Troyes (France)
These are made of calf mesentery, a heifer's udder, egg yolks, shallots, parsley, butter, nutmeg, pepper, salt and white wine.

Andouilles and Andouillettes—How to serve
If you buy either of these they are usually already cooked. *Andouilles* can be sliced and eaten cold, or slices can be grilled and served with mashed potatoes. *Andouillettes* are lightly slashed rather than sliced, and served whole. The President of the A.A.A.A. says that for the purist grilling is the only way

to cook them, and they should be served with mustard sauce. On no account should they be accompanied by fried potatoes because two greasy dishes do not go well together. Potatoes should be mashed, or rather puréed—there *is* a difference between English and French mashing—but better still a purée of lentils, beans (*haricots rouges*), celery or split peas. Recipes will be found on pages 100–102.

Ap Yeung Cheung (China/Hong Kong)

Ap means duck, *yeung* is liver, and *cheung* (which is sometimes spelt *cheong* or *chang*) is the word for sausage. This one—made by the King of King's Company—contains preserved duck liver along with the ingredients that go into most Chinese sausages—lean and fat pork, sugar, soy and Chinese wine. (See page 95 for further details of Hong Kong sausage-making.)

Armadillo Sausage (USA)

In research—even for a book on sausages—long hours of routine transcriptions are occasionally rewarded with a bizarre discovery that lifts one's efforts momentarily out of the rut. There was such a moment, when reading Theodora FitzGibbon's *Food of the Western World*, we found that armadillo sausages were once very popular in parts of Texas. We wanted to know more. Why Texas rather than anywhere else? What part of Texas? And, of course, how they were made? Only the last question is answered. 1.8kg (4lb) armadillo meat, finely minced, to 450g (1lb) breadcrumbs is seasoned with allspice, chopped sage, whole black peppercorns and salt. If the mixture is put into large casings it is smoked; if put into small casings it is fried or grilled or boiled.

Aufschnittwurst (Switzerland)

A *brühwurst* or scalded sausage (see page 85) for slicing, made of pork and beef.

Augsburgerwurst (Germany)

Ingredients
900g (2lb) lean pork
450g (1lb) hard back fat
cinnamon, cloves and nutmeg
1 teaspoon black pepper
1 tablespoon salt
saltpetre
beef runners

Method Chop the lean pork coarsely and roughly dice the fat in
5mm (¼ in) cubes. Add the spices and seasoning to taste, with
a pinch of saltpetre. Fill the runners and air-dry for 4 days at
approximately 15°C (60°F). Lightly smoke. To cook, simmer in
water for 15–20 minutes.

Baleron (Poland)
A smoked pork sausage from Poznan and Lublin.

Bauernbratwurst (Switzerland)
This country-style *brühwurst* (see page 85) is made for grilling
or frying.

Bavarian Sausage (Germany)

Ingredients
900g (2lb) pork
450g (1lb) veal
450g (1lb) back fat
sugar, salt, saltpetre
finely ground coriander, pepper
garlic, shallots
sheep casings

For this typical *brühwurst* the meat should be completely free
from sinew and finely minced. The flavouring is delicate; less
than 1 teaspoon each of salt, saltpetre, coriander and sugar—
rather more pepper. Finely minced garlic and shallots should
be added to taste. When the casings are filled, they are tied to
form links about 12 cm (5 in) long. These are air-dried for 24

hours, then warm-smoked till they are golden brown. They are simmered in water for about 8 minutes before serving.

Beef Cervelat (England/Scotland)
See *Cervelat, Beef*

Beef Sausage (Scotland)
This sausage is popular north of the border. The Scots seem to shun pork, preferring mutton or beef in pies as well as sausages. It is made from lean beef to which a bullock's heart is sometimes added, also fat or suet, bread, sausage meal and seasoning. Oddly enough, pig casings are often used. The proportions in one recipe consist of three parts lean beef, two parts fat, one part each bread *and* meal. We find beef sausage, even without so much stodge, most unappetizing and Cassell's *Dictionary of Cookery*, edited by A. G. Payne, ignores the bread and meal, using twice as much lean beef as suet, and adding any tasty condiments and shallots, chopped very fine. This sounds much better.

Beef Sausage, Smoked (Scotland)
(Meg Dod's recipe of 1826)
Beef is salted for 2 days and then minced with suet and onions. The recipe does not give proportions, but you could start with twice as much lean as fat, adding 2 medium-sized onions for every 450g (1lb) of meat. Any adjustments can always be made to suit individual taste. Pepper and salt are the seasoning and the forcemeat is put into fairly large casings, such as beef middles. These are then smoked. The Hebrideans are said to leave them up the chimney until required. Onions, however, should not be included if the sausages are to be kept after making. Garlic, one presumes, is a different matter.

Berliner Mettwurst (Germany)
A regional variety of *mettwurst*.

Berliner Riesen Bratwurst (Germany)
A giant *bratwurst*.

Berliner Rotwurst (Germany)

Rotwurst is a type of black pudding, and therefore a *kochwurst* (see page 85). It is dark red in colour. Black pepper is the keynote of this version, made of coarsely chopped meat and cubes of bacon.

Beskidzka (Poland)

A hard sausage, found all over Poland, made from pork and beef in natural casings.

Bierschinken (Germany)

This *brühwurst* (see page 85) is distinguishable by small chunks of cooked ham fat, and sometimes pistachio nuts. It is a large sausage and is usually eaten cold. One commercial recipe lists white pepper, nutmeg, paprika and mustard among the seasonings. The proportion of finely minced pork is two-thirds lean shoulder to one third fat belly; the amount of ham and seasonings seem to vary. This sausage should not be confused with the one that follows.

Bierwurst (Germany)

A spicy pork sausage—and often a mixture of pork and beef—with hard back fat, sometimes flavoured with garlic, but without the chunks of ham. Usually coarse textured.

Black Bear Sausage (Germany)

Sixty per cent lean bear meat and 40% shoulder of pork, minced fairly fine, flavoured with finely minced onion and garlic and then seasoned with black and white pepper, crushed juniper berries, light brown sugar, salt, saltpetre and paprika. The farce is stuffed into casings to form links about 30 cm (12 in) long and 3 cm (1¼ in) in diameter. The sausages are cool-smoked for 12 hours. Louis Szathmáry says the ideal bear for sausages is a one to one-and-a-half-year-old male, purchased in October or November. He also says that if, after smoking, the sausages are left for a day at room temperature and then wrapped in foil, they will keep for 6 to 8 months in a freezer.

Black Pots (England)
A Cornish black pudding (see below), made like gerty meat pudding with the addition of pig's blood.

Black Puddings (Great Britain/Eire)
(See also *Boudins*)
A hundred years ago, black puddings were relished by people from all walks of life. Today they have fallen from the grace that they enjoyed when Charles Elmé Francatelli made them specially for his royal and noble patrons. Traditionally, they belong to the Midlands and North of England, though they were made under different names in most regions. They can even be made at home if you have a Catermaster kit. Since 1973 this firm has offered the public a do-it-yourself black pudding mix, consisting of processed blood, cereal, onion, groats and seasonings. Beef runners are also provided and can be filled with the equipment in the basic kit (see page 69).

Black puddings have often been associated with the fox-hunting fraternity. In *Handley Cross*, you may remember, Jorrocks sits down to a meal in which 'the second course consisted of a brace of partridges and a snipe, and three links of black pudding. . . .' To this day they remain a part of the traditional fare of the Tarporley Hunt Club, which holds its annual dinners during the first week in November at the Swan Hotel in Tarporley. Gordon Fergusson, member and unofficial historian of the Club, sent us this description. 'The Hunt Room, with its fine portraits and magnificent chandelier, forms a unique setting for the dinners, at which the members wear scarlet coats with green collars, green breeches and green silk stockings. Naturally enough, "Foxhunting" is the principal toast of the evening and, after the speeches, the tables are reset for supper. At about midnight, devilled bones and black puddings are always served, washed down with mulled ale.'

This club, the membership of which is limited to forty, maintains its own cellar at the Swan, eats off its own china, and even has its own eighteenth-century mahogany chairs carved with foxes' masks. It was founded in 1762 and almost half the past Presidents have been Masters (though the Club refers to them as Managers) of the Cheshire Hunt.

A friend of ours who lives in that area was able to get the original recipe for the Black Pudding.

Black Pudding (as originally served at the Tarporley Hunt Club)

Ingredients
7kg (14lb) groats
3.5kg (7lb) leaf or back fat
2kg (4lb) fine oatmeal
1kg (2lb) rusk
1kg (2lb) onions
4.8 litres (1 gallon) pig's blood
25g (1oz) *mancu*
50g (2oz) bergice (dry antiseptic)
beef runners

Seasoning
350g (12oz) salt
175g (6oz) white pepper
100g (4oz) ground coriander
75g (3oz) ground pimento
50g (2oz) ground caraway seed
(175g (6oz) of this seasoning will flavour 7kg (14lb) black
    pudding mixture)

Method Put the groats loosely into a bag and tie. Boil until they are well swollen and thoroughly cooked. Empty into a large tub, add seasonings, bergice, rusk and onions and mix well while still hot. Add the back fat cut into 1 cm (½ in) cubes. This can be softened slightly to facilitate filling. Now add the blood and stiffen with the oatmeal. Fill the beef runners (or wide hog casings), allowing about four pieces of fat to each pudding. Tie up firmly and boil gently for 20 minutes. To obtain a rich black colour, add 25g (1oz) of *mancu* to the ingredients.

It is the seasoning that enables you to distinguish one black pudding from another. Here are the different recipes for seasoning the best known black puddings. The quantities are given in parts so they refer equally well to grammes or ounces.

The Far-famed Bury Four parts of rubbed marjoram to three of rubbed thyme, three of rubbed mint, two of rubbed pennyroyal and one of bruised celery seed.

The North Staffordshire Four parts of rubbed thyme to three of pimento, two of marjoram, two of rubbed pennyroyal and two of ground coriander.

The Stretford Six parts of ground marjoram to three parts of ground thyme, three of ground mint and one of ground pennyroyal.

The Yorkshire Six parts of ground marjoram to five parts of ground thyme, two of ground lemon thyme and one of ground savory.

In his *Handy Guide for Pork Butchers*, T. B. Finney says that 175g (6oz) of any of these seasonings will flavour 7kg (14lb) of black pudding mixture. Of course there are slight differences to be found in pudding recipes. We have found some which include stale bread, rice *and* oatmeal. The *boudin noir* is much less stodgy. Of the British recipes, we prefer the Scottish black pudding.

Black Puddings, Bulgarian
See Karvaviza, Karvaviza Drug Vid and Karvaviza Po Banski

Black Pudding, Caribbean (West Indies)
The BBC broadcast a recipe for this black pudding, and we were delighted to find it in their *Recipes for Far Away Food*. It has overcome the stodge problem in a most original way.

Ingredients
4 tablespoons salt
1 lime
2 spring onions
2–3 hot red peppers
100g (4oz) sweet potato (or the same amount of cooked
   rice)
50g (2oz) pumpkin
sprig of marjoram
black pepper
150ml (¼ pint) pig's blood
25g (1oz) butter
1m (3–4ft) hog casing

Method Wash the hog casing inside and out in water with the juice of half the lime and a tablespoon of salt. Rinse well and then place in a bowl of fresh water, again with salt and lime juice. (This is not necessary if prepared casings are used.) Chop the spring onions and crush the peppers. Peel and grate the sweet potato and the pumpkin and mix together with the onions, peppers, marjoram, salt and black pepper. Strain the pig's blood into the mixture, stirring well. Fill the intestine, tying one end first, and, when it is nearly filled, tie the other end leaving 2.5 cm (1 in) to allow for expansion. Join the two ends to form a circle, place in boiling water and allow to simmer for 20 minutes. Then prick the skin to prevent bursting. Cook gently for a further 30 minutes and serve hot.

Black Hog's Pudding
The following two recipes come from a handwritten family cookery book, compiled by Anne Skinner in 1689, now in the possession of Kemmis Buckley.

'To Make Black Hogs Puddings. Take a pint of Gritts, put it into three pints of milk, either steep them all night, or boyle it to ye thickness of a pudding, then put in it three pints of grated bread, take three or four eggs, a little salt, cloves, mace, sage, pennyroyalls, sweet fennell, a bitt of leecke, lime Savoury; & parboyle a little liver and grate in a pint & half of blood & strain into it, & a little pepper, mingle them well together, & if it be not soft enough put Some more milk, cut to it half a pound & half of lard, into long peices then fill them and boyle them.'

'To Make black puddings very good Mrs Hume. A quarter of Blood & Ditto of Milk, 1 pint of Oatmeal wch must be scalded in a pint of Milk before it is put to the other things, the crumb of a penny Loaf, 3 Egg whites & yolke well beat, a Tablespoonful of salt, Ditto of all spice half a nutmeg, a quarter of an Oz of cloves, ditto of Mace half a p^d of Pigs stake & a half, cutt in square bits. Mix all these ingredients well together, & when the guts are well wash'd & cleaned with salt, & water, put them in and tie them up in hanks, then boil them in a large pott, taking them out every five minutes to prick them with a pin, lest they crack, let the water be ready to boil when you put them in, let them boil for half an hour, remembering to prick them every five minutes, then lay them to cool & drain in a Tray or large Dish upon some very clean straw.

To dress them Prick them again & Broil them on a Gridiron.'

Black Pudding, Scottish
This is the version given by F. Marion McNeill in her *Recipes from Scotland*.

> **Ingredients**
> 1.2 litres (2 pints) fresh pig's blood
> 300 ml (½ pint) milk
> 450g (1lb) shredded suet
> onions to taste
> 25g (1oz) lightly toasted oatmeal
> salt, pepper
> beef runners

Method Let the blood run into a deep dish, stirring all the time. Add 1 teaspoon of salt, stir again and rub through a hair sieve. Then pour in the milk and mix well before adding the suet, minced onions, oatmeal, salt and pepper. Fill the casings, leaving room for the contents to expand, and tie at equal lengths. Have a pan of boiling water ready, and throw in a dash of cold water to bring it just off the boil while immersing the puddings. After simmering for 5 minutes, prick them all over with a large needle and continue to simmer for 2 hours. Hang them up to dry. Before serving, either heat them through in boiling water, or slice and fry.

Block Sausage

We are not sure where this originated. It could be German or American. We found it in Law's *Grocer's Manual*. It is made from streaky pork, chopped to the size of beech-nuts, and finely minced lean beef. It is seasoned with salt, saltpetre, white pepper, cane sugar, a little garlic, cardamon seed and the whole mixture moistened with rum before being lightly stuffed into ox casings. It is then air-dried, salted and cold-smoked.

Bloedpens (Belgium)

A form of *boudin noir* found in Brussels.

Blood Pudding, 'Pwdin Gwaed' (Wales)

> *Ingredients*
> the blood of a freshly killed pig
> 600 ml (1 pint) well water
> salt and pepper
> onions
> herbs to taste
> a little fat from the intestine
> oatmeal
> hog casings

Method Gather the blood into a big bowl while it is still warm and stir until it is cold. Add the well water and a little salt and leave the liquid to stand overnight. Wash the casing well and also leave to stand overnight in salt water.

Next day, chop the onions and the fat and coat them with oatmeal, season with herbs and pepper and stir into the blood. Push the mixture into the casing. Tie both ends with string; boil for about 30 minutes and then hang to dry. It can be served sliced and fried with rashers of thick, salty bacon.

Blood Pudding, 'Pwdin Gwaed Gwyddau' (Wales)
Goose blood is used instead of pig's blood.

Blood Sausage (Sweden)
The Swedish black pudding is made from pig's blood, rye meal and raisins.

Also see under: **Black Pudding** (English); **Blood Pudding 'Pwdin Gwaed'** (Welsh); **Blutwurst** (German); **Boudin Noir** (French); **Black Pudding** (Scottish).

Blood and Tongue Sausage
Frank Garrard gives a recipe for commercial manufacture in his book *Sausage and Small Goods Production*, but does not say where it originated. The proportions of the ingredients are one part of blood, one-and-a-half parts of cooked pork rind, three parts of cooked pork tongue and four-and-a-half parts of pork back fat, seasoned with salt, saltpetre, pepper, mace, marjoram, and onion powder.

Blue Sausage (Switzerland)
In 1903, the Council of State in Geneva ruled that sausage casings containing horsemeat should be dyed blue—hence the name.

Blutwurst (Germany)
There are many varieties of German blood sausage. One of them contains diced bacon, calf's or pig's lung, and pig's blood seasoned with cloves, mace and marjoram. This is filled into bullock runners and boiled.

Bockwurst (Germany/USA)
This *brüwurst* is, we understand, what a frankfurter is called in Frankfurt. In general it refers to a spicy sausage made of veal and pork, or spiced beef and pork, finely minced with hard back fat added. It is seasoned with pepper, salt, nutmeg, coriander, ginger and garlic. Sheep casings are filled with the mixture, and well smoked before scalding. In the United States,

eggs, and sometimes milk, are added, and it is flavoured with leeks or chives.

Boczek (Poland)
Pork, hard in consistency and smoked, but without the traditional casing.

Boerewors, Pork (South Africa)
Three parts of pork minced with two parts of bacon fat are seasoned with pepper, salt, nutmeg, coriander. After being moistened with vinegar, the ingredients are well mixed and allowed to stand for 2 hours before being filled into hog casings. They are served grilled. Sometimes beef is used instead of pork.

Boerewors, Lamb (South Africa)
Made of 40% lamb, 25% beef, 25% lean pork and 10% hard pork back fat, moistened with wine and brandy and sprinkled with ground, scorched coriander, pepper and cloves.

    Another recipe gives rather more beef than pork.

Boiled Beef Sausage
Law's *Grocer's Manual* lists lean beef, suet and bread (first soaked in water then squeezed) as the main ingredients, seasoned with white pepper, ground nutmeg and salt; all well mixed and filled into weasands.

Bologna (Italy)
This is one of the most famous sausages—possibly the origin of 'poloney' and probably of 'boloney'. One recipe includes pork, veal, anchovies, pistachio nuts and sheep's or pig's tongue, cooked in wine, all stuffed into a casing of beef bungs. Each sausage is wrapped in linen, bound with twine and boiled for 1 hour. An Italian manufacturer in Bologna, however, told us that he had never heard of anchovies being used.

    One American version is much simpler, while another is much more complicated.

Bologna (1)
Chop together twice as much lean beef as fat pork. Season with salt, pepper and coriander. Fill beef casings and smoke for 48 hours.

Bologna (2)
Of the total meat content three-fifths is beef, one-fifth fat pork and one-fifth cooked pork tripe. A little cereal (about 50g in 1.5kg or 2oz in 2lb) can be added, and as much water as fat pork. The seasoning consists of equal quantities of coriander, ginger, dry mustard and nutmeg, with seven times as much pepper. It is stuffed into beef bungs, tied into 7.5 cm (3 in) links and smoked at 40°C (110°F) increasing to 65°C (150°F) for three hours. After this it is simmered in water at a temperature of between 70° and 75°C (160—170°F).

Other recipes give onions and parsley amongst the ingredients.

Bonnachen (Scotland)
This Highland sausage is made of twice as much lean beef as suet and seasoned with salt, saltpetre, black and white pepper, sugar, ginger and cloves.

Boterhammenworst (Holland)
Three parts of veal from a fat calf, two parts of lean pork and five parts of back fat, coarsely chopped and cured for 48 hours in a mixture, of which the proportions are six parts salt, two parts cane sugar and one part saltpetre. The amount needed to cure 2.25kg (5lb) of meat would be about 75g (3oz). In commercial manufacture, the cured meat is minced, well mixed with a little farina paste and diced fat, and the seasoning added. This consists of pepper, ginger, nutmeg and mace. It is filled into ox bungs and warm-smoked for 4 hours, then cooked for 2½ hours in warm water at a temperature of 78°–80°C(169°—172°F)

Boudins (France/Belgium)
Pudding is so very English a word, that it always comes as a surprise to find its origin in the French word *boudin*. As far as

sausages are concerned, *boudins*, like puddings, are mostly black or white. Nancy may have the slight edge on other French towns for its *boudins noirs*, but excellent examples of *boudins blancs* and *noirs* are to be found in Albi, Auvergne, Bercy, Dijon, Limousin, Lyon, Paris, Rouen, Roussillon and Toulouse. But since this is an alphabetical list, we must first deal with:

Boudin Asturien (Spain)
See *Morcilla.*

Boudins Blancs (France)
They are made of many mixtures, which may contain pork and chicken, veal, rabbit, hare, cream, onions, eggs, and breadcrumbs or ground rice. The sausages are simmered in milk and water for 20 minutes or so, pricked with a needle as they rise to the surface, and sometimes left to cool in the liquid for 14 hours. Jane Grigson advises lowering them into the water in a salad shaker or strainer. They are gently fried or grilled, or wrapped in buttered greaseproof paper and baked. They are easy to make, and we have found them the most popular of all our homemade sausages.

The Breakfast Book says you should take equal parts of the white meat of cold fowl, breadcrumbs, boiled onions and cream. The meat is pounded to a paste, seasoned well and the other ingredients added. It is bound with the yolks of eggs, and the casings filled. These are boiled for 15 minutes; but should be fried in butter before serving.

Boudin Blanc à l'Ancienne Mode (France)
Curnonsky, in *La Table et l'Amour*, describes the following method, but he does not give the amounts of all the ingredients.

Chop the flesh of raw fish, breasts of chicken, calf sweetbreads and carp roes. Put this mixture into a mortar and pound it to a fine paste. Add some crustless bread which has been simmered in milk. Put as much butter as you have flesh and bread, and add a cow udder, previously boiled and chopped, about 100g (4oz) of rice boiled in milk, and the same amount of onion purée, and then, one by one, five or six egg yolks.

Whenever an ingredient is added it should be well beaten into the mixture before adding another. Put the mixture into a bowl with pepper, salt, nutmeg, and 1 litre (1¾ pints) of cream. Mix it well, then fill the casings which are simmered in milk. After cooling, they can be gently grilled.

Boudin Blanc d'Ourville (France)

Ingredients
600 ml (1 pint) fresh milk
handful of breadcrumbs
6 onions
225g (½lb) hard back pork fat
6 egg yolks
1 wineglass of cream
50g (2oz) butter
salt, pepper, French spice (see p.72)

Method Boil the milk. Throw in the breadcrumbs, then sieve the mixture and bring to the boil again, stirring all the time. Simmer until all the liquid is absorbed and the mixture is really thick. Leave aside to cool. Chop the onions finely and fry gently in butter until they are soft but not brown. Chop the pork fat and add a piece of butter, then the onions, the milk mixture, the cream, the egg yolks and the seasoning. Stir well between adding each ingredient. Cut the casings into the required lengths; tie one end and fill them three-quarters full. Tie the other end and repeat until all are filled. Lower the *boudins* very gently into boiling water. You can tell when they are cooked, as, when pricked with a pin, fat will appear. Take them out of the water with a skimmer and place in cold water to cool. Drain well, and grill them, each enclosed in a cylinder of greaseproof paper. Serve very hot.

Boudin Blanc de Paris (France)
This is a recipe we can thoroughly recommend. We have also used turkey breasts, instead of chicken, with excellent results.

Ingredients
225g (½lb) uncooked breast of chicken
225g (½lb) best loin of pork
675g (1½lb) chopped onions
25–50g (1–2oz) breadcrumbs softened in milk
150–300 ml (5–10 floz) cream
3 eggs
butter
pepper, salt, French spice (see page 72)
600 ml (1 pint) milk
beef runners

Method Mince the meat and fat finely. Soften the onions in the butter over a low heat. Soak the breadcrumbs in milk, season the meat and re-mince. Mix the breadcrumbs, onions and meat, and pound together with a pestle in a mortar if you have them. Then add the eggs and cream. Mix well and check seasoning. Fill the casings rather loosely as the stuffing will expand. Form links by tying with string or thread. Add 1.2 litres (2 pints) of water to the milk and bring to the boil. Lower the sausages gently into the liquid and barely allow them to simmer. As the sausages rise to the surface prick them with a needle. After 20 minutes, lift and drain, and set aside until the following day, when they should be gently pricked again and grilled or fried in butter.

Boudin Blanc Rennais (France)

Ingredients
3 onions
450 ml (15 floz) milk
cloves, a sprig of chervil
the white meat of an average-sized chicken
125g (5oz) fat pork
125g (5oz) fine breadcrumbs
2 eggs, pepper and salt
beef runners

Method Boil the milk with the onions, cloves and chervil for 10 minutes. Chop the pork fat and chicken, then add the breadcrumbs. Beat the eggs and stir into the mixture and season. Next, strain in the milk and mix well. Fill the casings loosely, and knot them every 20cm (8 in). Simmer gently in water for 45 minutes. To serve, fry gently.

Boudin Noir (France)

This must have been the type of sausage to which Homer referred, and against which Leo V brought in his legislation. The Assyrians are said to have made them and the inhabitants of Tyre excelled at their manufacture. They have the longest history of any sausage, and are as popular today as they have ever been. In some regions of France they are traditionally served on returning from midnight mass on Christmas Eve. In the village of Manziat, about 10 kilometres north of Mâcon, they hold a competition every year to see who can eat the most *boudin*. Two tons of it are eaten in one day, and a recent winner consumed a metre of this black sausage. But the biggest *boudin* festival is held at Mortagne-au-Perche, a town of 5,000 inhabitants, 165 kilometres west of Paris. Here the *Confrérie des Chevaliers du Goûte-Boudin* organize a competition which attracts some 600 entries from all over Europe, including 50 or more from Great Britain. A prize is given for the best black pudding from each country and another for the overall champion.

There are many different recipes, but the main ingredient of all of them is pig's blood. Henri Paul Pelleprat says that it should be taken straight from the hanging pig, and kept moving over hot embers to prevent coagulation.

Larousse quotes some verse by Achille Ozanne, a cook and poet. It is too vague to be of much use in the kitchen, but for those who are interested, here is our own doggerel translation:

> First take your onions and chop them fine
> In bacon fat let them gently stew
> Till they fill the air with a scent divine
> And turn to an exquisite golden hue.
> Stir in the blood, and strongly season—
> Keep spices, pepper, nutmeg handy—
> Forget not salt, and t'would be treason

Should you omit a glass of brandy,
All this, mixed well, must now be filled
Into a length of porcine gut—
But lest it on the floor be spilled
Be sure to see one end is shut,
Ends tied, then simmer (let them not boil)
For twenty minutes they remain
In trembling waters, now your toil
Is nearly done. Just simply strain.

The classical recipe given by *Larousse* is as follows:

Ingredients
900g (2lb) fresh pork fat
400g (14oz) chopped onion
50g (2oz) lard
salt, freshly ground pepper and spices
750ml (1¼ pints) pig's blood
200ml (8floz) cream

Method Dice the pork fat and let it soften slightly at the side of
the stove. Cook the onions gently in lard. Mix both these with
the blood, cream and seasoning. Pour into the casing. This can
be formed into links or left in a spiral. Lay it on a wicker or
wire tray and immerse in boiling water. Lower the heat and
cook at no more than 90°C (190°F) for 20 minutes. As the
boudins rise, prick them, and when a brown liquid rather than
blood appears, they are cooked. You can use dried blood.

Jane Grigson has a more complicated version which includes
3 litres (5 pints) of blood, 1.35kg (3lb) chopped onions and
the same amount of pork flare fat. She adds 100g (4oz) of
breadcrumbs soaked in 750 ml (1¼ pints) thick cream, 75g
(3oz) salt and 1 teaspoon each of sugar and French spice (see
p.00); chopped parsley and chives or sage are added to taste
and a liqueur glass of rum.

Boudin Noir à l'Ail (France)
This contains chopped garlic instead of spice, and the fat is
half flare and half back fat.

Boudin Noir Alsacien (France)
This contains apples as well as onions.

Boudin Noir à l'Anglais (England/France)
Add 450g (1lb) of either rice or pearl barley to the basic recipe.

Boudin d'Auvergne (France)
Pig's blood, onion and milk with both hard back and flare fat go into this sausage.

Boudin de Brest (France)
Although the method is the same as for the *Larousse* recipe, the proportions are slightly different: 2 litres (3½ pints) blood, 1 litre (1¾ pints) cream, 450g (1lb) back fat, 300g (11oz) onions (which are not chopped but boiled and then sieved to make a purée). These *boudins* are knotted every 20 cm (8 in).

Boudin Breton (France)
This version uses two parts of pig's blood to one part of calf's blood.

Boudin à la Crème (France/Belgium)
For this sausage, 1.2 litres (2 pints) of pig's blood and half as much cream are mixed with one egg, 150g (5oz) of butter and 450g (1lb) of chopped onion.

Boudin Créole (USA)
In this the blood is mixed with bread soaked in milk, and diced pork back fat, seasoned with parsley, chives, garlic, French spice, (see p.72) pepper, salt and a dash of rum.

Boudin à la Flamande (Belgium)

Ingredients
175g (6oz) raisins
300g (11oz) back fat
1 litre (1¾ pints) pig's blood
vinegar
3 onions
100g (4oz) lard
300ml (½ pint) cream
salt, pepper and parsley

Method Soak the raisins in warm water. Add a spoonful of vinegar to the blood to prevent coagulation. Chop the onions finely and sauté gently in the lard till they are tender. Add the cream, the back fat cut into dice, the blood, salt, pepper, parsley and raisins. Put the mixture into the casings which can be knotted or left in one piece. Simmer for 20 minutes or until no blood appears when pricked, then drain and hang to cool. Another version of this recipe uses 100g (4oz) currants and the same amount of sultanas, as well as the raisins, and 200g (8oz) brown sugar.

Boudin de Languedoc (France)
This has lean neck of pork, as well as fat, and is flavoured with caraway or aniseed.

Boudin de Lyon (France)
Chives, parsley, thyme, paprika and a lot of brandy give this a distinctive flavour.

Boudin de Poitou aux Epinards (France)
To 3 litres (5 pints) of blood, 1kg (2lb) chopped spinach and 350g (12oz) flare fat, add 150 ml (¼ pint) of vodka or gin and 3–4 tablespoons orange-flower water. Season with French spice (see page 72), thyme and salt.

Boule de Bâle (Switzerland)
The ingredients are lean pork, beef and fat pork, scalded *after* smoking over beechwood. It should be heated before eating.

Boutefa (Switzerland)
This big, Vaudois sausage is made from 80% pork and 20% beef, and is smoked.

Bräckkorv (Sweden)

Ingredients
900g (2lb) beef
900g (2lb) lean pork
900g (2lb) fat bacon
750ml (1¼ pints) cold boiled milk
2 boiled potatoes
2 tablespoons salt
2 tablespoons sugar
1 teaspoon saltpetre
1 teaspoon white pepper
pinch allspice
casings
curing salt (see page 79)

Method Mince the beef, pork and half the fat bacon two or three times, the final time adding the potatoes, then moisten with milk. Dice the rest of the bacon and stir into the meat mixture. Add the seasoning, then fill the casings and knot to form links. Leave to cool in cold water. Rub with curing salt and leave for 24 hours. After this you may smoke the sausage if you wish.

Brägenwurst (Germany)
A long thin, lightly smoked sausage, made of pig's brains, oats and flour.

Brain Sausage (USA)

Ingredients
calf's brains
lean pork
fat pork
4–6 grated onions for every 2 calves' brains
pepper, salt
casings

Method All the ingredients are chopped, mixed, then pushed into casings which are knotted into links. They are boiled for 5 minutes, then quickly cooled. They are fried in butter before serving.

Bratwurst (Germany)
This *brühwurst* (see page 85) originating in Nürnberg, is a fine-textured, rather pale sausage, made from pork and/or veal and lightly fried chopped onions. It is quite heavily seasoned with salt, pepper and mace, and filled into hog casings to form longish links (see *Rostbratwurst*). It is usually grilled or fried. In Thuringia, they grill their sausages over an open wood fire, and, just before they are cooked, splash them with cold water to make the skins crisp.

Braunschweigerwurst, 'Brunswick Sausage' (Germany)
Brunswick is a sausage-making centre, producing not only various types of sausage, but different recipes for each type. The straightforward Brunswick is made of pork, salt, saltpetre, white pepper and caster sugar. It is first air-dried, then smoked for a long time. It is usually eaten raw. However, some sausage-makers use pig's liver, fat pork trimmings (finely minced), onion, thyme, marjoram, ginger, salt and pepper. This is filled into hog fat ends (or bungs) and boiled or steamed. Yet another variation is the *Brunswick liver and sardine sausage* given below.

Braunschweiger Cervelat (Germany)
This is made of beef (free from all sinew), lean pork, fat bacon, salt, coarsely ground white pepper and cane sugar. Beef middles are used as casings, and the sausages are cured by hanging in a well-ventilated room at 15–16°C (58–60°F) for three weeks. They are cool-smoked over a fire of oak and beech sawdust, on to which a handful of juniper berries is thrown. They are classified as *rohwurst*, and George Ellwanger found them the biggest and best of all the cervelats.

Braunschweiger Mettwurst (Germany)
A smoky pork sausage which can be coarse or fine and may be eaten sliced and fried, either hot or cold.

Braunschweiger Schlackwurst (Germany)
Pure pork *cervelat*, which can be coarse or fine, and is usually eaten cold.

Brunswick Liver and Sardine Sausage (Germany)
The Seasonings are the same as those given in the first *Braunschweiger* entry. Sardines and pig's liver are mixed with lean and fat pork and bacon. These sausages are boiled and cooled rapidly in cold water.

Bread-and-Butter Sausage (England)
We are not certain that this sausage originated in England, nor why it is so called, unless it was eaten with bread and butter. It is made of veal and pork, finely chopped, together with salt, saltpetre, ground cloves, pepper and ginger, the whole worked into a stiff paste. Small pieces of scalded raw bacon are added. The mixture is put into ox casings, smoked quickly until it is red, then boiled for 30 minutes and finally cooled.

Breakfast Sausage (England)
One of the few sausages to make use of weasand as a casing is the English breakfast sausage, which is nowadays rarely, if ever, eaten for breakfast. We have known families in the past who always served Sainsbury's Breakfast Sausage with boiled eggs on Sundays; this was supposed to lighten the load on the domestic staff. It is usually eaten cold and thinly sliced, and we find it rather boring, although it is improved by frying. According to one recipe, the ingredients are equal parts of beef and lean pork chopped fine, bread, back fat, cut into small cubes the size of a kidney bean, white pepper, mace, nutmeg and salt. The sausages should be smoked for 2 hours and boiled for 45 minutes. In Sweden they are often eaten hot, after boiling, grilling or frying.

Brussels Mosaic (Belgium)
Whether this really originated in Belgium we do not know. It became popular there in the first quarter of this century. Lean pork and veal are first pickled in salt and saltpetre, then finely

minced and seasoned with pepper, mace, ginger and cardamom. Chunks of ox tongue, raw bacon fat, liver sausage and frankfurters are inserted to give the appearance of mosaic. It is smoked for 1 hour, then simmered and smoked again; this time juniper berries are added to the fire.

Budino (Italy)
Small Italian *boudin*, or *sanguinaccio*, popular in and around Aosta.

Bulviv Desros (Lithuania)
Pearl V. Metzelthin, in *The Worldwide Cook Book* describes how 6lb of potatoes, peeled and grated, 6oz of bacon, cut into ½-inch cubes, and one and a quarter cups of finely chopped onion (both lightly fried) are blended with two eggs and a cup of water. The casings are filled and formed into links 6–8 inches long. These are baked in a greased baking tin until done, which can take up to 2 hours, and basted from time to time with water. They should be served with sauerkraut.

Bündnerwurst (Switzerland)
Minced lean pork and diced fat, seasoned with ground cloves, salt and pepper, in a casing made from a pig's bladder. It is a smoked sausage which is boiled before serving, and can be eaten hot or cold. (*Bündnerplat*, however, is a dish of the dried beef from Les Grisons).

Burenwurst (Germany)
This sausage falls into the same category as *Braunschweigerwurst* and *dürre* containing beef, bacon fat and 3% potato starch.

Burgenländische Hauswürstel (Austria)
Burgenländ, lying along the Hungarian border, is a province of small farms. This sausage, for which it is famous, contains 55% lean pork and 25% bacon fat, the rest being made up of beef, water and seasonings.

Bury Pudding (England)
See under *Black Pudding*.

Butifarra (Spain)

A sausage from Catalonia, firm in texture and 10–12 cm (4–5 in) long.

Ingredients
900g (2lb) of pork, lean and fat, preferably from the loin and belly
1 glass of white wine
salt, pepper, garlic, cinnamon and powdered cloves
(oregano and cayenne are sometimes added)
casings

Method Mince the meat and mix well with the other ingredients. Fill the casings and tie with thread to form links. Hang in a cool place for 2 days, then cook in boiling salted water for 1 hour. Cool and air-dry. In Catalonia they are most often eaten with mushrooms of different kinds, or haricot beans.

Butifarra Negra (Spain)

This is the mixture as before, with the addition of pig's blood and chopped mint.

Cabanos

See *Kabanos*.

Cacciatorino (Italy)

These small *salami* weigh about 225g (½lb) each. They are made of pork and beef to which milk is sometimes added. Because of their size, rather less salt than one would expect is used in curing them, so they mature more quickly than most varieties. They are said to have originated near Como. *Cacciatore* means 'hunter' and seems to imply that these *salami* were made to a suitable size for a sportsman's pocket, when out hunting.

Caillettes de Foie de Porc à la Pugetoise (France)

The word *caillette* is simply a variation of *cayette* and *gayette*. They are a Provençal form of *crépinette*. Puget-Ville, together with Solliès-Pont and Le Luc in the province of Var, are famous for their *caillette de foie de porc*, so we give this recipe:

Ingredients
1kg (2lb) pig's liver
250g (½lb) pig's sweetbreads
250g (½lb) fat, green bacon
salt and pepper
7–8 cloves of garlic
chopped parsley
a pig's caul

Method Cut the liver and bacon into strips and place them in a dish together with the chopped sweetbreads, the finely chopped garlic and parsley, and the seasoning. Leave to marinate for 24 hours. Soak the caul in warm water, then roll it round the meat mixture to form a sausage about 10–12 cm (4½ in) in diameter. Tie it with string like a parcel. Roast gently in a moderate oven for 1½ hours. Let it cool in its own juices, then cut into slices and eat cold.

Caillettes Provençales aux Tomates (France)

Ingredients
450g (1lb) spinach
1 tablespoon lard
2 shallots
3 cloves garlic
400g (14oz) chopped lean pork
250g (9oz) chopped smoked belly of pork
400g (14oz) chopped pig's liver
large bunch of chopped parsley
thyme, pepper and salt
6 large, ripe tomatoes
2 eggs
2 tablespoons olive oil
a pig's caul

Method Wash and cook the spinach, then drain very well and chop finely. Peel and chop the shallots and two cloves of garlic and soften them gently in the melted lard. Add all the chopped meats and cook for 5 minutes, stirring all the time; now add the spinach, most of the parsley, the thyme and the seasoning and cook for another 5 minutes, continuing to stir.

Peel the tomatoes, cut in half, and de-seed them. Chop the remaining clove of garlic with the rest of the parsley and sprinkle over the tomatoes.

Beat the eggs very well and, at the side of the stove, add them to the meat mixture stirring them well in. Wash the caul and lay it out on a board. Make 12 little balls from the forcemeat and wrap each one in a piece of caul. Oil a large fireproof dish and put in the *caillettes* placing half a tomato between each one. Sprinkle the whole with olive oil and cook in a moderate oven for 20–25 minutes. Serve very hot.

Cambridge Sausage (England)

This is probably the most popular sausage in England. It is made of pork, with twice as much lean as fat. Scalded rice and sausage meal are added: the proportions vary, but we think there is usually too much binder. The distinctive flavour comes from the seasoning, which consists of sage, cayenne, ground mace, nutmeg, pepper and salt.

Caribbean Black Pudding

See under *Black Pudding, Caribbean*

Caserta (Italy)

Caserta is just north of Naples, and this *peperoni* sausage contains chili, as well as pimento

Cervelas, Cervelat (Europe)

This is the ancestor of our saveloy. Originally, it is said, it was made of brains, hence the name. If this was so, it seems strange that brains are not found amongst the ingredients in any country today. Although brain sausages are still made, they are not called *cervelas* or *cervelat*. The ordinary one is stumpy, and made of lean and fat pork, usually seasoned with garlic.

According to *The Breakfast Book* you should 'Chop together the lean of pork and bacon fat, letting the latter predominate by one fourth. Season with pepper, salt, coriander, allspice and nutmeg. Put into skins, make them into lengths, smoke them for three days, then boil them in a liquor seasoned with herbs, vinegar, etc., and serve them cold upon a napkin, or slice them and toss them in butter.'

In *Le Grand Dictionnaire de Cuisine*, Alexandre Dumas lists: *Cervelas de Milan, Cervelas Mortadelles dits Saucisson de Bologne, Gros Cervelas appelé Saucisson de Lyon*, and the following:

Cervelas Maigre à la Bénédictine (France)
This is made from eel and carp minced with fresh butter, Welsh onions, shallots, garlic and eggs, salt, pepper and spice. It is fed into fishgut casings, smoked for three days and then poached in white wine.

Cervelat (Germany)
The ingredients are finely minced beef and pork, smoked to a golden brown with pink flesh. The casings are usually beef middles or bungs, linked in fairly long lengths.

Cervelat, Beef (England/Scotland)
Although the final 't' in the word *cervelat* is inclined to make one think it is Continental, the detailed recipe given below is English. Again, there are several varieties. In one version only beef and bullock heart are used to fill sheep or narrow pig casings. The following recipe, however, strikes us as being more interesting.

> *Ingredients*
> 10 parts lean beef
> 3 parts fresh, fat pork
> black pepper, salt and saltpetre
> beef middles

Method Chop the two meats finely, and add the seasoning to taste. Fill the casings to form 25cm (10in) links. Allow to dry for 8 days, then smoke for 6 days. These sausages are often dyed with cochineal. Another recipe gives roughly the same proportions of meat, but adds coriander, nutmeg and cardamom to the seasoning. The mixture is left to cure before being stuffed into beef middles, tied in 35cm (14 in) lengths and then smoked for 12 hours at 50°C (120°F).

Cervelat Pølse (Denmark)

Two parts of lean beef and two parts of lean pork, both finely chopped, and one part of diced pork back fat, are seasoned with salt, saltpetre, pepper, sugar, ginger and nutmeg. Ox runners are used for casings, making sausages about 45cm (18in) long. These are air-dried for 24 hours, then hot-smoked and boiled till the sausage feels rather like a rubber ball and actually bounces slightly if dropped. The casings are then varnished red, and the sausage is usually eaten cold, in very thin slices.

Chasseur (France)

After travelling all over France we found this sausage in Exeter. It looks like a *chorizo*, but, in spite of the pimento, it has a flavour quite its own. We found it delicious and satisfying.

Chaurice (USA)

This is the Creole version of *chorizo* from New Orleans. Creole cooking is in many respects unique, being a blend of French and Spanish cuisine interpreted by Negro cooks. The basis is French, but Louisiana was handed over to Spain in 1768, who returned it to France in 1803, before it was sold to America. Here is a typical recipe:

> **Ingredients**
> 1.75kg (4lb) lean pork
> 900g (2lb) pork fat
> 2 large, finely chopped onions
> 3 teaspoons salt, 2 teaspoons black pepper
> 1 teaspoon paprika
> 1 teaspoon chili pepper
> 2 tablespoons chopped parsley
> generous pinch of thyme
> 2 chopped bay leaves
> ½ teaspoon allspice
> 4.25m (5 yds) sausage casing

Method Put the pork and pork fat through the medium plate of the mincer, and place in a large bowl; add the remaining ingredients and mix well. Push the mixture into the casings and tie the links. This makes about 2.75kg (6lb).

Chicken, Ham and Tongue Sausage (England)

The proportions are five parts of ham, two parts of veal, two parts of fat, two parts of chicken, two parts of ground rice, one part of ox tongue and one part of sausage meal. Eggs can be added. The mixture is put into weasands and boiled for 1 hour before being dyed with poloney colouring.

Another recipe simply gives the white meat of any fowl, tongue and ham, bound with an egg and seasoned with parsley, lemon thyme, mace, pepper and salt.

Chipolatas (England/Europe)

How the Italian word for stew containing onions (*cipolle*) became adopted by the French to mean a small sausage remains a mystery. Most people believe that chipolata refers merely to a size of sausage, and not to the contents, but Finney gives a special recipe which consists of six parts lean pork, two parts fat pork, two parts rusk, and one part scalded ground rice. The rice is coloured with Parisian Red, and the seasoning includes coriander, pimento, nutmeg, thyme, cayenne, white pepper and salt. Sheep casings are used and linked into short lengths, which are half the size of ordinary pork sausages—16 per pound instead of 8. Chipolatas are often mistaken for cocktail sausages, but the latter are just a miniature version of the ordinary pork sausage.

Chitterling (England)

This is not strictly a sausage, although it is the main ingredient of *andouilles* and *andouillettes* and is, after all, a section of the pig's intestines. As Sheila Hutchins says in her *English Recipes*, it neither was, nor is 'considered a delicacy for polite houses'. But it is well liked in East Anglia, Warwickshire, County Durham and the West Country. One can still find it in Bideford, both raw and ready to eat. The gut is cut into 10cm (4 in) strips, thoroughly cleaned, scalded, soaked in salt water for five days and then given a final rinse. Chitterling can be boiled, jellied and eaten cold, or fried. Jane Grigson says that 'it is usual, in Wiltshire at any rate, to plait the intestines after their soaking in salt water. They certainly look more attractive.'

Chorizo (Spain)

There must be as many *chorizo* recipes as there are Spanish pork butchers. As with all country sausages, each region may vary the proportions, flavouring or style, but the two things that are common to all are pork and pimento. Ursula Bourne, whose opinion we respect, says that the best come from Estramadura, near the Portuguese border, and Pamplona, not far from the French frontier, where the pigs feed on acorns. There are two main varieties—smoked and unsmoked.

> *Ingredients*
> 675g (1½lb) lean pork
> 225g (8oz) fat pork
> 1 sweet red pepper, de-seeded
> pinch of hot red pepper, salt
> casings

Method Chop the meats and pepper finely. Mix well with the seasonings and leave in a cool place for 48 hours. Moisten, if necessary, with a little stock. Fill the casings to form links weighing about 75g (3oz). Dry for 2 days in a cool, airy place, then smoke lightly.

Jane Grigson has a rather more elaborate recipe, which includes 100ml (3–4 floz) red wine, ¼ teaspoon each of granulated sugar and cayenne, a pinch of saltpetre and a large clove of garlic, as well as the ingredients given in the first recipe, but using only three-quarters the amount of meat. As usual, she gives beautifully meticulous instructions: 'Cut the pepper in half, remove all the seeds as well as the stalk and put through the mincer, coarse blade, with the lean and fat pork.'

We made *chorizos* following the basic recipe, but, having no sweet red pepper we used ground paprika, and to compensate for the resulting lack of moisture we increased the amount of wine. It seemed to us that the mixture needed testing for consistency and flavour several times, and we did this by taking a minute dollop and frying it in olive oil before we filled the casings. Although the flavour will mature, how much seasoning to use is very much a personal decision. We air-dried the *chorizos* and then cool-smoked them for 8 hours.

Chorizo Basquais (France/Spain)
This Basque version is softer and less highly spiced than the Spanish variety.

Chorizo de Catimpalos (Spain)
This contains quite large pieces of ham, in which it resembles the *chorizo de Salamanca*, although it is smaller.

Chorizo d'Estramadura (Spain)
According to Plummery, the seventeenth-century French writer, this strongly spiced sausage is made of a pork fillet, the same amount of pork fat and pig's liver, all chopped and pounded in a mortar. Sweet pimento, cayenne, crushed juniper berries, salt, spices and tomato purée are used for seasoning. The mixture is filled into beef casings which are tied in links and hung up in the chimney for 6 to 7 days. Every evening, when the fire is damped down, a few handfuls of juniper berries are thrown on top. Sometimes the sausages are rubbed with hot, red pepper before smoking. They are often served with a purée of chick peas.

Chorizo de Lomo (Spain)
Large pieces of loin of pork, highly spiced and pimento flavoured, are the ingredients of this sausage.

Chorizo de Pamplona (Spain)
From the capital of Navarre, this sausage is made of finely chopped pork, paprika, garlic, various spices and herbs. It can either be eaten in thin slices in an open sandwich with a glass of sherry, or added to traditional Spanish dishes.

Chorizo Piquante (Mexico)

Ingredients
900g (2lb) lean pork
2 small, finely chopped hot red peppers
2 teaspoons salt
3 cloves crushed garlic
2 tablespoons chili powder
1 teaspoon freshly ground black pepper
½ teaspoon ground cumin
4 tablespoons vinegar
1m (1 yd) sausage casing

Method Put the pork through the mincer, using the coarse plate. Place the mince in a bowl and add all the other ingredients. Mix very thoroughly, then push it into the casing, twisting into whatever lengths are required. These sausages may be hung in a cool place to dry and will keep for several weeks. Use as fresh sausages. This quantity will make about 1kg (2lb).

Chorizo from the River Plate (Uruguay/Argentina)

There are sausage fanatics just as there are balletomanes and circus buffs. When the original edition of this book first appeared we received letters from all over the world. One of the most constructive was from David Emmet, who wrote from Uruguay sending us a recipe which his wife had been given by her grandmother. Here it is:

Ingredients
1kg (2lb) lean pork meat
450g (1lb) back fat or unsmoked bacon
200g (7oz) lean veal or beef
1 glass of dry white wine
2 or 3 cloves of garlic finely chopped
1 tablespoon of paprika (sweet pimento)
½ teaspoon of hot red pepper
a generous pinch of marjoram
salt and pepper to taste
10g (½oz) saltpetre

Method Traditionally the lean meat and fat are chopped by hand as you want a fairly coarse texture. Add to the meat the other ingredients and leave to marinate overnight. The next day test for seasoning by frying a spoonful of the mixture, and then proceed to fill the casings which must be the wide ones and tied at approximately every 12 cm (5in). Once filled and tied, pierce each one with two or three dressmaker's pins pushed through a slice of cork, in order to let out any air. It is better to hang them for 2 or 3 days before cooking.

There are of course various recipes as some people prefer to use all pork meat, others use half pork, half veal and an equal amount of fat. The seasonings are the same, except for the amount of hot pepper which varies according to taste.

Chorizos may be eaten in the same way as any sausage— fried, grilled or in a stew, or in more complicated dishes. The length of cooking depends on the heat used.

Chorizo de Salamanca (Spain)
This is coarser in texture than the *chorizo de Pamplona*, and has its own particular flavour, though the main ingredients remain pork, paprika and garlic. See also *Chaurice* and *Chouriço*.

Chouriço (Portugal)
The Portuguese version of *chorizo*, but made of pork cured in brine and seasoned with garlic, pepper and red wine. Just before the casings are filled, paprika is added. The sausages are smoked and then kept in olive oil.

Chouriço de Sangue (Portugal)
The Portuguese variety of black pudding and *boudin noir*.

Coblenz Sausage (Germany)
See under *Koblenz Sausage*.

Copocolla (Italy)
The ingredients for this sausage consist of pork from the shoulder which is mildly cured and sometimes air-dried for as long as 7 to 8 months. It is mixed with red peppers and spices

and encased in beef bungs. The one we tasted was full of large pieces of lean meat, surrounded by fat; very different from the finely chopped *salami*, in which the lean meat surrounds larger pieces of fat.

Coppa (France)
This is a Corsican sausage which is made of shoulder of pork taken from a chestnut-fed pig.

Cornish Skinless (England)
If one defines a sausage as meat encased in pig, beef or sheep gut (or some other natural animal envelope), then skinless sausages should be excluded. They are, after all, no more than rissoles. If, however, the recipe could easily be used to fill a casing we think it may be included, especially if the mixture is as good as this one, recorded by Kathleen Thomas:

> *Ingredients*
> **450g (1lb) fat and lean pork**
> **450g (1lb) beef suet**
> **450g (1lb) lean veal**
> **225g (8oz) grated breadcrumbs**
> **½ lemon**
> **2 teaspoons salt**
> **6 fresh sage leaves**
> **a pinch each of savory, thyme, marjoram and nutmeg**

Method Remove all the skin, gristle and sinew from the meat and mince it. Pare the rind of half a lemon and add it, together with the herbs, salt and nutmeg to the meat. Mix well. If you are not going to fill the casings, press this farce into a dish until needed (for up to a week in the fridge) then take out a dollop, shape it and fry in butter.

Cotechino (Italy)
This speciality of Emilia-Romagna consists of lean and fat pork, moistened wth white wine and subtly spiced. Each sausage weighs 450–900g (1–2lb). As they are very lightly salted they are not meant for keeping and should be cooked before eating. Make a few incisions in the skin, wrap it in a cloth and boil for

2 hours. It is often served with beans, lentils or mashed potatoes, and is one of the ingredients in a *bollito misto*. Robert Carrier suggests that one should try slices of it with cooked spinach.

Cotto (USA)
Short for *salame cotto* or cooked salame. Made of pork, highly seasoned, flavoured with garlic, cooked and smoked.

Cou d'Oie (France)
The bones are taken out of the neck of a goose, which is then stuffed with goose meat, goose liver and truffles. This is cooked in goose fat, and preserved in an earthenware jar as a *confit d'oie*. It is eaten cold as an hors-d'oeuvre.

Craquelet (Switzerland)
A mixture of pork and beef, reduced to the consistency of thick cream. It is filled into natural casings, then smoked and cooked. It can be eaten cold, or boiled or grilled and eaten hot.

Crépinettes (France)
This opens up another great gastronomic vista. There are dozens of different kinds of *crépinettes*. The English equivalent is the faggot; but here you will find much less resemblance than there is between the *boudin noir* and the black pudding. Basically, it is a dollop of minced meat, about the size of a small roll, wrapped up in a piece of pig's caul. Occasionally, paper-thin salt pork is used as an envelope. It is sometimes coated with melted butter and breadcrumbs, and it can be baked, grilled or sautéed. Most of the recipes given in *Larousse* include truffles, which would certainly never appear in a faggot, and, nowadays, are so expensive that one doubts whether they often find their way into crépinettes. Here are some of the varieties:

Crépinettes d'Agneau (France)
Chopped lamb, truffles and mushrooms in a brown sauce.

Crépinettes d'Agneau à la Liégeoise (Belgium)

350g (12oz) chopped lamb, mixed with 100g (4oz) breadcrumbs, previously soaked in milk and then squeezed; one large, finely chopped onion, cooked in butter, pepper and salt, and a few crushed juniper berries go to make up the contents of this *crépinette*.

Crépinettes de Foie de Porc à la Vauclusienne (France)

Ingredients
450g (1lb) pig's liver
175g (6oz) bacon
100g (4oz) stoned black olives
a handful of spinach
1 onion
parsley
nutmeg, pepper, salt
a pig's caul

Method Chop very finely all the ingredients that can be chopped and season with pepper, salt and nutmeg. Wash the pig caul well, and cut into 12–15cm (5–6 in) squares. Place a spoonful of the mixture on each square, fold over the sides, and secure with thread. Bake in a hot oven. One recipe gives the baking time as 30 minutes, but this must depend on how finely the ingredients have been chopped and on the heat of the oven. We think that more time will probably be needed.

Crépinettes de St-Menehoulde (France)

St-Menehoulde refers to a place rather than an obscure saint, and is the home of one of the many gastronomic clubs of France, La Confrèrie Gastronomique du Pied d'Or de St-Menehoulde, where they cook pig's trotters until the bones become soft and edible. This form of meat, bound with a thick brown sauce and mixed with finely minced pork, is wrapped in pieces of caul.

Crépinettes Reine Jeanne (France)

Sheep's or calf's brain, blanched and cut into small pieces, is added to a very thick béchamel sauce, together with diced ham, chopped mushrooms and sliced truffles. A large spoonful of this is enveloped in a square of pig caul, which is then covered in egg-white and breadcrumbs and fried. It should be served with lemon.

Crépinettes de Volaille (France)
Chopped chicken, mushrooms and truffles in a velouté sauce are the ingredients for this filling. See also *Caillettes* and *Gayettes*.

Crespone (Italy)
This Milanese *salame* is made from equal quantities of lean pork, beef and pork fat, seasoned with garlic, pepper and white wine. It is usually about 5cm (2in) in diameter, and like other *salami*, is salt-cured and air-dried.

Csaba (Hungary)
A piquant sausage flavoured with hot red pepper and paprika. It will keep well without refrigeration.

Culatello di Zibello (Italy)
Zibello is a village in the vicinity of Parma which became famous several hundred years ago, when the Pallavicini family, Lords of Lower Parma, found the local *salame* so delicious that they sent it as a 'rare and precious offering' to the Sforzas. But the secret of the recipe has been lost.

Cumberland Sausage (England)
The distinguishing characteristics of this type are the coarse texture of the chopped pork, spiced with black pepper (though one source stipulates white), and the fact that in Cumberland the sausage is not twisted into links, but forms one continuous coil. It is sold by length rather than weight. One recipe gives four parts of lean pork to two parts back fat and one part belly. Commercial brands add almost the same weight of fibrisol and rusk as back fat. There are, of course, butchers in Cumberland who use 98% pork. There are also farmers who believe that real Cumberland sausage will never be tasted again. They got

their unique flavour from a special breed of pig, and the last old sow of the line died in 1960. The Cumberland sausage is now growing in popularity. For Cumberland sausage seasoning, see page 75.

Dampfwürstel (Austria)
This is a *bratwurst*, similar to *schüblinge* and *Salzburgerwurst*. It contains beef and bacon fat and a little potato starch.

Debowiecka (Poland)
This is a speciality of Poznan, made of pork and similar to *krajana* but with less fat. It is about the same size as *Krakowska*, but much darker in colour.

Debrecen (Hungary)
This town, about 120 miles east of Budapest, is famous for the spicy sausages which take its name. They are usually eaten by themselves, but also find their way into various stews; not only *gulyas*, but the lesser known *pörkölt* and *tokány*. They consist of 75% pork, two-thirds of which is lean. Beef and water, spice and seasoning make up the rest.

Debrecener Rohwurst (Hungary)
This is made entirely of pork, 70% lean and 30% fat.

Deer Pudding (Scotland)
F. Marian McNeill quotes a recipe 'from the kitchens of a highland Chief'. This gives venison, suet, oatmeal, onions, salt and pepper as the main ingredients, contained in deer-tripe skins.

Diot (France)
A fresh sausage found in the neighbourhood of Valloire, in Savoie, remarkable more for the vegetables it contains than the meat. Turnip, beetroot and carrots are all found in it early in the season, but as the turnip and carrot get scarcer, so the sausage gets redder as more beetroot is added.

Doong Gwoo Lap Cheong Jing Ju Yook (China/Hong Kong)

This rather complicated sausage is made of pork, chicken and mushroom. Three times as much breast of chicken as barbe-cued pork are both finely diced and mixed with Chinese mushrooms, bamboo shoots and water-chestnuts. Seasoning includes soy, pepper, sugar, ginger and garlic. The farce is inserted into wide casings. You will find Charmaine Solomon's meticulous instructions for making and cooking it in *The Complete Asian Cookbook*.

Domasni Nadenizi-Na Furna (Bulgaria)

The Balkan Cookbook gives the following ingredients: 2–3 onions, 2–3 tablespoons of fat, 700g (1½lb) meat, 1 tablespoon of rice, salt, paprika and pepper to taste, all packed into 50cm (20in) sheep casings. This is baked in a hot oven for 40 minutes in a pan containing 1 tablespoon of fat and 3 or 4 of water for frequent basting.

Drisheen (Ireland)

Sometimes written *droiseann*, this is an Irish black pudding made in Limerick with sheep's blood. It is filled into ox runners and flavoured with tansy. In Cork and Kerry it is made of pig's blood, and Theodora FitzGibbon says that in County Clare goose's blood is used, while turkey's and hare's blood are not unknown. It is made with two parts blood to one part cream and one part breadcrumbs, flavoured with herbs, filled into large casings and boiled for 20 minutes. It is as good as a *boudin*, and worthy of more subtle accompaniment than tripe with which it is often eaten. See *Packet*.

Dürre Rund (Austria)

This sausage, similar to a *Braunschweigerwurst*, is brown-skinned and of medium size.

Easternola (USA)

A sausage made of pork, mildly seasoned with black pepper and garlic.

Emmentaler (Switzerland)
A regional *brühwurst*.

Epping Sausage (England)
This was once famous. George Augustus Sala had a friend
whose cook used to send a pound of Epping sausages round to
the baker and have him insert them one by one into the dough
of rolls ready for the oven. 'They came home smoking hot and
saturated with the grease of the porcine compost.' Today they
are dismissed in one book as 'a variation of the Cambridge
sausage'. *The Complete Farmhouse Cookbook*, however, says they
are skinless and made of equal quantities of pork and beef
suet, very finely minced, seasoned with salt, pepper, nutmeg,
sage, and some bacon. The mixture is bound with beaten egg.

Erbswurst (Germany)
Described by Lorna Bunyard in *The Epicure's Companion* as
'prosaic . . . made with a definitive object, that of providing a
portable food with a high nutritional value'.

Extrawurst (Germany)
This is a moist *brühwurst* of beef and pork or bacon fat, also
known as *fleischwurst*. *Feine extrawurst* is very finely minced.
Feine extrawurst in stangen—sometimes shortened to *feine in
stangen*—means that it is sold in single lengths rather than in
links. It is fairly large and pale pink in colour.

Faggots (England/Wales)
Faggots, you may remember, were the cause of the Great Fire
of London. A batch of them caught fire in a baker's shop in
Pudding Lane, so they were certainly eaten in 1666. There is
no reason why they should not be as good to eat as *crépinettes*;
maybe they once were, but again, the introduction of the
cheapest kinds of meat and—as in black pudding—a large
proportion of bread or cereal, has led to the product being
downgraded. It is also known as Savoury Duck and Poor Man's

Goose. While some recipes make use of pig's fry, which consists of lights, liver and melts, the more refined ones limit the offal to liver. Here are recipes from the North, West of England, as well as the Midlands and Wales.

Faggots, Newcastle-upon-Tyne

Ingredients
225g (½lb) pig's liver
225g (½lb) very fat bacon
1 large onion
225 (½lb) stale bread
a small amount of stock
225g (½lb) medium oatmeal
2 eggs
pepper, salt
a pig's caul

Method Soak the caul in tepid water and the breadcrumbs in a little stock. Mince the meat and onion, stir in the breadcrumbs and oatmeal and season. Spread the caul out flat and cut into 10cm (4in) squares. Put a large spoonful of the mixture on each square and fold over to form an envelope. Pack the envelopes closely together in a baking tin and cook in a hot oven until brown.

Faggots, Shropshire

Ingredients
450g (1lb) pig's fry
3 onions, sliced small
75g (3oz) fresh white breadcrumbs or mashed potato
salt, pepper
a pig's caul

The method is the same as for **Newcastle Faggots**.

Faggots, West Country
This recipe comes from *A West Country Cookery Book* by Kathleen Thomas.

Ingredients
350g (12oz) pig's liver
100g (4oz) fat salt pork
1 egg, lightly beaten
fresh breadcrumbs
1 onion
mixed herbs, nutmeg, pepper and salt
rich gravy
a pig's caul

Method Chop the liver very finely with the salt pork and the onions, and season with the herbs, nutmeg, pepper and salt. Place the mixture in a saucepan and cook gently with the lid on for 30 minutes. The meat should not be browned. Drain off the fat, add the egg and just enough breadcrumbs to bind the ingredients. Form into small cakes and wrap each one in a square of caul. Place them side by side in a baking tin, add a cup of rich gravy or strong stock and bake in the oven until brown.

In variations of the above recipes, the fry and onions are simmered for 1 hour in water which barely covers them. The liquid is then drained off and used to soak the breadcrumbs. Ginger and sage are sometimes used in the seasoning. In Somerset, the ingredients are mixed raw and nutmeg included, and the faggots are put in a shallow dish half-filled with water and baked in the oven for 1 hour. See also *Ffagod*.

Falukorv (Sweden)
Falun is a town and district, 190 kilometres north-west of Stockholm. The local sausage, which has achieved national popularity, is thicker than most. It is made of beef, lean pork and pork back fat, to which dried milk is sometimes added. It is hot smoked, and can be eaten after boiling, grilling or frying, but often finds its way into stews and casseroles.

The Far-famed Bury
See under *Black Pudding*.

Färepølse (Norway)
A sausage made of mutton, beef and goat meat, cured in sugar, salt and alcohol.

Feine in Stangen (Austria)
See *Extrawurst*.

Ffagod Sir Benfro (Wales)
At first sight one might think this a reference to a Welsh
baronet, but *sir* means shire, and *Benfro* is Pembroke.

> **Ingredients**
> 675g (1½lb) pig's liver
> 2 large onions
> 75g (3oz) suet
> 100g (4oz) breadcrumbs
> 2 teaspoons salt
> ¼ teaspoon pepper
> 1–2 teaspoons sage
> a pig's caul

Method The liver and onions are minced raw and mixed with
the suet, breadcrumbs and seasoning. The procedure for
cooking is the same as described in the recipes for faggots.
Sometimes the mixture is cooked unwrapped.

Fidegela (Switzerland)
This sausage from the Tessin canton, is made of pig's liver,
pork rind and fennel.

Figatelli (France)
A Corsican sausage, it was originally made of pig's liver, but
nowadays lamb's liver is frequently used.

Filipino Red (Philippines)
Why red? The Filipinos say this sausage has always been red,
and, not satisfied with the pink tinge given by saltpetre, they
add a special colouring. Perhaps the influence of the Spanish
chorizo was a contributory cause, although pimento does not
now appear amongst the ingredients. This sausage consists of
raw pork, dried in the sun, then minced and mixed with garlic,
salt, saltpetre, brown sugar, monosodium glutamate, and a red
colouring agent. Sometimes ham is included. Narrow hog

casings are used. If these are not available, then flour is added as a binder.

Fish Sausages (England/Scotland)

These seem to have gone out of fashion. As *The Grocer's Manual* gives a 'typical' recipe, one can assume that the sausages were made from different kinds of fish at one time. The proportions appear to have been 80% fish, free from skin and bone, 10% suet and 10% farina, blended to a fine paste and seasoned to taste. Finney says haddock and mackerel are best, and should be seasoned with mace, nutmeg, cayenne, pepper and salt. We have made, and liked, kipper sausages.

Fläskkorv (Sweden)

Ingredients
3kg (6½lb) lean pork
900g (2lb) fat bacon
100g (4oz) potato flour
1.5–2 litres (2½–3½ pints) ham stock
2 tablespoons salt
1–2 tablespoons white pepper
1–2 tablespoons ginger
approximately 5m (16ft) casings

Method Cut the pork and bacon into small pieces and mince twice. Add seasonings and potato flour, moisten with the stock and blend well. Cook a sample and either stiffen with more flour, or moisten again with stock as necessary. Fill the casings loosely and knot into links. Cool in cold water and dry. Make a Swedish curing mixture (see page 000) and rub this well into the sausages and leave for 18–24 hours. If the sausages are to be kept for any length of time, they should be stored in brine.

Fleischwurst (Germany)

A German description of this reads: 'A juicy, hearty-flavoured sausage of finely chopped meat. It can be eaten hot or cold, is pink to light brown in colour and is flavoured with garlic.' In some stores you may see this described as *extrawurst*. The one we ate was bland to the point of boredom, but this had been produced by a large German export manufacturer and had been marked down from 39p to 29p. The label stated that it was made of minced pork and beef. *Fleischwurst* often contains veal as well.

Frankfurter (Germany/USA etc)

Strictly speaking, the genuine frankfurter really comes from Neu-Isenburg, a little town on the road from Frankfurt to Darmstadt. America adopted it, invented the hot dog and made it the best-known sausage in the world. Its growth is due in no small way to Nathan's Great Coney Island Frankfurter, which, however delicious you may find it, bears little resemblance to the original German product. The genuine frankfurter should be made of prime lean pork and a little salted bacon fat, finely chopped and blended into a smooth paste, then smoked. Some American frankfurters are made of nothing but beef, and Nathan's Great Coney Island Frankfurter is one of them. Most American versions use a mixture of pork and beef.

Whether the hot dog was invented on Coney Island by a German butcher called Charles Feltman, using frankfurters, or whether it can be more justly attributed to a pedlar called A. L. Feuchtwanger, who, in New Orleans in 1883, created a hot dog with a *Wienerwurst* is debatable. The history of America's most popular snack is festooned with decorative myth.

Just before World War I, Charles Feltman employed a delivery boy and roll-slicer called Nathan Handwerker. One day, a singing waiter, known as Eddie Cantor, and his accompanist, Jimmy Durante, both hot dog devotees, suggested to young Nathan that he should set up on his own, and sell hot dogs for a nickel, thereby undercutting Feltman. Nathan Handwerker opened his first five-cent hot dog stand on Coney Island in 1916. As his name was too long for the sign above his stall, he dropped his surname—and never looked back. Nathan's Hot Dogs are always made of a grilled sausage in a toasted roll.

The contents of a frankfurter should be 27% beef trimmings, 27% pork trimmings, 24% pig's cheek, 13% tripe and 9% pig's hearts. To this should be added one third of its weight in iced water, and this mixture can be flavoured with salt, onion, mace, white and red pepper, saltpetre, sugar, and thickened with flour. Narrow bullock runners are used for casing, tied off in 7cm (3in) links. (Nathan's frankfurters are 18cm or 7in long.) Of course there are other recipes. One gives 60% pork and 40% beef. Another gives 3oz bacon to 1lb of lean pork, moistened with red wine and seasoned with equal parts of black pepper and ground coriander with a sprinkling of nutmeg. 3oz of bread soaked in milk may be added.

Recipes for frankfurter dishes will be found on pages 36–37.

Frankfurters, Yellow (Germany)
This is a German variation, which uses 70% pork and 30% pig's or calf's brain. The seasoning consists of pepper, salt and nutmeg, and in winter an egg yolk is added to every 5kg (10lb) of meat. The ingredients are finely chopped and loosely fed into casings which are tied in 45cm (18in) lengths, and boiled for 45–60 minutes. They are then immediately painted with a mixture of one teaspoon of saffron, two tablespoons of rum and the same amount of boiling water. We were very disappointed with the result when we made them.

Frankfurt Tongue Sausage (Germany)
This is made from leg of pork, first coarsely chopped with salt, saltpetre, and cane sugar, and left to cure until the meat turns pink. It is then finely minced and seasoned with pepper, mace and cardamom. Diced tongue and pistachio nuts are added before filling bullock runners which are tied every 30cm (12in). After boiling in water for 90–100 minutes, it is smoked over oak sawdust strewn with juniper berries.

Frische Leberwurst (Germany)
Pork and pig's liver in links about the same size as an English sausage.

Frizzes (USA)
Choice pork, coarsely chopped, seasoned with garlic, black pepper and spices, filled into hog casings.

Fruit Sausages (England)

Sheila Black, journalist *par excellence* and sausage-maker extra-ordinary, describes in her *Black Book* how she makes sausages out of apples, apricots, cherries and even mashed bananas and sweetcorn, not to eat instead of meat but as an accompaniment to meat dishes—apple sausages with pork, cherries with duck, and banana and sweetcorn with chicken.

Game Pudding (England)

This is very similar to Game Sausage, but the flesh and liver of pheasant is bound with breadcrumbs and moistened with stock before being stuffed into casings.

Game Pudding à la Richelieu (England)

The only difference here is that potato and butter replace the breadcrumbs and stock.

Game Sausage (England)

Take the leftovers of any game. Remove any skin and sinew, mince, then pound in a mortar with 170g (6oz) of lean ham and 170g (6oz) of butter to every 450g (1lb) of game. Season with red pepper and mace. Fill casings in the usual way.

Gänselandleberwurst (Germany)

A rustic version of *Gänseleberwurst*.

Gänseleberwurst (Germany)

This *kochwurst* must be the Emperor of liver sausages, holding the same relative position as *pâté de foie gras* to ordinary liver pâté. The goose livers should, of course, be truffled and labelled *getrüffelte gänseleberwurst*. A simpler and less extravagant version for the home sausage maker is the Swedish *Gåsleverkorv*.

Garlic Sausage (England)

An English commercial recipe for this French sausage gives 35% pork cheek meat and 30% lean bull beef. The pork is put through the 2.5cm (1 in) plate of the mincer and left in a basic curing mixture for 36 hours at a temperature of 4°C (40°F).

The amount of the cure works out at 75g (3oz) to every 2.5kg (5lb) meat. Half is used for the pork and half for the beef which is put through the 1 cm (⅜ in) plate of the mincer. Both meats are then run through a 3 mm (⅛ in) plate with the garlic. Gerrard gives the proportion of 25g (1oz) garlic for 55kg (100lb) of meat, but to our mind this seems a very meagre amount. The forcemeat is filled into weasands, chilled at 4°C (40°F) overnight, then hot-smoked for 1½ hours at 60°C (140°F); the temperature is then raised and the smoking continues for another 2 hours at 70°C (160°F).

Gåsleverkorv (Sweden)

Ingredients
75g (3oz) rice
200 ml (⅓ pint) water
300 ml (½ pint) milk
1–2 goose livers
1 egg
1 tablespoon chopped and lightly fried onion
3 tablespoons raisins
1 tablespoon corn syrup
salt, pepper, marjoram
the sewn-up skin of a goose neck and about 50cm (20 in)
    beef casing

Method Boil the rice in the water until the water is almost absorbed, then add the milk and simmer until the rice is cooked. Put the mixture aside to cool. Chop or mince the goose livers. Mix all the remaining ingredients well, add the rice and pack loosely into the goose neck, filling the remainder into the casing. Simmer, in water or stock, for about 45 minutes.

Although slices of this sausage can be served on their own, they are an essential part of *Svartsoppa* (black soup), a traditional Swedish dish made from goose giblets and pig's blood. See also *Gefüllter Gänsehals*.

Gayettes (France)
By what some might call a queer coincidence, a *gayette* is a Provençal faggot. The word must surely be a local version of

caillette, for both are a form of *crépinette*. It is made of equal parts of pig's liver and green fat bacon, diced very small and seasoned with garlic, salt, pepper and spice. This mixture is formed into balls weighing roughly 100g (4oz), which are wrapped in pieces of pig's caul and fastened with thread. They are baked with a little lard for 20–25 minutes and eaten hot or cold. Another version gives 45% fresh pork, 35% green bacon and 20% pig's liver, wrapped as before but baked with half a wine glass of water and a bay leaf for 45 minutes.

Gefüllter Gänsehals (Germany)
This variety of goose-liver sausage, like the Swedish version, uses the skin of the bird's neck as a casing.

> **Ingredients**
> 1 goose's liver
> 1 goose's neck
> 225g (½lb) pork
> 1 egg
> breadcrumbs, salt, pepper

Method Remove the fat from the goose neck very carefully so that the skin remains intact. Sew up one end and fill it with the chopped liver and pork, bound with the egg and sufficient breadcrumbs to form a cohesive stuffing, seasoned to taste. The open end is then sewn up and the sausage fried in goose fat. It is usually eaten cold in slices.

Gehirnwurst (Germany)
Half the contents of this sausage consists of pig's brain, the rest is made up of equal quantities of fat and lean pork. These ingredients are chopped and well mixed, then seasoned with pepper, salt and mace. They are stuffed into pig casings and poached in pairs in boiling water for 5 minutes, then cooled. Before serving they are fried in butter.

'Gendarme' (France/Switzerland)
A chewy little brown smoked sausage made of beef, pork fat and rind, and seasoned with salt, spices and wine.

Genoa Sausage (Italy)
Extra lean pork and spices go to make this air-dried sausage, the best of which are reputed to come from St Olcese, a nearby village.

Geraucherte Bratwurst (Germany)
This is a smoked *bratwurst*. Six parts of finely chopped lean pork to one part of coarsely chopped fat bacon—a high proportion of lean to fat—goes into this sausage which is seasoned with salt, pepper and saltpetre.

German Sausage (England)
In spite of its name, this is our very English luncheon sausage. Sausage-makers, like ballet dancers between the wars, appear to think a foreign name provides an aura of expertise. It seems very probable in the case of the German sausage that the name was hastily replaced by luncheon sausage at the beginning of World War I. Anyhow, it is made of lean beef and salt pork, both minced, and studded with diced back fat. The mixture is bound with flour, cornflour and/or farina. The seasoning is provided by salt, saltpetre, sugar and spice. Cochineal is added to give colour and ox bungs are used as casings. It is cooked in water at 80°C (180°F) for 1 hour and at 75°C (170°F) for a further 2. It is then smoked until brown and rubbed with olive oil. The result is what you would expect, and one imagines that the Germans were not sorry when they found we had changed the name.

Gerty Meat Pudding (England)
The following recipe for this old West Country dish came from St Mellion, and is recorded in a Cornish recipe book compiled by the Cornwall Federation of Women's Institutes.

'Thoroughly cleanse the inside of a pig with salt and allow it to soak overnight in brine. Take the lights, melt, heart and kidneys, cover with cold water and boil till cooked (about ¾ hour). Cast down the fat and lard, mince the scallops with the cooked heart etc. Save the water they were boiled in. To every 3 quarts of liquid allow 1 quart of groats, and boil until cooked.

Add the groats to the minced ingredients and season with salt and pepper. Fill the skins with this mixture and boil gently for ¾ hour.'

(Scallops are the pieces of meat etc. which are left after casting, or rendering down the fat and lard.) Pig's blood added to the mixture turns gerty meat puddings into black pots.

Mrs Gilby's Sausages (England)
Mary Norwak and Babs Honey in their comprehensive work *The Complete Farmhouse Cookbook* quote Mrs Garden, whose recipe, originally written in an Eton College exercise-book and published in 1847, is as follows: '12lb sausage meat, 4oz salt, ¼oz mace, ½oz cloves, 10oz breadcrumbs, ½ pint water, or sufficient to make it a proper consistency.'

Glamorgan Cheese Sausage (Wales)
This was a favourite of George Borrow, who preferred it to the Epping sausage. Strictly speaking, neither should be called a sausage at all because both are skinless. The contents, however, are quite different. The Glamorgan variety is made of grated cheese, breadcrumbs, eggs, parsley, onion, and thyme or rosemary, blended together and formed into sausage shapes. Most recipes give twice as much breadcrumbs as cheese, and 1 or 2 eggs to 225g (8oz) of cheese and breadcrumbs together. For this amount half a fairly large onion would be sufficient. Dry mustard can be included with pepper and salt to taste. The sausages are fried in lard and served with apple rings and tomatoes, or tomato sauce.

Gloucester Sausage (England)
Traditionally, this sausage was made of pork from the Gloucester Old Spot pig, a breed which looks as if it is making a comeback. David James produces an excellent sausage consisting of over 90% pure pork, flavoured with sage, under this name at Cheltenham.

Gogue (France)
This is a speciality of Anjou, and traditionally made at Easter. It is a *boudin noir* made with pig's blood, cream, eggs, onions

fried in lard, breadcrumbs soaked in milk, and beet leaves. Seasoned with salt and white pepper, it is air-dried for several days. Before serving it is cut into slices and grilled.

Goose Blood Pudding (Scotland)

Mrs Glass's recipe of 1747 suggests that you chop off the head of a goose, drain the blood into a dish and mix with groats or barley. Season with herbs and spice according to taste. Remove the windpipe etc. from the neck and use the skin as a casing. This sausage 'is often placed in the middle of a goose giblet pie'. F. Marian McNeill says it is still made, but barley meal is always used and it is cooked in broth. The Welsh also made a goose sausage, using the skin of the neck as casing in the same way.

Goose Salame (Italy)

See *Salame di Oca*.

Goose Sausage (England)

Six parts of lean beef to one part of suet are finely chopped together and moistened with Madeira in which garlic has been steeped for 24 hours. The chopped lean meat of a roast goose is then added—how much depends on your taste—but there should be half as much goose as beef. The whole is filled into hog casings after seasoning with salt and pepper.

Göteborg (Sweden)

This is made mostly of beef, seasoned with salt, pepper and thyme.

Gothaer (Germany)

A fresh meat, air-dried sausage from Gotha in East Germany.

Göttinger (Germany)

A *fleischwurst* of which more than 70% is usually pork (45% lean and 25% bacon fat).

Grisoni (Switzerland)
This looks exactly like a small *salame* which is square in section. It is made of the salted, air-dried beef for which Les Grisons is famous. It is also expensive, beef costing twice as much as pork in Switzerland. The one we bought in London cost about 30p per ounce.

Grützewurst (Germany)
The French version of this is *saucisson au gruau*; and *gruau* mean 'groats'. The German word must surely be the origin of the American word 'grits'. The meat ingredient of this sausage is chitterling, cut into strips about 10cm (4in) long, mixed with groats or wheat meal which has been cooked in an aromatic broth. It is seasoned with salt, pepper and grated lemon peel. The sausages are steeped in boiling water for 3 minutes, dried, and lightly fried in butter before serving.

Gutsleberwurst (Germany)
A *kochwurst* of coarsely chopped liver, containing pieces of solid meat and cubes of fat, farmhouse style, but of high quality.

Gyulai (Hungary)
These are pork sausages in which sweet pepper dominates the seasoning. They are mildly smoked and are sold in pairs. Gyula, their place of origin, lies near the Romanian border.

Haggis (Scotland)
The Romans spread the idea of stuffing chopped meat and meal into some part of an animal's gut or gullet to many countries. They used pork in pig gut, but when they introduced the sausage to Scotland they found that the Scots much preferred mutton. The Roman idea was adapted to suit local taste by using mutton in a sheep's stomach. Here is a traditional recipe:

Ingredients
2 handfuls of oatmeal
2 or 3 onions
225g (8oz) shredded beef suet
1 tablespoon chopped parsley
grated nutmeg, black pepper, cayenne, salt
the paunch[1] and pluck[2] of a sheep

[1] Today the paunch is rarely used. Professionals use beef bungs.
[2] The pluck consists of the liver, lights (lungs) and heart.

Method Wash the paunch in several changes of cold water. Turn it inside out and plunge it into boiling water. Then scrape it and leave it overnight in cold, salted water. Wash the pluck and blanch it. Let it simmer for 1½ hours and reserve the cooking liquid. One recipe suggests leaving the windpipe hanging over the side of the pot so that any impurities may pass out freely. When cooked, cut out all gristle, veins and pipes. Mince the heart, lights, and half the liver (the other half is not needed). Then mince the onions and mix them with the suet. Toast the oatmeal slowly in a warm oven. Mix all the ingredients together, using plenty of freshly ground black pepper. Use enough of the water in which the meat was cooked to make the mixture 'sappy'. Fill the paunch five-eighths full. Press out the air and sew up the bag. Put it into fast boiling water. Pierce it with a darning needle when it first starts to swell and reduce the heat so that it boils gently for 3 hours without a lid on the pan. Neeps (turnips to the Sassenach) are the traditional accompaniment, and of course whisky.

Haggis Royale (Scotland)

The Cook and Housewife's Manual, written by Meg Dods (pseudonym of Isabel C. Johnson, and taken from Sir Walter Scott) was published in 1826. F. Marian McNeill considers it worthy of sharing a shelf with Brillat-Savarin's *Psychologie du Goût*. Meg Dods' recipe for Haggis Royale is as far removed from the ordinary kind as *boudin blanc de Paris* is from hog's pudding.

Chop 3lbs of leg of mutton and 1lb of suet, then stir in as much beef marrow as you like, the crumb of a penny loaf, 4 well-beaten egg yolks, ½ pint of red wine, 3 filleted anchovies and 'crystals of cayenne' to taste. This is well mixed, wrapped in a veal caul and baked in a fast oven. 'Serve as hot as fire, with brown gravy and venison sauce.'

Venison Haggis (Scotland)
Nichola Fletcher, author of *Venison, The Monarch of the Table* says this is the best haggis she has ever eaten. Her recipes for it and Venison sausages will be found under 'Venison'.

Ham Sausage (England)
Meat from the leg and shoulder of pork is chopped very fine. For every five parts of lean, add one part of fat and one part of rusk. The fat should be coarsely chopped. The mixture is moistened with water or stock and seasoned with mace, ginger, cayenne, white pepper, salt and saltpetre, before being packed tightly into weasands. A length of tape is tied to one end and wound diagonally round the sausage to the other and back, like cross-gartering, and made secure. It is simmered for 1 hour and smoked for 10 days.

Ham Sausage (Germany)
Mince very finely 2¼kg (5lb) of lean pork and mix with 450g (1lb) of coarsely chopped fat. Add 50g (2oz) pepper, 20g (¾oz) saltpetre and 75g (3oz) salt; moisten with 150ml (¼ pint) of claret or burgundy, and let the mixture stand for 6 hours. Fill the casings as tightly as possible, forming links 10–20cm long. Leave for a few hours then press the filling down again, before binding with tape, rather like cross-gartering. Cool-smoke for 12 days. They can be eaten raw; or gently simmered in water either before or after smoking.

Hamburger Gekochte Mettwurst (Germany)
Mettwurst is usually a *rohwurst*—a preserved sausage which is air-dried or smoked. In the case of *mettwurst* both processes are used. However, this Hamburg variety of coarsely chopped lean pork must count as a *kochwurst*, which is steamed or boiled.

Hammelwurst (Germany)
A mutton sausage.

Haslet (England)
This is a form of faggot. Two parts of pig pluck, one part of
pork fat and one part of lean pork are chopped and mixed with
three parts of finely chopped onion. This is seasoned with
sage, pepper and salt, wrapped in a piece of pig caul and baked
with little bits of lard dotted over the top, in the ratio of 50g
(2oz) to every 1kg (2lb) forcemeat.

Haslet, Lincolnshire (England)
This is a much more refined recipe. The main ingredients are
lean pork and rusk in the ratio of five parts to one. The
seasonings remain the same.

Hertzwurst (Germany)
Coarsely chopped pig's heart is mixed with finely minced
shoulder and belly of pork. It is seasoned with pepper, salt,
nutmeg and pimento, and filled into hog casings.

Hessian Leberwurst (Germany)
Hesse is sausage country. Frankfurt lies within its border and
with Thuringia to the east and Westphalia to the north and
west, one feels surrounded by *wurst*; yet we have not managed
to find out what makes this liver sausage different from other
local varieties.

Hildersheimer Streichleberwurst (Germany)
A Hanoverian speciality of pig's liver and pork, which, as the
name implies, can be spread.

Hog (or Hog's) Pudding (England)
This is a West Country dish, and one version could well be
called the Sassenach type of haggis, since it contains the pig
pluck (i.e. liver, heart and lungs).
   A more delicate recipe gives five parts of lean pork to two
parts of fat, two parts of rusk (or four parts of groats or

unpolished barley), chopped very fine and filled into wide hog casings which are dried and boiled for 30 to 50 minutes. The difference between Devon and Cornish Hog's Pudding is found in the seasoning. Finney gives the Devonshire seasoning as white pepper, salt and minute quantities of mace, nutmeg, thyme and cayenne, while the Cornish seasoning contains white pepper and salt, with traces of rubbed parsley, thyme, mace and nutmeg. In both cases 15g of seasoning to 450g (½oz to 1lb) is suggested.

Compare the above with this 1689 recipe from Anne Skinner's book (see *Black Hog's Pudding* page 110).

'To Make White Hogs Puddings. Take a pound of Bisketts, & cut them pieces & grate a peny loafe, then boyle a quart of cream, & put it to ye bisketts and bread to swell them, take a pound of blanch'd Almonds & beat them very small with rose water, then put in Eight Eggs, leave out four whites, & some beaten nutmegs, mace and ye marrow of ten Bones, & cut half very Small, & ye rest in pretty Small pieces, to put in as you fill them, then cutt some cittron. A little Amber greess, a little fatt, then fill ye gutts being well dried, but fill them not to full. Bullock gutts are best. Sweeten them with good sugar.'

The recipe for making the modern variety is as follows: Simmer the pluck and trimmings in water for 1 hour. Remove the meat and soak the groats or barley in the stock for 12 hours, then boil until tender. Mince the meat, season and mix with the groats or barley. Lengths of large casing 30cm (12in) long are filled with the mixture and tied into rings. They are sliced and fried, if eaten hot.

There are several variations on this recipe. Rice can be used instead of groats or barley. Raw eggs and even currants are sometimes included. One early 19th-century Cornish recipe replaces the offal with fresh fat and lean pork, and the cereal with breadcrumbs, which makes it indistinguishable from a sausage.

Holsteinerwurst (Germany/America)
This sausage, originally from north-west Germany, is made of equal parts of minced fresh beef and cured pork, highly spiced

with pepper, coriander, nutmeg and cardamom, sugar and salt. It is a *kochwurst*. The ones found in the United States are heavily smoked, and in rings. They often contain fresh pork cheek meat as well as pickled pork trimmings.

Investiture di Parma (Italy)

This seventeenth-century *mortadella* was a great feature of Parmesan gastronomy. Now, alas! it is of historical interest only.

In the second half of the seventeenth century the Italians played a game known as The Kitchen of Cockaigne, that legendary land of luxury and idleness. A board was marked out in twenty squares, each representing an Italian city, together with its gastronomical speciality. The drawing representing Piacenza shows cheese; Cremona depicts nougat; Modena features fresh sausages and Parma has the *investitura*, a *mortadella* so named because it was 'dressed'—or straightened perhaps—with lashings of string, much as many dried and smoked sausages are today.

Although the Parma *Investiture* has now disappeared, 300 years ago it was probably the most famous local dish, and remained so for more than a century. The Duke of Este's court cook, Cristoforo Messiburo, reprinted the recipe in his book *Epulario* (Ferrara, 1549).

'Take the throats of pigs, keeping those glands which are smooth and clean, but removing all traces of fat; the loins, and slice them small; the ears which have been well scrubbed and singed, and the snouts; the tongues which have been peeled and thoroughly cleaned in hot water; the trotters boned, well scrubbed, and singed, and the testicles.

'Take a clean crock and line the bottom with the trotters, ears and snouts, and layer with coarse salt. On these place the tongues, covered with fine salt, and then the throats, loins, and testicles, sprinkling all with a little fine salt. Leave for three days and then wash everything well in red wine. Steep all the ingredients in a clean crock of red wine for another day. Drain them well and remove all traces of salt, rinsing thoroughly several times. Finally pat everything dry with a clean white cloth.

'Then make the "mortadelle", making sure the ingredients are tightly packed together. These can be used immediately or stored for the future.'

Although this may not appear very appetizing, it does show the elaborate preparation which went into making sausages more than 400 years ago.

Irish Pork Sausages (Ireland)

Most of the Irish people to whom we have spoken say that there are no indigenous sausages except *drisheen*, which puzzled us since the Irish are so fond of pork. We found a recipe by Myrtle Allen in the American magazine *Gourmet*, which is very similar to one for English pork sausages, the main ingredients being twice as much lean as fat pork, fresh breadcrumbs and eggs; but the seasoning contains many more herbs and includes garlic, thyme, marjoram, basil and rosemary as well as salt and pepper.

Isterband (Sweden)

This is a beef and pork mixture to which parboiled barley— and sometimes potato—is added. It is usually salt-cured and air-dried, but can be hot-smoked. To cook it, you either score it lengthways, and fry with the scored side down, or split and grill. In either case it is often accompanied by fried onion and pickled beetroot.

Italian Sausage (Italy)

The Breakfast Book gives this recipe: 'Take the leg and shoulder of a young porker, remove the fat and rind, and with a sharp knife scrape the lean into a paste. Add half its weight of bacon fat, roughly cut up; season with pepper, cloves, mace, and nutmeg. Stuff the mixture into skins, and smother them in pounded saltpetre for eight days. Smoke them till sufficiently dry, and afterwards rub them with olive oil and the ashes from burnt vine branches.'

Jagdwurst (Germany)
The hunter's sausage is a large *brühwurst* of finely minced pork with diced pork fat. It is sliced and eaten cold. (See page 53 for Brunswick Salad).

Játernice (Czechoslovakia)
A small sausage, dark in colour, made of liver and lungs, which is easily recognized because the casings at the ends of each link are twisted round sticks. They are sold fresh and should be boiled and/or fried before eating.

Jausenwurst (Austria)
In Vienna, *jause* is, or was, a ladies' tea-party, starting at 5 p.m. and continuing till 7 p.m., two hours of gossip and chit-chat during which sweet and savoury canapés were served. We have not found out whether *jausenwurst* was offered at these get-togethers, but it is made of beef, lean pork, pork head meat, and bacon fat to which 2% of potato starch is added.

Jelita (Czechoslovakia)
Similar in appearance to the *játernice* and cooked in the same way, but it is in fact a blood sausage.

Jésus (France)
A very large pure pork *saucisson*, sometimes weighing as much as 3kg (7lb). It is coarsely chopped with quite large pieces of fat and matured for a long time. The *Jésus de Morteau*, eaten hot with *pommes à l'huile*, was a speciality of the Restaurant Moissonnier, Paris.

Jewish Sausages (Israel/International)
These little sausages, made of beef, egg, onion, carrot and matzos meal, are served at Passover.

Judru (France)
A speciality of Chagny—26 kilometres south-west of Beaune—rather like a *salame* and made of pure pork.

Kabanos (Poland)

This is a hard sausage made of coarsely minced pork. It is smoked and its natural casing is twisted to form thin links about 30cm (12in) or more in length. It is found all over Poland, but we have seen it in some London stores spelt with an initial 'C' and wrongly described as being Spanish. Although originally Polish and taken on hunting expeditions, it is now also made in Belgium and eaten at home.

Kälberwurst (Switzerland)

Literally 'veal sausage'. A speciality of the Glarus canton is to cook this sausage in a thick sharpish sauce, flavoured with nutmeg.

Kalbsbratwurst (Switzerland)

This white sausage is bland in flavour. It is made of veal, bacon, milk and spices. It is another speciality of the Glarus canton and is grilled before serving.

Kalbsleberwurst (Germany)

Calf-liver sausage, very finely minced. (See *Leberwurst*, page 172).

Kalbsroulade (Germany)

A mixture of pork and veal studded with diced pork fat and pistachio nuts.

Kantwurst (Austria)

This is a *rohwurst* consisting of ⅔ lean pork and ⅓ fat. Beef is sometimes mixed with the lean pork. The most noticeable thing about this sausage is that it is rectangular in section.

Karlovska Lukanka (Bulgaria)

Twice as much beef as bacon and twice as much pork as beef is seasoned with equal amounts of sugar, salt, caraway seeds and oregano and pepper. (*The Balkan Cookbook* gives 7 teaspoons of each to 7 kilos (15lb) of meat in all. This is filled into wide casings and twisted and tied into 25cm (10 in) links. These are pricked with a needle and air-dried. After 2 or 3 days they are rolled into shape and allowed to dry off completely. Wrapped in paper and stored in a wooden box of wood ash, they are said to keep for a year.

Karvaviza (Bulgaria)
This Bulgarian black pudding uses the lung, heart and kidney of a pig as well as meat from the neck and belly, and, of course, the blood. It is seasoned with allspice, caraway and oregano and smoked.

Karvaviza Drug Vid (Bulgaria)
Another version of Bulgarian black pudding which is boiled rather than air-dried.

Karvaviza Po Banski (Bulgaria)
This is very similar to the black puddings described above, but includes the spleen.

Käsewurst (Austria)
65%–85% of this sausage is the same as the farce for *Tirolerwurst*, the remainder being diced cheese, usually Emmental or Bergkäse.

Kasseler Leberwurst (Germany)
This Westphalian speciality originally came from Kassel, and since the hams from that part of Germany are famous, one can expect other pork products to be of high quality. It is a dark-coloured sausage of pig's liver and diced lean pork.

Kaszanka (Poland)
This is a soft sausage made from pork, pig's liver, lungs and blood. Buckwheat groats are used as a binder and it is well spiced. The links are knotted, and it is found all over Poland.

Katenrauchwurst (Germany)
This black-skinned *rohwurst* is about 45cm (18in) long and 10cm (4in) in diameter, and contains pieces of smoked pork. It is dark in colour, and coarse, but firm in texture. It got its

name because it was originally produced in the peasant huts called *katen*, where it remained in the chimney being smoked for a long period. The Germans cut it at an angle to produce thick oval slices.

Kentish Sausages (England)
Two parts of lean pork to one part of fat, seasoned with sage, mace, nutmeg, pepper and salt are the ingredients of this sausage, which is fairly coarse in texture. The best ones we have tasted come from Tunbridge Wells and were made by W. J. Hill & Sons. Their 100-year-old recipe is given under *Tunbridge Wells Sausage*.

Kielbasa (Poland)
We first came across this sausage watching *Kojak* on television. On making enquiries we found that *kielbasa* is simply the Polish word for sausage, but in the United States it is used to denote a special ring sausage made of pork, beef and fat, seasoned with spice and garlic and filled into hog casings. It is particularly popular in Pittsburgh which has a large Polish population. It is 4cm (1½in) in diameter, and can be fried and served with potatoes, or boiled and accompanied by lentils. (Recipes on page 60).

Kipper Sausages (England/Scotland)
The trouble with kippers is the bones. If one could have those delicious smoky fish, crisp on the outside, soft and buttery on the inside, without all the boredom of removing every minute bone, what a dish they would make. Well, the answer is the kipper sausage. As we have already pointed out, they could be bought in London before World War II, and we have heard they can still be found in Scotland; but obviously, the best thing to do is make them yourself. After many experiments we decided that the following recipe gave the best results:

Ingredients
3 pairs of good fat kippers
75g (3oz) butter
75g (3oz) shredded suet
2 large slices of bread
pepper, mace, salt
casings

Method Put the kippers in a baking tin with a little water and dot them with butter. The water need not cover the fish. Bake in a moderate oven until the flesh comes away from the bones. Skin and bone them. Put the bread to soak in the buttery water. If you have too much water, reduce it by fast boiling. Mix the fish, bread and suet in a bowl and season to taste. (Mace is a personal choice, but you could try a little lemon instead. The great thing to remember is to experiment.) Now put the farce through the fine plate of the mincer, twice. Test for consistency and flavour, and adjust if necessary. If it is too sloppy you will have to add more bread. It should be loose and sticky, but not at all runny. You can fry a small lump in hot fat to get an idea of how it should taste. Fill the casings, twisting into links.

Some of the ones we made were too dry, and we used butter, oil from a tin of sardines and other fats and liquids before we came up with this recipe. The sausage needs a little bread or cereal to hold the moisture, and the suet helps to enrich it without distracting from the flavour.

Kishka (Hungary)
This is similar to a *kielbasa*, but more highly spiced and contains rice. It is stuffed into either beef runners or hog casings. When fried it bursts, which, apparently, is what it is supposed to do.

Cecil Gysin tells us that *kishki* is the Russian word for casings and *baranyekishki* means sheep casings.

Klobás (Czechoslovakia)
A red-skinned sausage spiral, not formed into links, juicy, with a thick skin. It is made of smoked pork or veal and wine.

Kloepfer (Switzerland)

The name given by the citizens of Basel to their own form of *cervelat* made of beef, pork, bacon, pork rind and spice. It is about 10cm (4in) long, and 3cm (1½in) in diameter. A mild sausage with a pleasant smoky taste, it can be brought in the Swiss Centre in London.

Knackerli (Switzerland)

A sausage from Appenzell, made of beef, pork, veal and spice.

Knackwurst (Germany)

This stumpy sausage is made of 50% lean pork, 30% beef and 20% fresh fat pork, all finely minced and flavoured with salt, cumin and garlic. Saltpetre is added to give the meat a good colour. The casings are beef runners which are tied and air-dried for 4 days before being cool-smoked. They may be poached in boiling water for 10 minutes before serving. (A recipe for serving will be found on page 54.)

Knoblauchwurst (Germany)

Knoblauch means garlic, and this sausage is highly flavoured with it. It is made of fat and lean pork, salt, pepper, and spice. In the United States it is sometimes known as *knoblaugh*. This sausage is considered by some to be a good alternative to *knackwurst*.

Knockpølse (Denmark)

Forty per cent lean beef, 25% lean pork, 25% veal and 10% pork back fat are used to make these sausages which are flavoured with salt, saltpetre, nutmeg, cinnamon, ginger, pepper, garlic or shallots. The beef and veal are roughly chopped together before adding the pork, then all the lean meats are finely chopped together. The fat is diced in 5mm (¼in) cubes and added to the meat which is then seasoned and well mixed. Hog casings are loosely filled and twisted to form links 12cm (5in) long. These are air-dried for 1 day, then hot-smoked. This is the Danish version of Knackwurst.

Koblenz Sausage (Germany)

Veal and pork are pickled in brine for some days. The meat is minced and seasoned, onions and garlic dominating the pepper and salt. The farce is fed into narrow pig casings, fairly loosely, to form links, 6 of which weigh 450–500g (about 1lb). The sausages are air-dried for a few hours before being smoked over a fire of oak and beech at 38°C (100°F) until a yellowish red. They are simmered for 6 to 8 minutes before serving.

Kochbratwurst (Germany)

See *Bratwurst* and *Kochwurst*.

Kochwurst (Germany)

Larousse gives *kochwurst* or *mettwurst* as *saucisse à bouillir*. While this is not inaccurate, as both *can* be boiled, the Germans tell us that they look upon *kochwurst* as one of the three basic types of sausage (see page 85). They claim *mettwurst* as *rohwurst* and *bratwurst* as a *brühwurst* that should be fried or grilled. All of which only goes to show that it is better to put sausages into frying-pans than pigeon-holes.

Kolbasa (USSR)

The Russian word for a type of sausage. Theodora FitzGibbon says there are many different varieties, amongst them *kolbasa Ukrainskaya*, or Ukrainian sausage, which is very thick and about 1.25m (4 ft) long.

Kolbasz (Hungary)

This word obviously comes from the same root as *kolbasa*, *kielbasa* and *klobás*, which all mean sausage. This Hungarian type keeps well hanging in a cool place. It does not need refrigeration.

Kolska (Poland)

A firm pork sausage from Poznan and Lublin. The modern variety contains glucose, ascorbic acid and polyphosphates as well as salt and spice, and usually comes in an artificial casing.

Königwurst (Germany)

A royal sausage made of equal parts of chicken and partridge, to which are added chopped truffles and mushrooms. The whole is bound with egg, seasoned with salt, pepper and mace and moistened with Rhine wine. It is braised, allowed to cool and then sliced and eaten cold.

Koprivstenska Lukanka (Bulgaria)

This sausage is made of twice as much pork from the neck and breast as beef from the leg. The meat is chopped and allowed to drain. It is then minced (although *The Balkan Cookbook* says that traditionally it was beaten with a club). The mixture is seasoned with salt, white pepper, sugar and caraway seeds and allowed to stand overnight. It is stuffed into beef casings, twisted into links about 15ins long and air-dried for 10 to 12 weeks. It is said to keep for a year.

Kosher Salame (Israel)

Here, lean and fat pork are replaced by kosher-killed bull beef and brisket fat. White peppercorns, cardamom, nutmeg, coriander and garlic provide the flavouring, and weasands—or a cellulose imitation—form the casings.

Kraine (Austria)

This is similar to *Burgenländische hauswürstel*.

Krajana (Poland)

Another firm pork sausage originating in Poznan. The knotted links are smoked.

Krakowska (Poland)

This medium-sized, slicing sausage, in which lean beef is blended with lean and fat pork then smoked, must have originated in Cracow, but it is now found all over Poland. The texture is so close and firm that at first glance the meat looks almost solid and not chopped at all. It has a pleasant smoky flavour. In the Austrian *Krakauer*, chunks of lean meat can be seen.

Kranjska Kobasica (Yugoslavia)

Kranj is a town north of Ljubljana from which comes this local variety of pork sausage. Six times as much pork as bacon is used in this sausage. The meat is cut into cubes and seasoned with sodium nitrate, pepper, salt and garlic. The mixture is kneaded together for about 30 minutes and filled into small casings. These are tied in pairs and smoked for up to 3 days if they are to be eaten hot with sauerkraut, but they should be smoked for longer if they are to be eaten cold.

Kräuterwurst and Krautleberwurst (Switzerland)

This is derived from *kräuter*, meaning herbs. It is a Swiss liver sausage featured in a speciality of the Waadt canton, called Kräuterwurst à la Montreux, in which they are laid on baked leeks and covered with rich brown gravy.

Lamb's Blood Pudding (Scotland)

A recipe dated 1775 gives lamb's blood, fat from around the kidney chopped small, cream, salt, pepper, spice, a sprig of mint and chopped onion or chives as the main ingredients of this black pudding, which the Scots consider to be the best of its kind. It is not usually put into a casing.

Lancashire Pork Sausage (England)

The proportion of lean to fat pork varies in different recipes. Some give equal parts of each to which should be added half the amount of either in stale breadcrumbs. Others say three times as much lean as fat, and as much bread as the latter. Sage, thyme, salt and pepper are usual seasonings, but Mrs Chaplin of Finsthwaite used to add 1 teaspoon of anchovy essence to every 450g (1lb) of sausage meat. Another recipe omits the herbs but adds ginger and mace to the finely minced mixture.

Landjäger (Germany)

The interesting thing about this Swabian speciality is that it is one of the very few sausages that is square in section. The main ingredient is beef, with sometimes up to 40% pork, flavoured with caraway seeds and garlic. When the casings are full, they are pressed into a wooden frame with square battens between them. They are cured, cold-smoked and air-dried. The ones we tasted were rather greasy, but had a surprising aftertaste of cherries, which we subsequently found was due to the addition of cherry wine to the forcemeat. They should be hard, and are eaten raw.

Landmettwurst (Germany)
A country variation of *mettwurst*.

Lap Cheong (China/Hong Kong)
This is the ordinary Chinese pork sausage. *Lap* means dry (or wax) and *cheong* means intestine. The Chinese process differs in many ways from the western method and we have given that used by the King of King's Company in Hong Kong on page 95. Alas! his delicious sausages have not yet travelled as far as Europe, but a variety of *lap cheong* can be bought in London, and some are even imported from Canada. They contain pork, soy sauce, paprika, sodium nitrate, grain and alcohol.

Lebanon Bologna (USA)
This sausage does not come from the Levant, or Italy, as one might at first suppose, but from Lebanon County, Pennsylvania. The early German settlers, who became known as Pennsylvanian Dutch in the second half of the last century, used to make Bologna sausages. In 1885 Daniel Weaver started producing an all-beef, smoked Bologna. The pre-cured meat is coarsely ground and stuffed into casings which are hung in the smoke of specially matured hardwood for 4 to 6 days.

Leberstreichwurst (Austria)
This is a rather small liver sausage of pork and pig's liver. It has a fairly coarse texture and nowadays is often found in an artificial casing. It can be spread.

Leberwurst (Germany/Austria, France, Hungary etc.)
(See also *Leverkorf, Liver Sausage, Saucisse de Foie de Porc etc.*)
This word for liver sausage covers a vast range of products

from the truffled goose-liver variety (see *Gänsleberwurst*) to a Hungarian type which is made of the heart, liver and lungs of a pig as well as its neck. The lungs and heart are boiled until tender and then minced with the raw liver and neck. Four or 5 bread rolls and 1 or 2 onions are also put through the mincer. The mixture is well seasoned with pepper, salt and garlic and moistened with the stock in which the meat was cooked.

The Swiss canton of Les Grisons produces a local speciality called *le leberwurst*; and the German varieties—apart from *gänsleberwurst*—include *pfaelzer* and *gutsleberwurst*. Many liver sausages contain onion, but *Douglas' Encyclopaedia* cautions British sausage-makers against adding it in summer as the onion may 'easily cause acidity'; however, we have not found this warning elsewhere.

Here is the recipe for a liver sausage, scaled down from a commercial German-style version:

> **Ingredients**
> **1.5kg (3½lb) pig's liver**
> **450g (1lb) pig's cheek**
> **450g (1lb) salted pork fat**
> **550g (1¼lb) pig's snout**
> **100g (4oz) onion**
> **salt, pepper, ginger, marjoram**
> **cinnamon and/or cloves**

Method The snouts are simmered in just enough water to cover them for two hours, the cheeks for 45 minutes and the fat for 15 minutes. The onion is fried in lard and finely minced with the raw liver. The snouts and cheeks are first coarsely ground, then blended with the liver, onions, seasoning and fat. All is pounded to a smooth, fine paste, being moistened as necessary with the stock in which the ingredients were cooked. Hog fat ends (known as bungs in the USA) are used as casings, and the sausages are boiled for 1 hour at about 70°C (160°F), chilled, air-dried and smoked for 3 hours at approximately 45°C (110°F).

Leoni (Germany)

We thought this was an Italian sausage, but failed to find it on our Italian tour and only discovered when we returned that it is what the Bavarians call a *saucisse de Lyon*. We imagine that it is the same as *leona*, which the magazine *Meat* says is made of coarsely ground beef, pork trimmings and back fat, seasoned with sugar, pepper, ginger, coriander and nutmeg, in a casing of sewed beef middles.

Leverpølse (Denmark)
This is a firmer version of *leverpostej* (see below). One Danish recipe includes veal as well as pork in equal quantities added to the pig's liver, and the seasoning has nutmeg with the salt and pepper. Stock is used instead of milk, but the method is basically the same.

Leverpostej (Denmark)

> **Ingredients**
> 1 pig's liver
> 450g (1lb) lean pork
> 900g (2lb) flare fat
> 2 or 3 anchovies
> 2 eggs
> salt, pepper, nutmeg and cinnamon

Method All the meats and the anchovies are minced, then mixed with the eggs and the seasoning. Beef runners are recommended for casings and the sausage is simmered for 2 hours.

Leverkorv (Sweden)
This Swedish liver sausage differs slightly from other varieties in this book, and is comparatively easy to make:

> **Ingredients**
> 900 (2lb) pig's liver
> 225g (½lb) fat bacon
> 450g (1lb) veal
> 450ml (¾ pint) milk (cold, boiled)
> 2 tablespoons chopped onion
> salt, pepper, marjoram
> casings

Method First mince the liver and then push it through the sieve. Mince the veal two or three times until it is really fine, combining the bacon with it in the final mincing. Mix all the ingredients together, gradually stirring in the milk and seasoning. Do not fill the casings too full, as there must be room for expansion. Simmer gently for 30 minutes.

Lincolnshire Haslet
See *Haslet, Lincolnshire.*

Linguica (Portugal)
A coarse, pungent sausage, usually grilled over charcoal.

Linköping (Sweden)
The Östergotland town, 100 miles south-west of Stockholm, gave its name to this salt-cured sausage, made from pork and beef, which is an excellent spread for sandwiches.

Liver Sausage (England)
Douglas' Encyclopaedia gives ten recipes for liver sausage, but most of them are variations of *leberwurst, leverkorv, saucisse de foie de porc etc.*, and one is actually for an imitation liver sausage made out of tripe and fat from the intestines. The oddest, however, is raisin liver sausage. So far we have failed to find out where this sausage originated. The recipe has a Roman ring, but although the existence of sugar was known to the Romans, it was not brought to Europe until AD 625, and if, therefore, it replaced honey, the original recipe was stranger still. The ingredients are pig's liver, calf's brain, onions, currants, raisins, sugar and blanched almonds.

Lo Chou Cheung (China/Hong Kong)
Lean and fat pork are the main ingredients, but extra sugar is added to the sausage, which contains concentrated soy sauce, in contradistinction to *pak yau cheung*. It also contains wine, and is filled into dry hog casings. (See page 95 for full details of Chinese sausage-making.)

Lomo (Spain)

Unlike other sausages, this is made from a solid, lean loin of pork in a casing, not minced or chopped meat. It should be cut into very thin slices, and, although it can be fried like bacon, in our opinion it is best appreciated when eaten cold. It is the most expensive Spanish sausage to be imported into Britain.

Longaniza (Spain)

Some people consider this large *chorizo* the nearest Spanish equivalent to an English pork sausage, but we have yet to find a British brand which contains *pimentón*, and this powdered pimento is an essential ingredient. You may also read that it is always fried, but this is not so; there is a Spanish version of *oeufs en cocotte* in which the eggs, nestling in their buttered fireproof dish, are covered with slices of *longaniza*, sprinkled with fried breadcrumbs and baked in the oven.

Longeole, La (Switzerland)

A speciality of Geneva, made of chopped pork in a natural casing, dried for 48 hours and cooked for 2 hours before serving.

Loukanika (Greece and Cyprus)

Belly of pork is cut into small pieces and marinated in red wine, with salt added, and coriander and other herbs to taste. It is kept in the marinade for about a week, then stuffed into hog casings and hung to dry in a warm place, in the sun if possible, for about 2 weeks.

The Cyprus version, according to Tess Mallos, is made of shoulder of pork and the wine is port. She does not suggest drying, but simply storing in a refrigerator.

Lou-kenkas (France)

A small spicy Basque sausage, eaten hot, with cold oysters.

Lübecker Saucisson (Germany)

According to George Ellwanger, these were 'tiny sausages', but he gives no recipe, and *The Pleasures of the Table* was written 75 years ago, so things may have changed.

Lufttrockene Mettwurst (Germany)
A Westphalian *mettwurst* which, as the name explains, is air-dried.

Luganeghe or Luganiga (Italy)
One of the few fresh pure pork sausages that is not twisted into links. This speciality of northern Italy is sold by the length, like a true Cumberland sausage, and the cook cuts it to the size she requires before frying. Accompanied by *polenta*—another speciality of northern Italy—tomato sauce and parmesan cheese, it makes a delicious main course, simple, subtle, and satisfying.

Lukanka (Bulgaria)
A spicy pork sausage, slightly salted, which can be eaten raw or cooked. See *Smedovska Lukanka, Koprivstenska Lukanka,* and, *Karlovska Lukanka.*

Luncheon Sausage (England)
See **German Sausage**

Lyoner (Germany)
This is a German version of what was originally the French sausage from Lyon. It consists of beef, pork, veal and small pistachio nuts. It is a *brühwurst*, finely minced and mildly seasoned, and can be eaten hot or cold. The meat in the American version is 93% pork to 7% beef.

Lyons Sausage (France)
Another recipe from *The Breakfast Book* gives 500g (1lb) of beef, 1kg (2lb) each of bacon and fresh pork. The beef and pork should be chopped very fine, but the bacon cut into cubes. This is seasoned with saltpetre and pepper, filled into casings, tied in links and put in a dish. They are sprinkled with saltpetre and left for a week. They are then smoked for 3 days, steeped in red wine for 48 hours to which sage, thyme, and bay leaves have been added and smoked again, before being wrapped in paper till wanted.

Mährische (Austria)
Forty-five per cent lean pork and 25% bacon fat are the main
ingredients of this sausage, the rest being made up of beef,
water and seasoning.

Makkara (Finland)
The Finnish word for sausage. They are usually large.

Manchester Sausage (England)
For the seasoning of this sausage see page 74.

Mandaliya (India)
Indian sausage recipes are rare, and judging by this description
of a North Indian dish, extremely imprecise: 'entrails stuffed
with marrow and spices, then usually grilled'.

Mayence Red Sausage (Germany)
The ingredients are 75% neck of pork, 20% chopped pork rind
and 5% pig's tongue, seasoned with white pepper, peppermint,
cloves, marjoram and mace. The mixture is moistened with a
little pig's blood, filled into a pig' stomach and plunged
immediately into boiling water. If, when pricked, no blood
appears, but only white fat, the sausage is cooked.

Mazzafegati—sometimes spelt Mezzifegati (half liver) (Italy)
In this delicious pork liver sausage from Norcia in Umbria, you
will find pine kernels, but its distinctive flavour comes from
fennel and garlic.

Mealie Pudding (Scotland)
This is sometimes called white pudding. A sliced onion is fried
in pork dripping then mixed with 100g (4oz) of toasted oatmeal
and seasoning. It is cooked for 10–15 minutes before being
filled into hog casings. Sometimes the mixture is not put into
casings; it is then called skirlie.

Mecklenburgerbratwurst (Germany)
Equal parts of lean and fat pork, seasoned with spices, salt,
pepper and brandy.

Mecklenburgerleberwurst (Germany)

The fresh liver of a pig is minced and passed through a coarse sieve. This is mixed with half its weight of breast of pork, which has been boiled till tender, and chopped (not minced) together with the kidneys, tongue and a little back fat. Season this with pepper, allspice and powdered sage. Fill the casings only three-quarters full and boil for 30 minutes in the water in which the pork was cooked. Plunge into cold water and hang to dry or smoke.

Medister Pølse (Denmark)

Med means 'with', *ister* means 'fat' and, as many readers may already realize, *pølse* means 'sausage'. It is usually made of pork, sometimes mixed with beef or veal or both, and is packed into casings 4cm (1½in) in diameter. It is hot smoked and may be fried, grilled or boiled before serving.

Medvurst (Sweden)

A Swedish version of *Mettwurst.*

> *Ingredients*
> 900g (2lb) lean beef
> 900g (2lb) lean pork
> 900g (2lb) fat bacon, diced
> 150 ml (¼ pt) brandy
> 150 ml (¼ pt) stock
> salt, saltpetre, pepper, cloves
> casings

Method Mince the lean meat two or three times, mix well and season. Moisten gradually with the brandy diluted with an equal amount of stock. Now add the diced bacon fat. Fill the casings and knot them to form links. Cool them in cold water, then dry and place them in an earthenware dish. Rub them with the simple curing mixture described on page 80. Let them lie in the dish for 2 days, turning and rubbing them once after 24 hours, and again before taking them out. Having pressed the meat down you will find it has shrunk which means that the links must be re-tied. Although these are traditionally knotted, it is really easier to twist the ends, so long as they stay that way. One version includes veal, and is hot or cool-smoked over juniper berries. *Medvurst* is an extremely useful sausage as it can be grilled, fried, boiled or used cold for sandwiches.

Merguez (Algeria)
A highly spiced, short, stumpy beef sausage which is usually grilled. Its popularity is growing in France, both in Paris and the provinces, and it can even be bought in some London shops.

Mettwurst or Metwurst (Germany)
This *rohwurst*, like the Swedish version, is basically a mixture of pork and beef. The German sausage differs slightly and, again, the recipe changes from region to region. The seasoning usually includes sugar, paprika and nutmeg. The mixture is filled into beef runners or hog casings and then cool-smoked. There is *grosse mettwurst* and *feine mettwurst*, the former being very coarse in texture and red, the latter smooth and pink. The consistency can vary from spreadable to hard. They can be used successfully in pizzas and the last one we had was delicious fried, its extremely soft texture making it rather gooey to eat raw.

Milzwurst (Germany)
This Bavarian veal sausage is usually eaten after being fried in butter.

Mocetta, La (Italy)
A large *salame*.

Morcels (Portugal)
The Portuguese version of *morcilla*.

Morcilla (Spain)
The Spanish version of the *boudin noir* has almost as many variations as its French counterpart. The most famous, however, comes from Asturia. The Asturian breed of pig is black and

produces delicious ham and sausage. This province is also famous for its apples, with which pigs seem to have a special affinity. The *morcilla* is an essential ingredient of *fabada*, the national dish of Asturia, which includes *chorizos* as well as bacon, belly of pork, onions and white beans. There is a less famous *morcilla negra* from Andalucia, made of pig's blood, minced almonds, pimentos and parsley.

Morcilla Blanca (Spain)
Just as you will find *boudin blanc* in France, so you will find the Spanish equivalent, which is made of chicken and hard-boiled eggs.

Morpølse (Norway)
A sausage made of beef, mutton and reindeer.

Mortadella (Italy)
This is the original Bologna sausage. Its ancestry goes back to a date before 1376 (the year in which the Guild of Sausage Makers was formed) when, in the monastery kitchens, pork was broken down with a pestle and mortar. The mortar, it is said, was known as a *mortaio della carne di maiale*, which became shortened to *mortadella*. In those days it is said that the meat had to be still warm from a freshly slaughtered pig. Be that as it may, today there is an enormous variety of recipes for this type of sausage. It is cooked by boiling and then hung up to dry for a few days. Elizabeth David rightly says that the best are made of pure pork, but the cheaper ones may well contain veal, tripe, pig's head, donkey and soya flour. Coriander and white wine may be used as seasoning.

In Bologna, we learnt that Signor Tamburini uses only pure pork. He scoffed at the list of seasonings which I read from one recipe we had collected in England. 'Aniseed? No! Cloves? No! Cardamom? No! Rum? Good Heavens no!' he said. 'Nothing but pork, garlic, pepper and salt.' Other manufacturers may use some of the more exotic seasonings to disguise the cheaper meat, but they all have one thing in common—the size of the *mortadelle*—they are one of the largest types of sausage, and beef or pig bladders are used as casings. Elizabeth David does not care for the ordinary *mortadella*; Robert Carrier puts it amongst his favourite sausages. Jane Grigson prefers the French version and gives an excellent recipe in *Charcuterie and French Pork Cookery*. Good as some may be, we still prefer *salami*.

Mortadelle (France)
The French version of the above, using 47% lean pork, 30% salt pork fat and 23% fresh pork fat. It is steeped in wine and smoked for 4 days.

Mui Kwai Cheung (China/Hong Kong)
Mui kwai means 'rose', and like many of the sausages made by the King of King's Company in Hong Kong, takes its name from one of the ingredients, in this case the rosé wine which is added to the basic ingredients of lean and fat pork, soy, salt and sugar.

Mulhouse Sausage (France)
This is illustrated in *Larousse* and is obviously an Alsatian delicacy, but we have not yet tasted it.

Mumbar (Iraq)
There is nothing like working for an oil company if you want to see the world, except perhaps joining the Navy. It was oil that took me to Baghdad, but how Mumbar was made I had no idea until Tess Mallos, in her *Complete Middle East Cookbook*, told me. The main ingredients are lamb and rice, which is easily recognizable, and her recipe is impeccable. If, however, it was included here we would have to describe what one teaspoon of *baharat* contains—and that alone is a blend of eight different spices.

Münchener Weisswurst (Germany)
Invented on 22 February 1857, by a Munich butcher, this *brühwurst* has become a legend. Although the basic ingredients should be veal and parsley, you may find that now it contains beef. The description 'white sausage' really refers to its outward

appearance. Some say it should be grilled and served with sauerkraut and potato purée, while others prefer it gently steamed, but both insist that it must be accompanied by the sweet Bavarian mustard. The dyed-in-the-wool *Münchener* never eats this sausage after 11 am. For years we wondered why this was one sausage you could *not* find at Dallmayr's. We recently learnt from one who lives there that it is not an 'aristocratic' sausage. Apparently it would be rather like expecting to find faggots at Fortnum's.

Mushroom Sausage (England)

We cannot do better than give the recipe set out in Finney's *Handy Guide for Pork Butchers*. 'A first-class mushroom sausage may be made by using half a pound of well bruised button mushrooms, and one pound of rusk to every seven-pound block of meat. The mushrooms used for the purpose must be quite fresh and as dry as possible. Sweaty and flabby ones should not be used under any circumstances. These sausages should be eaten quite fresh, and should only be made to order, as they will not keep for any length of time. They should be placed in hot water for five minutes before cooking, which will help prevent them from bursting during the process.'

Mutton Sausage (England)

Here is a West Country recipe:

> *Ingredients*
> 450g (1lb) lean mutton
> 100g (4oz) mutton suet
> 100g (4oz) breadcrumbs
> 50g (2oz) boiled bacon or ham, roughly chopped
> stock
> pepper and salt

Method Mince the meat and suet, mix in the breadcrumbs and bacon, moisten with stock if necessary, and fill into casings. (Another recipe gives five parts of mutton to two parts of pork and one of rusk, moistened with fresh sheep's blood.)

Mysliwska (Poland)
This smoked pork sausage is found all over Poland. It contains the usual salt and spices, and the natural casing is twisted to form links.

Neuenburger (Switzerland)
A Swiss *rohwurst* we have heard about, but not yet tried.

North Staffordshire Black Pudding
See under *Black Pudding*.

Nürnburgerwurst (Germany)
Minced or finely chopped lean pork is mixed with diced bacon fat, steeped in kirsch. Salt, pepper, thyme and plenty of marjoram provide the seasoning. The filling is stuffed into casings which are tied to form links, each weighing about 100g (4oz). They should be lightly fried in butter before serving.

Oberland Leberwurst (Germany)
Remove the rind and bone from a shoulder of pork and boil it with 1–2kg (2–3lb) of diced back fat according to the size of the shoulder. Mince the pork with half its weight of raw pig's liver. Mix this with 2 or 3 finely chopped onions, add the diced back fat and season with salt, pepper and nutmeg. Add a little lard if the mixture seems too stiff. Fill the casings and boil gently for 45 minutes. Then steep the sausages in cold water until they are stiff, and finally hang them in a cool, airy place to dry.

Oderberger (Austria)
A sausage in the same category as *Braunschweiger*.

Ogonowa (Poland)
A skinless spiced and smoked pork sausage, found all over Poland.

Onion and Liver Sausage (England)
This is made of 25% liver, 20% lights, 15% back fat and 40% lean pork, flavoured to taste. Pepper, salt, nutmeg and marjoram

are the usual seasonings. The liver is minced, the onions shredded and the lights are sliced like runner beans. All these are gently fried and mixed with the chopped fat, which has, if necessary, been softened in hot water. The casings, hog fat ends (or bungs), are filled with the seasoned mixture and simmered for 30 minutes. They are then put under cold, running water and dried.

Ossocolla (Italy)
A kind of Copocolla.

Oxford Sausage (England)
Once again, there are several different versions. The following one is basically Mrs Beeton's recipe of 1861.

> **Ingredients**
> 450 (1lb) lean veal
> 450 (1lb) young pork
> 450 (1lb) beef suet
> 225g (½lb) breadcrumbs
> pepper and salt
> peel of half a lemon
> grated nutmeg
> 6 sage leaves
> thyme, savory, marjoram or basil

Method Chop the meats and suet finely together and add the breadcrumbs. Mince the lemon peel and chop the sage very finely. Mix these, with the grating of nutmeg and the other herbs and seasoning, into the sausage meat. In Mrs Beeton's day these sausages were not always stuffed into casings.

One of the variations cuts the beef suet by half, but adds anchovy.

Miss Parker's Oxford Sausage (circa 1800)
This comes from a family recipe book belonging to Kemmis Buckley.

'I p^d & half of Pork, half a p^d of Veal one p^d of Beef suet chopped very fine mix them together with one handful of sage shred fine, one ounce of salt, not quite ¼ of an ounce of

Pepper, a little nutmeg, 1 egg, near half a pint of water, they
are to be rolled without flour and fried without butter, the pan
must be made quite hot before they are put in, then keep
shaking them till they are a fine brown.'

Oyster Sausages (England)
The following recipe comes from *The Breakfast Book*. 'Beat a
pound of veal in a mortar, season it; beard and cut in pieces
two dozen oysters, add them to the veal, as well as some
breadcrumbs soaked in the oyster liquor. Put them in skins . . .
and fry as sausages.'

Another recipe says that large stewing oysters are best, and
goes on 'Open two dozen and mince them finely. Mix them
with 170g (6oz) of grated breadcrumb which has been soaked
in the oyster liquor, and 170g (6oz) of finely shredded beef suet.
Season with a saltspoon of powdered mace, half a saltspoon of
salt, half a saltspoon of pepper, a pinch of cayenne and moisten
with the well-beaten yolks of two eggs.'

Packet (Ireland)
A southern Irish black pudding which comes from Limerick,
and is very similar—if not identical—to *drisheen*. It is eaten
with tripe from a sheep's stomach. At one time the packet and
tripe trade was a speciality of the parish of St Mary in Limerick,
and was very lucrative. Packet is also popular in Cork.

Paphos Sausage (Cyprus)
In *The Tenth Muse*, Sir Harry Luke gives this country recipe:
'Take eight to ten pounds (4–5 kilos) of young pork, preferably
leg, separate the lard and pass the lean through the mincing
machine. Chop the lard up small, to about the size of peas, and
mix together with the minced meat, adding pepper and salt.
Add pounded coriander seeds and herbs to taste. Place the
whole paste in an earthenware casserole, cover with red wine
and soak for 48 hours. Clean the gut well and soak in vinegar
for two to four hours, then fill, tying at intervals of two-and-a-
half to three inches. Wrap in a muslin bag and hang out to
drain for four to five days after puncturing the casings with a

pin. The sausages may be eaten after seven to ten days, fried or grilled. If boiled in lard for ten minutes and then allowed to cool and remain in the lard, the sausages will keep for three to four months.'

Parisian Ham Sausage (France)
We suppose this must be of French origin, but the name does not ring true. It could easily be an Englishman's idea of a French sausage. There is, however, a special kind of cooked ham called *jambon de Paris*, also known as *jambon demi-sel*, *jambon blanc* or *jambon glacé*, which may have been an ingredient of the original version, but a contemporary English source says that it now consists of one-third beef and two-thirds fairly fat pork from the ham or shoulder, flavoured with leeks. This sausage is first smoked and then boiled.

Párky (Czechoslovakia)
Párky actually means 'pairs' and, because these frankfurter-like sausages were sold in pairs, they have become known as *párky*. Boiled or steamed (but rarely fried or grilled) they are a great favourite with the inhabitants of Prague, who will drop into one of the numerous *uzenazstvi* or sausage shops, at any time of the day or night for a snack.

Pasztetowa (Poland)
A soft, unsmoked sausage made from pig's liver and veal in a natural casing. It is found all over Poland.

Pea Sausage (England)
This is a vegetarian sausage, and, if you find nut cutlets as succulent and satisfying as lamb, you may well relish this mixture, which is 85% yellow peas 12% grated carrot and 3% onion, seasoned with salt, white pepper and nutmeg. Presumably the casings are artificial. The sausages are boiled. Although we have not made these sausages, it does strike us that the addition of a little fat, either vegetable oil or margarine, would be a great improvement.

Peperone (Italy)
The ingredients are 40% pork and 60% beef, coarsely chopped and highly seasoned with red peppers, fennel and spice.

Pfaelzer Leberwurst (Germany)
A liver *kochwurst*, medium to coarse in texture, which originated, we presume, in the Palatinate.

Pieds Cendrillons (France)
These are small *crépinettes* made of pork meat from the trotters, mushrooms and truffles, all minced and bound with a strong stock, then wrapped in a pig's caul. Originally, the mixture was wrapped in greased paper and the little packet was cooked in ashes, which were replenished during the cooking to maintain the heat. Today, if a caul is not used, the forcemeat is wrapped in thin pastry and baked in the oven.

Pikantwurst (Austria)
A spicy sausage with plenty of sweet red pepper.

Pinkel (Germany)
This sausage comes from Bremen and is made of groats, bacon and onions, seasoned only with pepper and salt, and lightly smoked. It is chiefly used in casseroles and stews, but can also be eaten with kale. It is a local variety of *grützwurst*.

Plockwurst (Germany)
There seems to be a wide variety of recipes for this *rohwurst*. A high proportion of beef gives most of them their dark colour; three parts beef to one part pork is quite usual. They are smoked. There is also a ham *plockwurst*, which is made of pickled pork. It is a large sausage, air-dried as well as smoked, and particularly suitable for slicing.

Poledwica Lososiowa (Poland)
A speciality of Gdansk, this is made of pork and back fat. It has a hard consistency and is smoked. The artificial casing, which is now generally used, is knotted.

Poledwica Sopocka (Poland)
This is also a speciality of Gdansk, made of pork and smoked, but not put into a casing.

Polish Sausage (Poland)
Of course, if one were meticulously accurate, one would say that there is no such thing as *a* Polish sausage, any more than there is *a* French *saucisse* or *an* English sausage. A number of recipes are, however, to be found under this title. One authority lists pork, garlic, pepper and nutmeg as the ingredients, which are well mixed and filled into casings, dried, then smoked over beechwood. Another stipulates coarsely chopped lean pork and finely chopped beef, seasoned with mace amongst other spices, and stuffed into beef runners. A third recipe states that there should be two parts of lean salted pork to one part of fat. These are chopped and mixed and put into casings which are tied in pairs of links 38cm (15 in) long, and hung to dry for 24 hours, and finally smoked 'till cooked through'. Then there is a commercial recipe, which uses hog casings filled with 30% lean fresh beef, 40% lean pork trimmings, 10% fresh pig's head meat and 20% pork trimmings. One assumes that the second lot of pork trimmings are fat. The seasonings and additives in this case are salt, dextrose, sodium nitrate, pepper, coriander and garlic. Finally, there is a German recipe for *Polnischerwurst*: 'Two-thirds of lean pork should be minced and mixed with one-third of fat, salt, pepper, pimento and cloves. This is bound with pig's blood in the proportion of 300ml (½ pint) to each 1kg (2lb) of meat. The sausages are air-dried, smoked and poached in water before serving.'

Poloney (International)
This word is usually considered a corruption of 'Bologna', synonymous with 'boloney'. *The Oxford Dictionary*, however, suggests as an alternative that it may be derived from 'Polonia', which may well be the case, as this sausage is more like the Polish than the Italian product. It was once very popular in England, and the clowns in small tenting circuses would always refer to ponies as 'polonies', and get a laugh. In those days it

was 'a sausage of partly cooked lean pork, fat pork and rusk in the ratio of four, two, one, chopped very fine.'

Nowadays it is usually made of a beef and pork mixture and is hot-smoked. But what distinguishes one poloney from another is the seasoning:

Bath Poloney seasoning: 27% white pepper, 1% cayenne, 2% mace, 1% ginger, all ground, and 69% salt.

Yorkshire Poloney seasoning: 26% white pepper, 2% mace, 2% nutmeg, 1% cinnamon, 2% coriander, all ground, and 67% fine salt.

Other poloney seasonings contain trace elements of cloves, cassia, thyme, etc., but all are used in the proportion of 15g to 450g (½oz to 1lb) of farce. Polonies can also be made of other meat, including chicken, ham and tongue, chopped very fine, seasoned and filled into weasands. Whatever the ingredients, all polonies are coloured by being dyed, after cooking, with Saupolon, Magenta crystals and Bismark Brown. The Swedes, amongst others, use them for frying and grilling. See *Bräckkorv*.

Pork Sausages (International)
90% of the sausages in this book contain pork, and many of them no other meat but pork, so we use the term to refer only to the product made in English-speaking countries. There is a difference between English and American pork sausages, not only in the legal meat content, but also in the seasoning. The Americans use cardamom as well as pepper, salt, coriander and nutmeg. While sage is the most popular herb in England today, a recipe of 1800 'for a private family' contained pennyroyal.

For a pure pork sausage the proportions are three parts of lean meat to one part fat. In a good fresh sausage, you may find 30% beef, 60% pork (half of which is fat), 5% cereal and 5% iced water. Lady Harriett St Clair suggested, in 1866, that you use nothing but ham trimmings and griskin, and Jane Grigson also ignores binders in her recipe.

Pork Sausages for Eating Cold
Put 1kg (2lb) of pork, lean and fat, and the same amount of lean beef in a pickle, as for pickling pork, for 10 days. Then

wash, dry and mince the meat finely. Season with salt, pepper and allspice. Fill the casings and tie into convenient links. Wrap in one layer of muslin and smoke until red. When needed they are simmered for 30 minutes; left to get cold and then cut into thin slices.

English Country Pork Sausages

Ingredients
450g (1lb) lean pork, neck or shoulder
225g (½lb) hard back fat
1 level tablespoon salt
freshly ground black pepper
parsley or thyme and sage

Method Mince the meat and mix well with the seasoning. Fill into hog casings. It is worth remembering that by mincing the meat, it is possible to use an overweight pig which has more flavour. (Left whole, pork from this kind of pig would normally be tough in texture.)

See the list of English sausages in the index. Many of these are called after a county or town and contain a high proportion of pork.

Porkinsons (sic) Banger (Tobago)

We did not think that many people know that Norman Parkinson, famous as a photographer, is also a highly successful sausage-maker in the West Indies; but a few years ago, as he and Wenda, his wife, were walking down the via Veneto in Rome, a complete stranger greeted him with 'Aren't you Norman Parkinson?' When Parks replied 'Yes, that's me,' the stranger seized his hand saying 'Gee! I'm so pleased to meet you at last. You're the guy who makes those fantastic sausages in Tobago!'

It all started when Norman Parkinson, who is no stranger to farming, realized that pigs would thrive in the cool Tobago hills, 250 metres above sea-level. They did indeed do well, and provided him and his wife with sausages, bacon and ham. A decade or so ago the Parkinsons gave a party and regaled their guests with these sausages. Everyone wanted to buy them and Parks was persuaded to put them on sale in the market. It was hard work keeping up with demand, as all the chopping was done by hand until revenue from some photographs he had taken of a royal betrothal enabled them to buy a machine. Then they started to supply the hotels on the island. To ease any labour problems that might arise, a co-operative was formed in which all the Tobagan workers have a share.

The recipe is as follows: 85% pure pork meat, half lean and half fat; 10% rusk, and the remaining 5% made up of water and seasoning, which consists largely of freshly chopped sage. This is filled into natural casings and formed into links, six of which weigh 450g (1lb).

Porpoise Sausage (England)

This is really a black pudding, and is given in *Food and Drink in Britain* by C. Anne Wilson. It dates from the fifteenth century.

'Take the blood of him [the porpoise] and the grease of himself, and oatmeal and salt and pepper and ginger, mix these well together and then put this into the gut of the porpoise and then let it seethe easily, and not too hard, a good while; and then take him out and broil him a little and then serve forth.'

Potato Sausage (Sweden)

Equal quantities of cold boiled potatoes, lean beef and pork (half fat and half lean) are minced together with onions. The weight of the onions should be half the weight of the lean pork. The mixture is seasoned with salt, pepper, mace, ginger and sage, then filled into narrow hog casings. The sausages should be boiled for 20 minutes before serving. See *Värmlandskorv*.

Prawn or Shrimp Pudding (England)

Here is a recipe from 1865.

'Pick the flesh from a sufficiency of fish, mince it pretty small. Dry and pound the shells in a mortar, together with some fresh butter; add to this the mince with an equal quantity of cold chicken, veal or sweetbread chopped small. Mix with the yolks of raw eggs, add a few breadcrumbs, a little gravy or cream, and white pepper to taste; put it into skins, prick them with a needle, and fry in butter when wanted. The flesh of lobster, crayfish, sardines, anchovies or tunny fish is equally good done thus.'

We wonder if pricking is really necessary.

Presskopf (Germany/Austria)

This is very similar to *presswurst*, but the chunks of meat are larger.

Presswurst (Germany)

This looks like a large sausage-shaped brawn. There are also Hungarian, Austrian and other versions.

> **Ingredients**
> **900g (2lb) streaky, pickled foreleg of pork**
> **1.35kg (3lb) pig's head meat**
> **450g (1lb) salted pig's tongue**
> **900g (2lb) salted pork rind and calves' feet**
> **strong stock, pepper, salt, nutmeg**
> **coriander and shallots**

Method Cut the pickled foreleg, the head meat and the tongue into pieces the size of beechnuts. Then add the rind and calves' feet, mix well and chop down to size of peas. Work the mixture together, binding with strong stock. Add the seasoning and fill loosely into a pig's stomach. Simmer for 1½–2 hours.

Presswurst (Hungary)

The trotters, neck and head of a pig are boiled with a bay leaf and seasoned with salt, pepper, paprika, marjoram, garlic and onions. When the forcemeat is cold, pig's blood is added and it is filled into casings. It is then boiled for 1½–2 hours and finally pressed under a heavy weight.

Puddenskins (England)

We think that one recipe in the vernacular is quite enough for any cookery book, and perhaps more justified in a book about sausages than any other. So here it is, taken from *The Cornish*

Recipe Book, compiled by the Cornwall Federation of Women's Institutes.

'Some brave, big slices of taties, turmuts (turnips) and onions, all mixed together with pepper and salt and put in a pie dish with a tidy piece of flesh from Mawther's Bussa (a piece of slightly salted pork). Put 'em to cooky, and have some skins (same as they do have for Hogs Puddens) and mix flour, suet, oatmeal and figs (old Cornish for raisins) and an egg, mixen like batter, lookey see! and shove batter into the skins, twist'en round the flesh and cook till light brown. Same to us down-along as Haggis be to they up-along.'

Punkersdorker (Germany)
This name strikes most English people as improbable; nevertheless, it is the name of a strong juicy German *salame*. It is popular with our family.

Puss, La (France)
A speciality from La Béarn.

Pwdin Gwaed (Wales)
See *Blood Pudding*.

Rabbit Sausage (England)
These sausages can be made out of boiled or roasted rabbit. The meat is picked off the bones and mixed with a third of its weight of coarsely chopped bacon. For 1.35kg (3lb) of rabbit you will need 45g (1½oz) of salt, 7g (¼oz) white pepper, 2 finely pounded cloves and a pinch of powdered mace. Filled into casings, they can be either boiled or fried. Or if a larger casing is used they can be boiled and eaten cold.

Regensburger (Germany)
This Bavarian regional speciality is a small, stumpy, spicy sausage made of minced beef and pork, speckled with pieces of bacon. Some of the ones we have eaten contain a high proportion of paprika, but this is not essential. They come in

links joined by string, and can be eaten cold, but are better added to soups or stews, or eaten hot with sauerkraut.

Reinsdyrpølse (Norway)
Made of reindeer meat, seasoned with sugar, spice, salt and spirit.

Reiswurstchen (Austria)
The distinguishing feature of this sausage is the casing. If one discounts the archaic wrappings of *pieds cendrillons*, it is the only product to be wrapped and cooked in paper. Cold boiled rice is mixed with lean veal, cooked and minced, bound with egg and seasoned. The forcemeat is then wrapped in rice paper, egg-and-breadcrumbed and fried. It is used in soups such as *kohlsuppe* and *brotsuppe*.

Resterwurst (Germany)
'A mixture of meat and fat with groats of various descriptions,' is how Lorna Bunyard describes it.

Rindfleisch Kochwurst (Germany)
Three parts of beef to one part fresh pork fat, seasoned with pepper, salt and saltpetre. The sausages are tied in pairs and dried for 48 hours. They are poached in water for 10 minutes before serving.

Rindfleischwurst (Germany)
Lean beef, with a little lean pork and bacon fat, seasoned with garlic, cloves, salt, saltpetre and black pepper. It is simmered for 1 hour.

Rookworst (Netherlands)
A popular, spicy, smoked sausage, which is used in a number of Dutch dishes.

Rosette (France)
A sausage similar to *salame*, but belonging to the Lyon region. Elizabeth David reports the best examples as coming from Lamastre, which is about 100 kilometres south of Lyon and to

the west of the autoroute. It is made of chopped shoulder of pork in a fatty casing, which dries and matures very slowly. The size varies from 1.25–2kg (2½–4lb).

Rostbratwurst (Germany)
Four parts of lean pork to one part of fat pork and one part of veal are finely chopped and seasoned, then filled into narrow hog casings. These are twisted into double links, each weighing around 200g (7oz).

Rotwurst (Germany)
A kind of black pudding, like Thuringian *blutwurst*. It contains large chunks of meat and is seasoned with black pepper. It is eaten in slices on bread, or cut into cubes.

Roulades (France/Switzerland)
These meat rolls are sometimes contained in casings, so may count as sausages, though you may also find them covered with egg and breadcrumbs. *Roulade de jambon* (smoked ham), *roulade de tripes* and so on are proliferations.

Ruegenwalder Teewurst (Germany)
Teewurst is a smooth, mild, paste-like sausage, suitable for spreading. The Ruegenwald version is made of minced pork and spare-rib bacon, smoked over beechwood.

Rullepølse (Denmark)
More of a sausage-roll than a sausage, in which a piece of belly of pork or veal, lamb or beef is flattened out and spread with minced onion, spices, herbs and finally, after being tightly rolled, sprinkled with salt and saltpetre. It is then dry salted for a week and simmered in water.

Sacherwürstel (Austria)
A *bratwurst*, made chiefly of beef and bacon fat.

Salam (Switzerland)
This should not be confused with *salame*, because *salam* is a *cervelas*, which is categorized as a *brühwurst*, while *salame* is a

rohwurst. It is apparently similar to *klopfer*, but so far we have not been able to track it down.

Salame (Italy)

Germany, Austria, Switzerland, Denmark, Hungary, Romania, Bulgaria and Spain all make traditional *salami*, but for us this type of sausage remains essentially Italian. We feel the same way about German or Danish *salami* as we do about Cyprus sherry or Canadian cheddar cheese. They can be delicious, but one wishes that people did not have to use a name made famous by somone else.

In Italy we tasted more varieties of *salami* than we would have thought possible. Some were pure pork; some were a mixture of meats; some were moistened with red wine; some were said to contain rum in which garlic had been soaked; some were pickled in brine and air-dried; some were smoked. Here are a score of them.

Salame Calabrese (Italy)

A short stumpy *salame* of pure pork, about 18 cm (7 in) long and 6 cm (2½ in) in diameter, weighing about 225g (½lb). The further south you go, the stronger the seasoning, and Calabrese *salame* is very peppery. It contains quite large pieces of white fat, and the links are tied with twine, which runs up the side of the sausage from one link to another.

Salame Casalingo (Italy)

Robert Carrier, in *High Life*, wrote, 'Look for the deep cherry red of the meat, and the white waxiness of the fat when it is fresh.' This is excellent advice, but do not think that *casalingo* refers to a place, it simply means 'home-made type'.

Salame Cotto (Italy)

See *Cotto*.

Salame di Cremona (Italy)

Larger than most, and similar in content to the Milan variety, but not so finely chopped.

Salame Fabriano (Italy)
This regional speciality from Ancona and Marche, is made of half pork, and half *vitellone*, which is meat from three-year-old cattle, somewhere between veal and beef.

Salame di Felino (Italy)
Felino is a village 16 kilometres south-west of Parma. Here, at the factory, you can buy the *salame*. It is made of pure pork, of which up to one fifth is fat. It also contains white wine, garlic and whole peppercorns. Sizes vary; the one we bought was 25cm (10in) long and 5cm (2in) in diameter. It is fairly expensive, but so succulent that we both agreed it was well worth the price.

Salame Finocchiona (Italy)
This large, pure pork *salame* is similar to the Florentine variety, with fennel added. Although we are both fond of fennel, neither of us was sure how it would go down in a sausage, but the taste was delicious: it blossoms on the palate like a flower, and is not too strong, so one can appreciate the subtlety of this sausage.

Salame Fiorentino (Italy)
Larger than average, about 10cm (4in) in diameter, this *salame* often consists of pure pork mottled with big pieces of lean meat as well as fat, which makes it different from some of the other Tuscan *salami*.

Salame Genovese (Italy)
There are a dozen or more *salamufici* in Genoa, all making the strong local *salame*. It is usually made from a mixture of pork and *vitellone*. Proportions vary, but they are usually half *vitellone* and half pork, with rather more fat than lean in the latter. Incidentally, Genoese *salame* is the most popular in the USA. See *Salame San Olcese*.

Salame Iola (Italy)
A Sicilian *salame* made of pure pork, seasoned with garlic and doubly wrapped in twine.

Salame Milanese (Italy)

The ingredients of this *salame* should be at least 50% lean and 20% fat pork. The remaining 30% can be beef or *vitellone*. The meat is chopped and seasoned with garlic, whole white peppercorns, salt and sometimes a little sugar. It is packed into hog fat ends, air-dried, bound with twine and left in a cool airy place for 2 to 3 months.

Salame Montenero (Italy)

This is one of Signor Tamburini's Bologna specialities. It is a particularly good pure pork sausage, subtle and succulent.

Salame Napoletano (Italy)

Pork and beef are the main ingredients of this long, thin sausage, as they are in *crespone*. The Neapolitan *salame*, however, is seasoned with red and black pepper and has a much stronger flavour.

Salame di Oca (Italy)

This is a goose-flesh *salame*, and finding it was, in fact, almost a wild-goose chase. It all started in a bar in Monterosso, where the proprietor told us that this 'exquisite sausage' could only be found in Valenza, Po. Unfortunately, no one in Valenza seemed to have heard of it. Weary of traipsing from shop to shop, we went into a bar for rest and refreshment. The barman had not heard of it, but some of the customers had: '*Si! Si! Salame di Oca!* You will find it at Mortara, 40 kilometres from here to the north!' And sure enough, it was there. It is made of chunks of pure goose flesh and fat, and was pleasant, though bland, and very rich.

Salame San Olcese (Italy)

Most people consider this the best of the Genoese *salami*. It is made in a small village just north of the city. The ingredients are pork and pork fat, but *vitellone* can provide up to half the meat. The local people are fond of eating it as an hors d'oeuvre, accompanied by Sardinian ewe's milk cheese and broad beans.

Salame Saporito Stagionato (Italy)
This again, is not a regional speciality, but, like *casalingo*, a description. It is spicy and so soft that it can be flattened on two sides.

Salame Sardo (Italy)
Sardinian *salame* is made of pork and strongly flavoured with red pepper.

Salame di Sorrento (Italy)
The recipe followed by the Americans gives 80% pork and 20% beef, with slightly less salt than *Milanese*, and no garlic.

Salame di Toscana (Italy)
(See *Salame Fiorentino*, which is the most famous of all Tuscan *salami*.) The Tourist Information Centre, however, gave Greve and Panzano as manufacturing centres near Florence, Norcia, close to Arezzo, Montalcuro, in the vicinity of Siena, and Grosseto as other places producing Tuscan *salami*.

Salame Turistico (Italy)
We gathered that *turistico* is another adjective, like the word 'prime' stuck on a joint of beef in an English butcher's shop. Perhaps its significance is similar to 'export' used in describing beer. The one we ate was certainly of excellent quality.

Salame Ungherese (Italy)
Having started this section on *salami* by expressing disapproval of countries copying another's national product, we find the Italians—of all people—actually making Hungarian *salame*. It is made of finely chopped lean and fat pork, beef, paprika, garlic, pepper, salt and white wine.

Salame Val d'Ostana (Italy)
A small rustic sausage, about 15cm (6in) long and 2 cm (1 in) in diameter, made of pork and beef, soft in consistency and slightly garlicky.

Salamini di Cinghiale (Italy)

A small *salame*, made of wild boar meat, usually kept in brine or oil. It has a strong flavour, which we found interesting at first. Unfortunately we bought rather a lot of them, and after having them for picnic lunches four days running, they began to pall.

Other Italian *salami* have their own special names, so see *Soppressa*, *Crespone*, *Cacciatorino*.

Salame (Austria)

We were most surprised at the variety of Austrian *salami*. However, as they all contain around 70% lean pork and 30% fat, we will merely list their names. *Mailändersalame*, *Jagdsalame*, *Touringsalame*, *Edelweissalame*, *Heurigensalame*, and *Haussalame*.

Salame (Denmark)

The Danes have been making their own version of *salame* since before the fifteenth century. It is called *spegelpølse*. It is therefore wrong to suppose that the Danes merely copied the Italians. The modern, bright red Danish *salame*, however, is not quite the same as the original *spegelpølse*. It is a mixture of pork, beef, veal and pork fat, well blended, seasoned with spice, and sometimes garlic, and colouring is added. It is dry-salted for 12–30 days, or steeped in brine for two days. Air-drying lasts 1–2 weeks and it can then be smoked. It is usually eaten raw in thin slices.

Salame (Hungary)

The Hungarians were making *salame* over a century ago. It is said to have been made first in 1859 in Szeged. The meat of very fat pigs is used together with a secret blend of seven spices. Both natural and artificial casings are lightly smoked. Hungarian *salame* keeps well and its flavour grows sharper with age.

Salami (Spain)

The contents of the Spanish *salami* are much the same as the Italian, but they are usually milder in flavour.

Salami (Switzerland)
The Swiss variations include *chämi salame*, *salame nostrano*, and *salametti*.

Salame, Kosher (Israel)
See *Kosher* and also *Venison Salame*.

Salceson Wloski (Poland)
This is a hard pork sausage in a natural casing. Unsmoked, it is found all over Poland.

Salchichas (Spain)
These are fresh sausages, small, darkish and fairly coarse in texture but delicate in flavour. They are made of pork, lamb and sometimes beef. They can be eaten raw but are also found in many dishes, including *paellas*.

Salchichas Estremeña (Spain)
This sausage contains equal parts of liver, belly of pork and lean pork meat.

Salchichón (Spain)
These are large sausages made of lean pork and belly, seasoned with spice, salted and lightly smoked. The best known come from Vich in Catalonia, and *Douglas' Encyclopaedia* says that they are the finest sausages in Spain.

Salpicão (Portugal)
The main ingredient of this sausage is fillet of pork, smoked and spiced.

Salsiccie (Italy)
This is really little more than the Italian word for 'sausage'. It is not, however, quite as vague as the English equivalent, because it does refer to pure pork sausages, with what Robert Carrier describes as a 'rustic flavour'. He finds that the best way of cooking them is to prick them first with a needle, then poach in water for a few minutes before drying them and sautéing them in a mixture of butter and oil.

Salsicha (Portugal)
The Portuguese variety of *salchicha*.

Salsiz (Switzerland)
A *rohwurst* of lean pork, beef and pork fat, similar to *alpiniste* but smoked as well as air-dried. It is eaten raw. There is also a *lebersalsiz* which contains pig's liver as well as pork and beef, but is otherwise the same.

Salzburgerwurst (Austria)
A *bratwurst* similar to *schüblinge*.

Sanguinaccio (Italy)
This is the Italian version of *boudin noir* or black pudding.

Saster (Scotland)
Three parts of lean to one part of fat pork, preferably from the neck and foreleg of a young pig, are chopped, mixed and seasoned with salt, pepper and cloves. The filled casing is air-dried. It is very similar to the *Westphalian sausage*, but it is not smoked.

Saucisses (France)
This usually refers to fresh sausages, while *saucissons* can either refer to the large *saucisson-cervelas* which are boiled, or the *saucisson sec*, which is eaten sliced, like *salame*. With one or two exceptions, *saucisses* must be cooked before serving. You can buy them ready-made, as in England, though they are more likely to be made on the premises in France, or you can make them at home. Here is a translation of a typical professional recipe, given us by Raymond Landes, the *charcutier* in Duilhac-s/-Peyrepertuse, a small village some 30 kilometres north-west of Perpignan. 'The most important point to remember is that only the very best cuts are carefully selected from prime pigs. Only the meat surrounding the shoulder and the upper part of the hind leg is used, and it should not contain more than 5% fat. To make it more juicy you can add some of the breast, if necessary with some fat removed. This meat, with the rind

removed, is cut into bits weighing between 50 and 80g (1¾–2¾oz). After weighing all the meat it should be seasoned with 20g (¾oz) of salt and 3g (¹⁄₁₀oz) of freshly ground pepper to every kilo (2lb) of meat. Let the pieces rest for 1 hour, then mince, using the 8mm (⁵⁄₁₆) plate, and fill casings of approximately 25mm (a full inch) in diameter.

'This sausage should be grilled over a fire of holm oak or the trimmings of a vine after pruning. And of course it should be accompanied by a glass or two of Corbières—the excellent *vin du pays*.'

And here is a recipe for a typical home-made French *saucisse*.

Ingredients
900g (2lb) pork (hand is best)
450g (1lb) pork back fat
freshly ground pepper, French spice (see page 72), salt
sheep or hog casings

Method Chop or mince the meat coarsely, mix well and add the seasonings. Tie one end of the casing and fill with forcemeat. Tie the other end and twist into links of whatever size you require. If you don't want to twist them into links, the casing can be left like a *boudin noir*, in a spiral.

Saucisses d'Ajoie (Switzerland)
This speciality from the Jura, made of chopped pork in a natural casing, is smoked. It can be boiled in water and eaten hot, or air-dried and eaten cold.

Saucisses d'Alsace-Lorraine (France)
These are made of pork in the well-established proportion of two parts of lean to one of fat. It is the seasoning that makes the difference. Apart from French spice, pepper, salt and saltpetre, you should add a little ginger. After being filled, the casings are twisted into links 10 cm (4 in) long, and then air-dried for 24 hours. These are Christmas sausages, and Jane Grigson describes how you paint every third link with red dye or caramelized sugar, and wrap the ones between in gold and silver foil to form a garland for the Christmas tree. They are

eaten on Christmas Eve, either fried or simmered in stock, and served with hot potato salad—reminding one of the German influence—or with potato purée, which is more traditionally French.

Saucisses d'Arosa (Switzerland)
Two thirds of chopped pork and one third of 'blitzed beef'. (*Viande de boeuf blitzée* means that the beef is put through a multi-bladed machine which reduces it to the consistency of cream.) They come from the Canton des Grisons, and are virtually the same as *Saucisses de Davos* and *de Schaffhouse*. All are eaten hot.

Saucisses d'Auvergne (France)
These are like small *saucissons secs*.

Saucisses de Bordeaux (France)
Small pork sausages, eaten very hot with very cold oysters. As X. Marcel Boulestin once said, 'The burnt pork fat, the smell of the sea, the heat and the cold would revive any jaded appetite.'

Saucisses Bretonnes (France)
These are made of fairly fat, pure pork chopped together with parsley and chives, seasoned with salt, pepper and French spice, filled into casings and twisted to form links roughly 20cm (8 in) long.

Saucisses de Campagne (France)
Two parts of lean pork to one part of fat bacon is a good basis for this sausage. Pepper, salt and garlic are, we think, essential and so is red wine in the proportion of 3 tablespoons to every 450g (1lb). *Larousse* gives a number of other spices and herbs that can be added, such as pimento, savory, coriander, marjoram, thyme and bay leaf. Beef runners are used as casings and the sausages are air-dried. As an alternative method, you could try two parts of lean beef to one part of green bacon, with the same variety of seasoning. These are lightly smoked.

They are specially good in *potées*, those delicious thick soups which are a meal in themselves. One recipe is given on page 46.

Saucisses au Champagne (France)

There are two recipes for these, one old and one new. The eighteenth-century version simply says: 'Coarsely chop lean pork and dice the same amount of fat. Mix together and season with salt and spice. Add half a bottle of champagne and work this into the farce, then let it marinate for 10–12 hours. Drain, fill the casings and smoke them for two days in the chimney. They should be grilled.'

The contemporary version is more specific, but also more complicated:

> *Ingredients*
> 900g (2lb) leg of pork
> 900g (2lb) pork back fat
> 200g (7oz) truffles
> 4 eggs
> ½ bottle of champagne
> sugar, French spice (page 72), salt, ground white pepper
> sheep casings

Method Remove the sinews and tendons from the meat as soon as the pig is killed and cut the meat while the carcase is still warm as it will absorb the seasoning better; for the same reason it is a good thing to place the utensils you use for chopping in boiling water beforehand. Mix all the ingredients together, except the truffles, moistening with the champagne and stirring with a wooden spoon. Chop or mince the truffles and add these just before filling the casings. Let them hang for 24 hours so that the flavours blend properly. Deep fry before serving.

The interesting thing about this recipe is the importance attached to adding the seasoning while the flesh is still warm. This is not easy for the home sausage-maker, and may well terrify Americans, who are always trying to find ways of lowering the temperature throughout the sausage-making process.

Saucisses Croquantes (France)
These are also known as *saucisses au cumin*. They are cumin-flavoured frankfurters, and are made of three parts of lean pork, two parts of lean beef and one part of hard fat pork. For 1.35kg (3lb), you need 50g (2oz) cumin seed, crushed with a pestle in a mortar, 2 large cloves of garlic, salt, ground black pepper, chopped red pepper and a pinch of saltpetre. The beef is finely minced; the pork not so finely, but still finer than for ordinary sausages. Jane Grigson suggests using an electric mixer for blending, so that you can slowly add 275ml (8 floz) of water more easily. Fill the casings, twist into 12 cm (5 in) lengths, tie together in pairs and hang them to dry in a cool airy place for 4 days. Then cold-smoke them for 2 days. They should be poached in water for 10 minutes before serving. (See *Knackwurst*)

Saucisses de Davos (Switzerland)
See *Saucisses d'Arosa*.

Saucisses d'Engadine (Switzerland)
These are *rohwurst*, and therefore eaten raw.

Saucisses Espagnoles (France/Spain)
Equal parts of lean pork and hard back fat, seasoned with French spice, pimento, and, strangely enough, raisins.

Saucisses au Fenouil (France)
Little cork-shaped sausages, flavoured with fennel, which are either poached in water for 25 minutes, or poached for 15 minutes and then grilled on a skewer.

Saucisses au Foie (Switzerland)
A speciality of Vaud, obviously containing liver, but the rest of the ingredients remain obscure.

Saucisses de Francfort (Germany/France)
Larousse says that the *saucisse de Francfort* and *saucisse de Strasbourg* are similar, and Jane Grigson has a very good recipe

which covers both names. Every country seems to have its own version. See *Frankfurter* and also *Saucisse de Strasbourg*.

Saucisses au Gruau (France)
See *Grützewurst*.

Saucisses Juives (France)
Rather like the Algerian *merguez* but made entirely of calves' liver. See also *Kosher sausages*.

Saucisses Madrilènes (France)
Were these originally invented in Madrid? If so, they should come under Spain, but we have not come across them there, and *Larousse* does not say where they originated. They are made out of veal, fresh pork fat and fillets of sardine in oil; all chopped, seasoned and stuffed into beef runners, which are tied into rings before being poached in veal stock, then cooled. They should be fried in butter before serving.

Saucisses de Montbéliard (France)
Montbéliard is one of a group of towns south of Strasbourg and east of Dijon, near the Swiss border, each of which has produced its own special sausage. Dole, Thann and Morteau are others.

The Montbéliard sausage is made of pure pork, lightly smoked. It is cooked in a pan of cold water which is brought almost to the boil; as soon as the water starts to tremble the sausage is removed and usually served with *choucroute* or a purée of lentils.

Saucisses de Morteau (France)
Morteau sausage is similar to the *saucisse de Montbéliard*.

Saucisses au Paprika (France)
This is a type of frankfurter, very short and seasoned with paprika. It can be fried, grilled or poached, or it is sometimes served *en brochette*, or as an accompaniment to poultry.

Saucisses de Périgord (France)

Almost as much back fat as lean pork goes into this sausage—350g (12oz) to 450g (1lb); 50g (2oz) truffles, white wine, French spice, salt and saltpetre. The meat is minced or chopped and mixed with the seasoning. Three or 4 tablespoons of white wine are used to moisten the mixture and the truffles are added last. It is left for 24 hours before being filled into casings.

Saucisses de Schaffhouse (Switzerland)

See *Saucisses d'Arosa.*

Saucisses Soudjouk (Levant)

This is originally an Armenian sausage made of beef and quite highly spiced. It is served as a *mézé* or hors d'oeuvre.

Saucisses de Strasbourg (France)

Similar to *saucisse de Francfort,* and there is a small version which is a *knackwurst,* for which *Larousse* gives the equivalent of *saucisse croquante.*

Here is Jane Grigson's recipe for *saucisses de Strasbourg/ Francfort:*

> **Ingredients**
> **675g (1½lb) shoulder or leg of pork (salted in brine for 3 days if possible)**
> **450g (1lb) hard back fat**
> **1 tablespoon salt**
> **1 heaped teaspoon mixed white pepper and coriander**
> **1 scant teaspoon mace (or nutmeg and cinnamon, mixed)**
> **a tiny pinch of saltpetre, if the meat is unsalted**

Method Mince the meat twice—the first time coarsely—then add the seasonings and mince again with a finer plate. Add 250 ml (8 floz) cold water while stirring well. An electric mixer is ideal for this part of the job. Separate the skins into lengths of 30–45 cm (12–18 in). Fill the skins, tie them at each end and twist in the middle to make two long thin sausages. Hang them up to dry in a cool airy place where the temperature is not above 15°C (60°F) for a whole day and then smoke them for 8 hours. If the timing is awkward, it is better to leave them to dry for a longer rather than a shorter period.

Saucisses de Thann (France)
See *Saucisses de Montbéliard*, not that they are exactly the same, but we think they must belong to the same family.

Saucisses de Toulouse (France)
These sausages are found all over France. They usually have three times as much lean pork as hard back fat and are coarsely chopped by hand. Salt, white pepper, sugar and saltpetre make up the seasoning. In size they are like a large English sausage, but they are much more expensive. It is possible to buy them in a continuous length if you prefer it.

Saucisses de la Tremblade (France)
A small *locale* in Charente gives its name to these little sausages, similar to those of Bordeaux, which are eaten with oysters.

Saucisses Viennoises (France)
These, as Jane Grigson points out, are from Vienne, just south of Lyon, and not from Vienna in Austria. They are made from equal parts of lean pork, veal and fillet steak, very finely minced and seasoned with pepper, salt, saltpetre, cayenne and coriander, moistened with warm water. They are lightly smoked and poached in simmering water for about 10 minutes before serving. They should be pricked with a needle as they rise to the surface to prevent bursting.

Saucissons (France)
The Lyon gourmet and poet, Gabriel Paysan, had this to say:

LE SAUCISSON

Des hors-d'oeuvres? Admettons! Pourvu qu'on se limite
A l'entr'aide du 'cher ange' de Monselet,
Qui des tendres douceurs que sa chair recélait
Nous livre le meilleur dans son boyau d'ermite.

Apporte un saucisson, tiré de la marmite,
Qu'il bouille encore! Apprends que tel il ne me plâit
Que s'il fut façonné dans la ferme, et qu'il ait
Aux poutres de longs mois figuré stalactite.

Là, comme pour le vin, savoir vieillir est l'art . . .
Sous le fer du couteau qui le tranche en rondelles,
Sa chair rouge, pleurant, se constelle de lard.

Au diable salamis, bolognes, mortadelles!
Et vous pourrez sans pleurs suivre mon corbillard
Si je sais qu'on en mange au champ des asphodèles.

There are really three types of *saucissons*; they are all large,
but one kind, which includes saveloys and *cervelas*, are boiled
before eating, while the other two (*saucissons secs* and *saucisson
fumés*) are eaten raw. The boiling sausages are usually referred
to by the name of their place of origin, and sometimes they
seem to be called *saucisses*. This may be a question of size.
There appears to be no hard or fast rule in this category,
whereas the dried and smoked varieties are much more clearly
defined. Of course, the *saucisson de Lyon* is probably the best
known, but since we must maintain alphabetical order, the first
one is:

Saucisson à l'Anis (France)
A speciality of the *charcutier* in the village of Gémenos, 24
kilometres from Marseille. We have not heard of this being
made anywhere else.

Saucisson d'Arles (France)
Raoul Ponchon was so overcome when a friend sent him a
saucisson d'Arles as a present, that he wrote a poem of ninety-six
lines in its honour, much too long to quote here. But he was
not the only poet to be inspired by this sausage. Charles
Monselet, to whom Gabriel Paysan referred in the poem *Le
Saucisson* (see above) wrote:

ODE AU SAUCISSON D'ARLES

Provision fort utile
Sans cesse et dans tous les temps,
Indispensable à la ville
Aussi bien que pour les champs.

Si chez vous il se présente
Un convive inattendu,
La ménagère prudente
N'est pas prise au dépourvu.

Et si, dans l'huile épurée,
Vous voulez les tenir au frais,
Sur la partie entamée
Ils ne ranciront jamais!

Mais combien ont plus de charmes
Ceux qui sont à deux boyaux!
Car ils font couler des larmes
Sur la lame des couteaux!

What invokes such raptures?

As with other *saucissons*, proportions are apt to vary, but the meat is a mixture of pork and beef. Some recipes give half and half, others 60% lean leg of pork, 15% hard back and 25% lean beef. The pork is usually coarsely chopped and the beef finely minced and sometimes pounded. The fat is cut into short strips. If equal quantities of beef and pork are used, it is a good idea to add diced bacon at the ratio of 100g to 450g (4oz to 1lb). The mixture is seasooned with garlic, ground black pepper and peppercorns. French spice (page 72), paprika, salt and a pinch of saltpetre feature in some recipes. A sprinkling of granulated sugar and moistening with red wine are optional. The longer this is air-dried the better. Six months is not too long.

Saucissons Bernois (Switzerland)
This speciality of Berne is eaten hot.

Saucisson de Bourgogne (France)

The usual proportions: twice as much lean pork—preferably from the neck or shoulder for this sausage—as hard back fat; the lean is finely minced, the fat chopped more coarsely. These two ingredients are well mixed and seasoned with ground white pepper, salt, French spice (page 72) and sugar. The main difference between this and other sausages is that a little brandy or kirsch is added. After being filled into beef middles and tied into 45cm (18 in) lengths, the sausages are strung and hung in a cool airy place for 4 to 6 months. Jane Grigson says that they should be kept at a temperature of just under 15°C (60°F) for the first few days. As the contents dry out, the sausages will need restringing. Six months, at least, must elapse before they are ready to eat.

Saucisson de Bretagne (France)

A medium-sized pork sausage.

Saucisson de Campagne or de Ménage (France)

This is very similar to *saucisson de Bourgogne*, without the brandy or kirsch, but with garlic added. For an unsmoked sausage, add 1 teaspoon of saltpetre and the same amount of pepper, French spice and sugar is a reasonable basis on which to work for 1.35kg (3lb) of meat—lean and fat together.

Saucisson de Campagne Fumé (France)

A smoked version of the above, but it will probably need 3 teaspoons of sugar, 2 of pepper and at least double the amount of garlic.

Saucisson-cervelas (France)

We find the use of this phrase tautological and involved. It tends to complicate things, but since you will find it used quite extensively in France, it seemed a good idea to include it here with an attempt to explain the kind of labels that are to be found. *Cervelas* is the origin of the English saveloy; in size it comes between a *saucisse* and a *saucisson*. It is usually boiled, rather than fried or grilled, but of course there are exceptions.

The forcemeat is put into beef casings, usually about 4cm (1½ in) in diameter, and each link is between 20–30 cm (8–12 in) long. They are sometimes formed into loops, in which case the link is longer. They can be salted in brine and are usually lightly smoked. The meat of a really good *saucisson-cervelas* will consist of 50% lean pork, 25% fillet steak, 25% green bacon, and be seasoned with garlic, shallots, black pepper, salt and saltpetre. It is usually simmered in water, stock or red wine before being served, though it can equally well be eaten cold.

Larousse gives a basic recipe which consists of five parts of lean meat to one of fat, and confines it to pork.

Local variations include: *saucisson-cervelas de Lyon*, *saucisson-cervelas de Nancy* and *saucisson-cervelas de Paris*.

However, we found that there can be a greater difference between two sausages from the same town than between those from different cities. The main difference between the three mentioned above is that the *saucisson-cervelas de Paris* contains cayenne.

Saucisson Chasseur (France)
A small sausage of high pork content, weighing 125–225g (5–8oz). Useful for slipping into one's pocket when going out shooting.

Saucisson de Cheval (France)
A sausage made of 50% lean pork, 25% fat pork and 25% horsemeat.

Saucisson au Foie de Porc (France)

> *Ingredients*
> 900g (2lb) pork liver
> 900g (2lb) lean pork
> 900g (2lb) pork back fat
> 225g (8oz) onion, sliced
> pepper, salt, spice, cayenne, kirsch
> lard for frying

Method Chop the liver, pork and fat, each separately. Fry the onion in the lard over a gentle heat, until it is softened but not browned. Mix the meat, liver and fat with the onions, add the seasoning and spice and moisten with 1–2 tablespoons of kirsch. When it is thoroughly mixed, re-chop. Stuff the forcemeat into hog casings making sure that it is well packed down. Knot the casings every 12 cm (5 in). Hang them to dry in a cool airy place for 24 hours. Plunge them into boiling water, reduce the heat and let them barely simmer for 1 hour. Take the pan off the stove and let the sausages remain in the water for another 15 minutes. Wrap each one in muslin, tied at both ends. Serve cold.

In *La Charcuterie à la Campagne*, there is another recipe which incorporates diced tongue, but has less liver. It also has truffles and pistachio nuts, and sounds delicious. A third recipe, which may be English, gives three parts of pork (half lean, half fat) to one part of pig's liver. The liver is parboiled and chopped with the pork, seasoned with salt, pepper and spice, and moistened with pig's blood—about 2 tablespoons per 900g (2lb). The mixture is filled into beef casings and twisted to form links of about 12 cm (5 in).

Saucisson Gris (France)
See *Saucisson Lorrain*.

Saucisson d'Italie (France)
This French version of an Italian sausage uses two parts each of lean pork and lean veal to one part of hard back fat. The mixture is seasoned with salt, pepper, nutmeg, cinnamon, and ginger, and moistened with pig's blood and white wine (twice as much wine as blood). It is put into a pig's bladder, air-dried, and smoked over juniper for several days. The final process is to coat it with olive oil.

Saucisson de Jambon (France)
A speciality of Strasbourg, although it is also made in other places.

Saucisson de Lièvre (France)
A gamey hare sausage popular in Savoie.

Saucisson Lorrain (France)

This is similar to a *saucisson de Lyon*, with two parts lean pork, one part fat pork and one part beef. The lean pork comes from the shoulder and the fat from the throat.

Saucisson de Luchon (France)

Another local variation, which comes from the Pyrenean health and winter sports resort. We have not yet tracked it down.

Saucisson de Lyon (France)

As this is the basis of most *saucissons secs*, such as those from Arles and Lorraine, we will give a detailed recipe, with alternatives, for, as so often happens, there is no single basic recipe:

> **Ingredients**
> **900g (2lb) leg of pork**
> **125g–225g (5–8oz) hard back fat, either diced in 5mm (¼**
>   **in) cubes, or cut into long strips. This can either be**
>   **bacon, or pork which has been dry-salted for 10 days.**
> **salt, saltpetre, white peppercorns, ground white pepper**
> **French spice (page 72) and garlic**
> **hog casings**

Method Chop the lean meat finely, or it can be pounded to a paste. Add the fat and seasoning to taste. Mix well and stuff into the casings, which are tied to form links 45cm (18 in) long. Hang in a cool, airy place for at least 48 hours—some recipes say for as long as 6 days. Consolidate the filling by pressing it down firmly to one end and then stringing the sausage. The purpose of this is to straighten out the natural curve of the casing. Four strings running down the length of the sausage should be bound with twine running round it. The tension of the long strings on the outside of the curve should be greater than those on the inside. Some people make half-hitches down the sausage, with four strings. The point to remember is not to cut and tie, as the re-stringing process will have to be carried out several times. Then hang the sausage in a cool airy place for 3 to 6 months. The ones we made were not good, because although the temperature was constant, the humidity here, where we live, does not allow them to dry properly. The longer they mature, the better they will be.

Saucisson Cuit au Madère (France)
This is an example of the boiled rather than smoked or cured variety of *saucisson*. It is made of pork fillet, finely minced with half as much back fat, seasoned with white pepper, French spice and salt, moistened with Madeira wine and enriched with truffles or blanched pistachio nuts. The ingredients are stuffed into one of the larger casings, such as beef casings or hog fat ends, and gently simmered for 45 minutes.

Saucisson de Ménage (France)
The same contents as *saucisson de campagne*, medium coarse in texture.

Saucisson de Metz (France)
We found this recipe in an English book but, as we were unable to visit Metz on our French tour, we could not check locally. It does not sound French, but is interesting because of the amount of beef used; 70% fresh lean beef, 10% pork, both cured, salt and saltpetre, and 20% well-cured bacon, which is all finely minced, seasoned with ground black pepper and coriander, and filled into beef middles. These are air-dried for 5 days and cool-smoked for 3 days.

Saucisson de Montagne (France)
A coarsely chopped, pure pork, dried sausage.

Saucisson de Morue (France)
The only place that we know where you find cod-fish sausage is *Le Bistro de Paris*, in rue de Lille, Paris. This fashionable—and expensive—restaurant is, or was, run by Michel Oliver, who has presented cookery programmes for children on television, invented many dishes and designed a barbecue for Le Creuset.

Saucisson Neuchâtelois (Switzerland)
This sausage is smoked and boiled. It can be eaten hot or cold.

Saucisson d'Oyonnax (France)
This sausage from the Jura is traditionally cooked in ashes.

Saucisson de Paris (France)
This is a coarsely chopped and cooked pure pork sausage, with little fat, and when flavoured with garlic is known as *Paris-ail*. It is small for a *saucisson*.

Saucisson au Poivre Vert (France)
A pure pork sausage made at St Chamond, which lies in the narrow strip of land between the Rhône, running south, and the Loire, running north. The green peppercorns give it a very special flavour, and as you can now get them in Britain, it is well worth experimenting with them when making your own slicing sausages, both air-dried and smoked.

Saucisson Provençal (France)
This is an interesting variation, because of the high proportion of lean to fat: 85% to 15%. The meat is pork from the leg or shoulder. It is seasoned with salt, saltpetre, ground pepper and peppercorns, and French spice (page 72). It is air-dried for several days and lightly smoked.

Saucisson à Trancher (France)
Generally speaking, all the air-dried or smoked *saucissons* are slicing sausages. This one is made of belly of pork, half fat, half lean, seasoned with black pepper, garlic and chopped parsley. It is boiled in salt water for 2–3 hours before being air-dried for a month or more at 15°C (60°F).

Saucisson Vaudois (Switzerland)
Chopped pork and cured back fat, well spiced, is filled into hog casing, air-dried and then smoked for 4–5 days. This speciality is eaten with cabbage or leeks.

Sausage Meat (England)
Although we intended to include nothing but sausage in skins, several skinless ones have crept in, and this gives an excuse to

use this early recipe from a family cookery book in the possession of Kemmis Buckley, compiled by Anne Skinner in 1689.

'**To Make Sausage Meat my Mothers**. Take a loyn of Porke, cut ye leane into pieces & way as much of ye leafe fatt as ye lean, and shred ye meat very well with a shreding knife, then beat it with a rolling pin till you cannot discern ye fat from ye lean, then season it very well with pepper and salt. Shred a little red sage & mix with it then make it up into roles & have Some Slices of fat and lard it as you put it into your pott. Cover ye pott very close & set it in an oven with bread. When it comes out pour of ye clear fat & put your meat down well with ye back of a Spoon then pour on ye fatt againe and let itt stand till it is cold.'
     It will keep for 4 months.'

Saussiska (USSR)
The Russian word for sausage. It is made of pork, usually smoked, and often cooked in tomato sauce before serving. It is frequently eaten as a snack between shots of vodka.

Saveloy (England)
The English translation of *cervelas*. The modern commercial saveloy may contain practically every part of the pig except the brain, which originally gave the sausage its name: salt pork, lights, rind and pig cheek must be well cured. Saltpetre gives the meat its red tinge, but the sausages are smoked as well. One recipe gives half the weight of the meat in bread or biscuits. Home-made saveloys are not to be despised when made from tender, lean pork, very finely chopped and seasoned with sage, pepper, salt—and onion too, if you don't intend keeping them. Here is one recipe. Take 1½kg (3lb) of tender pork free from skin and sinew; rub it well with 14g (½oz) saltpetre and 250g (8oz) salt. Leave for 3 or 4 days rubbing and turning it every day. It is then minced finely, mixed with 250g (½lb) of fine breadcrumbs and seasoned with 1 heaped teaspoon of white pepper and 6 young sage leaves, chopped

very small. This fills the casings. They should be boiled and
smoked, and are sometimes baked before serving. One reference book suggests that the French equivalent of saveloy is
andouillette, with which we profoundly disagree, in spite of
some of the ingredients.

Schachtwurst (Germany)
Similar to *plockwurst*.

Schinkenwurst and Schinkenplockwurst (Germany)
These are Westphalian specialities in which the ham is flaked
rather than chopped, which is inclined to make it uncohesive.
The sausage is smoked over beech and ash wood, strewn with
juniper berries. When the time comes to slice it, chilling the
sausage in the fridge helps to keep it from falling apart.
Schinkenplockwurst contains large pieces of fat, and is firmer
than *schinkenwurst*. You may also find a sausage labelled *gekochte
schinkenwurst*, which contains beer and coarsely chopped lean
pork.

Schlackwurst (Germany)
This is a sausage resembling a *cervelat* in size and shape, though
usually a shade darker. It is listed as being made of finely
chopped pork, but you can also find the meat coarsely chopped,
and occasionally it is made of beef.

Schüblinge (Switzerland/Austria)
A mild sausage, from St Gall; it is about 15–17cm (6–7 in)
long and 2.5 cm (1 in) in diameter, made of beef, pork, bacon,
bacon cubes and spices. It is smoked, and eaten hot. Obtainable
at the Swiss Centre, London.

Schützenwurst (Switzerland)
From eastern Switzerland, and apparently very similar to *boule
de Bâle*. A *brühwurst*.

Schwäbischewurst (Germany)
A finely minced and pounded mixture of two parts of lean to
one of fat pork, seasoned with garlic, pepper and salt, then
boiled and smoked.

Schwartenmagen (France)

An Alsatian black pudding or blood sausage. It is sometimes called a *blut schwartenmagen* and is made of lean pork and blood. It is short and dumpy in shape.

Schwartwurst (France)

Another Alsatian black pudding, more like our own in shape and size.

Schwartzwurst (Germany)

This is a black pudding made with four parts lean pork to one part of fat, and one eighth of the total quantity of meat in breadcrumbs. It is seasoned with garlic, cloves, pepper and salt, and moistened with the pig's blood in the ratio of 600 ml (1 pint) to every 2kg (4½lb) of meat mixture. The filling casings are boiled for 30 minutes, then air-dried and smoked.

Schweinsbratwurst (Switzerland)

A pork *brühwurst* made for grilling or frying.

Schweinskopfwurst (Austria)

This sausage is made of 80% pork head meat, the rest being beef, water, seasoning and 1% potato starch.

Schweinswürste (Germany)

These Bavarian pork sausages are scalded in the making and flavoured with marjoram.

Schwertenmorgen (Germany)

George Ellwanger lists this, in *The Pleasures of Taste*, as coming from Thuringia, but gives no ingredients. It is presumably the same as *schwartenmagen*.

Selchwurst (Austria)

This sausage is similar to *Burgenländer hauswurstel*.

Seymour's Sausage (England)

In *Self-Sufficiency*, that admirably practical manual for enjoyable survival, John and Sally Seymour give an excellent recipe for a smoked sausage, and point out that you *must* use a large casing. The ordinary casings, which are used for sausages one grills or fries, will not allow the contents to remain moist while maturing. They suggest two parts of lean pork to one of fat, but they also use equal amounts of lean pork beef and belly of pork. The lean meat is minced and the fat diced. The meat is marinated in elderberry wine for 12 hours beforehand. When the casings are filled, they bind them with twine and hang them to dry in an airy place (near a solid fuel stove, such as an Aga) at a temperature of 15°C (60°F). After a week they are smoked for 24 hours, then left to mature for 6 months. The only attention needed is to squeeze down the forcemeat, which—as we have already explained—will shrink, and to re-string the sausages so that the casings are kept well filled, any empty space coming between the links.

Sheftalia (Cyprus)
The content of these sausages is not stuffed into casing but wrapped in caul fat like a *crépinette*. Half fairly fatty pork and half veal or lamb is finely minced, seasoned with finely grated onion, salt and freshly ground black pepper. About 1 table-spoonful of this mixture is wrapped up in a 10 cm (4 in) square of caul fat, and grilled over charcoal.

Si-Klok (Thailand)
Sixty per cent finely minced pork is mixed with 40% crabmeat. This is seasoned with chopped onion, finely chopped coriander leaves and roasted peanuts. Charmaine Solomon in *The Complete Asian Cookbook*, gives 2 tablespoons of each for 310g (10oz) of the pork and crab mixture. She also gives 2 teaspoons of red curry paste and tells you how to make it; but as there are 15 ingredients, it seems hardly worthwhile making it if you can buy it at your nearest Chinese emporium. You also need 2 teaspoons of fish sauce and 2 tablespoons coconut milk which you add to all the other ingredients. Do not form into links. *Si-Klok* is like a Cumberland sausage, cooked in a coil. The Thais apparently do prick their sausages, and they also throw some of the coconut remaining after the milk has been extracted on to

the charcoal. Charmaine Solomon says they are delicious 'and will spoil you for ordinary sausages for a long time to come'. We agree, although we had to make the coconut milk out of desiccated coconut, and replace the Thai spices with the nearest Chinese version.

Sin Ap Yeung Cheung (China/Hong Kong)
Sin means 'fresh', so in this sausage the duck (*ap*) liver (*Yeung*) is not preserved. Fat pork, salt, soy, sugar and Chinese wine are the other ingredients.

Shetland Sparls (Scotland)
These are highly spiced beef puddings. The meat is finely minced and seasoned with salt, black, white and Jamaica pepper (allspice), cloves, ginger, mace and cinnamon. The mixture is sewn up in 'sparls'—broad sheep casings—and smoked.

Slonina Paprykowana (Poland)
Pork back fat and paprika are used in the composition; but as it is not contained in a casing, this is not a true sausage.

Smedovska Lukanka (Bulgaria)
These smoked sausages are made of twice as much pork as beef and seasoned with salt, sugar, ground pepper, and caraway seeds in the ratio 5, 3, 2, 1. Wide beef casings are used, and pricked before smoking for 3 or 4 days.

Smoked Scots Sausage (Scotland)
This is another of Meg Dod's recipes of 1826. Beef is salted for 2 days and then minced with suet and onions. The recipe does not give proportions, but you could start with twice as much lean as fat, adding 2 medium sized onions for every 450g (1lb) of meat. Adjustments can always be made to suit individual tastes. Pepper and salt are the seasonings and the forcemeat is filled into fairly large casings, such as beef middles. These are then smoked. The Hebrideans are said to leave them up the chimney until required. However, onions should not be

included if they are to be kept after making. Garlic, one presumes, is a different matter.

Smyrna Sausages (Turkey)
Sometimes these are served with the skins removed; but of the sausages which we have tasted, the small, highly spiced variety, about 10 cm (4 in) long and 1.5 cm (½ in) in diameter, usually have a subtler flavour than the coarser, darker, thicker variety.

Sobresada (Spain)
The meat in this is very finely ground, chopped or minced, so it is smoother than the ordinary *chorizo*. The only difference in content is that a great deal more pimento is used in *sobresada*.

Sobresada Mallorquina (Spain)
A Majorcan version, this is milder, but still has a paste-like consistency; in fact, it makes a delicious spread.

Soppressa (Italy)
A *salame*, made of pork and beef, found in Verona, Padua and the surrounding countryside.

Sosij (Wales)
Believe it or not, this is Welsh for sausage.

Soudzoukakia (Greece)
Minced veal or pork, garlic, eggs, onions, parsley, breadcrumbs, salt and cumin go to make these sausages, which are usually fried in olive oil.

Speckblutwurst (Germany)
This sausage, usually about 5 cm (2 in) in diameter, contains lean pork, pig's blood and a high proportion of diced pork fat.

Spegelpølse (Denmark)
A dried sausage, similar to salame, which was being made in Denmark five centuries ago. There are many different recipes. One lists 35% lean beef and 35% lean pork, both chopped and free from gristle and sinew, 20% finely chopped pork fat

and 10% diced pork fat. These ingredients are well mixed, seasoned with pepper, salt, saltpetre and a little sugar, then left for 24 hours before being filled into ox runners as tightly as possible. They are tied at 45 cm (18 in) to form links, laid in a crock and covered with salt. When the salt has turned to brine, they are hung in a cool, airy place to dry. They are then cool-smoked till they are brown. Different types of wood are used to impart different flavours. They keep well, and—obviously—are sliced and eaten raw.

Spekepølse (Norway)
A lightly smoked mutton sausage.

Staburpølse (Norway)
A Norwegian black pudding.

Stångkorv (Sweden)
A sausage made of beef, pork offal and barley. It is usually coiled in a long casing and fried before serving.

Strasbourg Puddings (France)
This is an English version from a Victorian recipe:
'Chop up the livers of two fat geese, add an equal weight of pork fat, minced very fine and four onions boiled in gravy; sprinkle in a little dried sage, add pepper and salt, mix together with breadcrumbs and cream; put it into skins, and treat in the usual way.'

Strassburger Trüffelleberwurst (Germany)
A German version of the French *saucisson au foie truffé* from Strasbourg.

Streichwurst (Germany)
A name given to any spreading sausage, which is, of necessity, finely minced and pounded to a paste.

Stretford Black Pudding
See under *Black Pudding*.

Stuttgarter Presskopf (Germany)
Pork, veal, and beef are the main ingredients.

Suffolk Sausage (England)
A fairly coarsely chopped pork sausage, with a pronounced flavour of herbs.

Sülzwurst (Germany)
This would not have been included, had the word not ended in *wurst*. It is really a brawn with chunks of meat from a pig's head and leg, which together with sliced mushrooms, comes set in a pale jelly. We found it rather insipid.

Summer Sausage (USA)
An American term for a sausage that is meant to be kept for a long period. It is, for instance, made in the winter for summer consumption, and was originally introduced by German immigrants. It is usually semi-dry. One recipe gives 60% lean beef and 40% pork of which half is lean and half fat. Ground white pepper, black peppercorns, salt, coriander, mustard, garlic and red wine form the seasoning. The meat is first cut into 5 cm (2 in) cubes and cured in a sweet brine pickle for 12 days. It is then dried and minced through a 5 mm (¼ in) plate. The sausages are cool-smoked and left to mature for 2 weeks.

Szynka Sznurowana (Poland)
Szynka is Polish for 'ham', and this hard, smoked sausage is popular all over Poland.

Taliany (Czechoslovakia)
This word is derived from *Italiani*, and is the name of a sausage of supposedly Italian origin, similar to a *vursty*, but with diced fat bacon in the forcemeat.

Teewurst (Germany)
This is a sausage that has to reach the highest standard. It is always made of the best meat, and is strictly controlled for quality. It is often salmon-pink in colour and is a mixture of

finely minced pork and beef. It can be highly spiced, and is one of the many varieties that is spreadable. It is a *rohwurst*. (See *Ruegenwalder*)

Thuringer Blutwurst (Germany)
Streaky belly of pork is parboiled and diced, then mixed with finely chopped pork rind, raw liver and lung. Cooked tongue and heart is sometimes used. Pig's blood is heated and the meat added to it. It is seasoned with marjoram, caraway, cloves, pepper and salt. While still warm the mixture is loosely filled into large casings. It is then boiled and cooled, dyed red and cool-smoked over sawdust and juniper berries.

Thuringer Rostbratwurst (Germany)
A regional *bratwurst*—for frying or grilling—made of pork or veal.

Tiroler (Austria)
A *fleischwurst* made largely of lean cured pork, with a little veal and beef.

Tlacenka (Czechoslovakia)
A large, brawn-like sausage.

Tomato Sausage (England)
A great favourite with Midlanders. Recipes of course vary, but tomatoes constitute roughly 10% of the whole, 50% of the content is lean pork, 20% fat pork and 20% rusk, half of which is soaked, and half sprinkled on to the mixture during chopping. The main seasoning, tomato apart, consists of pepper, cloves, mace, sage and salt; but nutmeg, ginger, coriander and cayenne are found in some recipes.

Tongue Sausage (Germany)
Whole tongues are sometimes used in this slicing sausage. See *Zungenwurst*.

Touristenwurst (Germany)
Three-quarters beef and one-quarter pork, made up in links about the same size as an English sausage. See *Salame Turistico*.

Tripes à l'Djotte (Belgium)

This sausage is traditionally eaten between Christmas and the New Year. It consists of 450g (1lb) borecole (a kind of cabbage, or kale), 450g (1lb) of greaves (the fibrous bits of meat left over when rendering down fat to make lard), and 450g (1lb) of finely chopped raw pork. These are seasoned with salt, grated nutmeg, 10 cloves and 2 chopped onions. All is lightly mixed and usually stuffed into 50 cm (20 in) of hog casing, although Belgian farmers prefer to use the 'fat end'. This they call *le cra-boya*, which is immortalized in a song of that name. Unfortunately it is in a dialect which is quite incomprehensible to the ordinary French scholar.

Trüffel Leberwurst (Germany)

Pork, pig's liver and truffles.

Truffle Sausages (England)

We cannot resist quoting this nonchalant recipe from *The Breakfast Book*:

'To one pound of lean pork add half a pound of bacon fat and three ounces of fresh truffles; season with salt and spices; chop it fine; mix with a glass of champagne or some lemon juice, and proceed as with other sausages.'

Tuchowska (Poland)

One of the many regional sausages, similar to that of *Krakowa*, but in a natural casing.

Tunbridge Wells Sausage (England)

Pigs always do well in orchards, and in areas where fruit is grown you may well find good sausages. In research—even for a book about sausages—one occasionally comes across something rare and rewarding. We first heard of W. J. Hill's sausages made in Tunbridge Wells from a Russian friend of the old régime. 'They are the best in England, and the only place you can get them in London is at Paxton & Whitfield in Jermyn Street.' They were indeed delicious, and we wrote to Mr Frank Hill and told him so. We also asked how long he had been making them and if he considered them to be traditional, etc. etc. This was his reply ten years ago.

'. . . Our business is very much a family one, the writer's parents having purchased the original in August 1902, for the princely sum of £35, which included a lease, fixtures and fittings, and, what is more important, a number of recipes for various pork pies, smoked sausages, etc., including our Special Pork Sausage which has not changed during the whole of the 75 years.

'The recipe is quite simple: 50lb lean English pork, 25lb pork fat, 10lb bread crumb; seasoning includes white pepper, sage, mace and several other herbs. We claim that this recipe is the original Tunbridge Wells one having been used for at least 100 years, and so is different from the modern factory variety, the meat being fairly coarse cut, not in a bowl chopper which reduces the product to something akin to meat-paste, also we guarantee that *no* chemical preservatives, artificial colouring, pork rind emulsion or vegetable protein are used.

'It is interesting to note that in spite of being 'old-fashioned' our Xmas sales were in excess of 6 tons, all being sold over the counter in the above shop, except for a few hundred pounds supplied to Paxton & Whitfield of Jermyn Street, London.'

There is only one thing that has changed and that is the breadcrumb. Another quote from Mr Frank Hill:

'. . . Regarding breadcrumb, this was copied from the old recipe; we have, in fact, used a yeastless bread rusk for the last 30 years. It would not have been possible to use stale loaves nowadays in the quantity involved, and modern bread, which is not very well baked, would cause problems.'

Värmlandskorv (Sweden)

Ingredients
900g (2lb) pork
900g (2lb) beef
900g (2lb) potatoes
3 onions
1–2 tablespoons salt
1 saltspoon white pepper
1 saltspoon allspice
450 ml (¾ pint) water or ham stock
4 m (4 yds) natural casing

Method Mince the meat three or four times, the last time with the raw potatoes and onions. Mix well with the seasoning and moisten with the water or stock to get the right consistency. Fill the casings very loosely and knot into links. Rub the sausages with a salt cure and leave for 18–24 hours. They can be kept for several days in a brine made of 1 litre (1¾ pints) water, boiled up with 100g (4oz) coarse salt and 1 tablespoon sugar, then allowed to cool.

Veal Sausage (England)
This English, or Scottish, sausage seems to have completely disappeared. One English recipe is extremely simple. Take twice as much sinew-free veal as bacon. Mince finely, season with pepper, salt and nutmeg and mix well. Moisten with milk, and fill into narrow casings. However, other recipes give the equal quantities of pork and bacon; and one Victorian recipe adds, the hard-boiled yolks of 4 eggs and 4 anchovies to each 450g (1lb) of meat.

Veal Sausage (Scotland)
The Scottish version is more interesting. It comes from Lady Harriett St Clair's *Dainty Dishes*, published in 1886 and consists of equal parts of lean veal and fat bacon, a handful of sage, salt, pepper and three or four anchovies. The ingredients are reduced to a paste by chopping and then pounding with a pestle in a mortar.

Venison Sausage (Scotland, USA, England)

English sausage-makers seem very reticent about the contents. Fortunately Peter Crawley put us in touch with Nichola Fletcher, author of *Venison, The Monarch of the Table* and of *Game for All*, and venison expert. She most generously sent us these recipes from Scotland.

Ingredients
2kg (4lb) lean venison (neck or shoulder)
700g (1½lb) shoulder of pork
450g (1lb) pinhead oatmeal
570ml (1 pint) hot water or stock
45g (1½oz) salt
30g (1oz) salt
30g (1oz) coarsely ground black pepper
15g (½oz) chopped fresh sage

Method Soak the oatmeal in the hot water or stock overnight. This softens it and prevents the skins from bursting. Soak the skins overnight if they are dry-salted. Mince the venison and pork as fine or coarsely as you wish, add the rest of the ingredients and fill the skins. Leave them to dry in a cool place for a few hours.

A Richer and Darker Venison Sausage

Ingredients
2kg (4lb) lean venison
450g (1lb) venison heart and liver
700g (1½lb) belly or shoulder of pork
60g (2oz) salt
1 teaspoon black peppercorns, crushed
1 teaspoon juniper berries, well crushed
(opt) 30g (1oz) crushed garlic
red wine to moisten

Method Mince all the meat together and stir in the rest of the ingredients. If using the wine, moisten the mixture well and leave overnight. This meaty sausage takes a little longer to cook, but is very good baked.

Her notes are also of interest. 'The pinhead oats give the first sausage a nice nutty bite, but on no account use anything finer or it will look like porridge. The second is very dark and rich and you can add an awful lot more spices if you like e.g. nutmeg, cloves, ginger etc., etc. A sausage is such a personal thing. . . .'

Venison Sausage (USA)

The American version uses 40% pork and 60% venison, seasoned with onion, garlic, salt, saltpetre, black and white pepper, juniper berries, brown sugar and lemon. Both the juice and zest of lemon is used.

The Breakfast Book stipulates raw venison and 'half its weight of very sound bacon fat.' It also includes brandy in the seasoning.

Venison Haggis, Barry Burns' (Scotland)

'There are three vital points which if followed should prevent the skins from contracting and bursting. Firstly fill the skins only half full to allow for the contents swelling. Secondly, prick the skins all over with a needle before (and occasionally during) cooking. Thirdly, when using ox bungs, do not cut into individual haggises until after cooking. In other words, make them like a string of giant sausages with two strings tied between each haggis. Admittedly you need an enormous pan to cook them in, but it saves a lot of frustration.

We also have to thank Nichola Fletcher for Venison Salami and for managing to persuade her butcher to divulge the secrets of his Venison Haggis, which she says 'beats all other haggis she has ever eaten'. We thank Barry Burns too, for allowing us to include his personal recipe. The Scots are certainly more generous than the English when it comes to sharing recipes.

'*Ingredients* *(to make 6 x 1lb haggises)*
450g (1lb) lean venison
450g (1lb) venison heart
450g (1lb) venison liver
450g (1lb) venison lights
450g (1lb) beef suet
225g (8oz) pinhead oatmeal
300 ml (½ pint) water
4 level tablespoons salt
4 level teaspoons ground black pepper
4 level teaspoons ground ginger
4 level teaspoons nutmeg

'*Method* Soak the oatmeal in water overnight. Mince all the meat, offal, and suet and mix them well together with the soaked oatmeal and seasonings. Fill the skins, tying the ends securely as described, and pricking all over with a needle. Cover with cold water in a large pan, bring to the boil and simmer gently for 3 hours.

'After cooking, the haggises can be frozen or will keep in a fridge for several days. The cooking liquid, once skimmed of fat, makes an excellent foundation for soup or else can be used to warm the haggis for serving. To heat them up, just put some broth or water in a pan and simmer the haggis gently in it for ½ hour, or else put into a covered dish with some liquid and warm through in the oven. If your haggis looks as though it might burst the second method of warming is safest.'

Venison Salami (Scotland)

Ingredients
2kg (4lb) venison
450g (1lb) lean pork
450g (1lb) belly of pork
450g (1lb) hard pork back fat
180g (6oz) salt
1 dessertspoon brown sugar
a pinch of saltpetre, nutmeg, ginger, white pepper
1½ tablespoons black peppercorns
1½ tablespoons juniper berries
6 large cloves garlic

Method Mince the lean pork and the venison together very finely and then mince the belly of pork coarsely. Cut the back fat into tiny little cubes—the exact size is up to you—a variety of sizes will give you a more interesting pattern. This is easier to do when the fat is well chilled. Thoroughly mix all the meats with the rest of the ingredients and then pack as firmly as you can into a thick casing. It will shrink as it dries. Then hang the lengths of salami up to dry and mature until they have acquired that lovely white bloom. (It is essential that the atmosphere is both dry and cool; 15°–18°C (60°–66°F) is the ideal temperature.)

Verscheworst (Netherlands)
The Dutch word for 'fresh sausage'.

Vursty (Czechoslovakia)
Just as the Czechs borrowed *Taliany* from the Italian, so they borrowed *vursty* from the German as a name for their short fat sausage.

Waadtländer Bratwurst (Switzerland)
A frying or grilling sausage from Waadt.

Waadtländer Saucisson (Switzerland)
This canton also produces this *rohwurst* speciality.

Waldviertler (Austria)
Beef, lean pork, pork head meat and bacon fat are the main ingredients of this sausage.

Weisswurst (Germany)
A veal sausage. See *Münchener Weisswurst*.

Westphalian Sausage (Germany)
Three parts lean to one part fat pork are the main ingredients, being taken from the neck and foreleg of a young pig. The sausages are simply seasoned with pepper, salt and cloves, and air-dried until they are yellow.

White Pudding (England)

There are many recipes. The simplest gives three parts each of Scotch groats (or pearl barley) and suet, to two parts leeks and two parts rusk, moistened with fresh milk and seasoned with thyme, marjoram, pepper and salt.

White Pudding (Ireland)

Very similar to the Scottish version given below, but sometimes cloves are included in the seasoning, and the beef runner casings are usually tied in a horse-shoe shape.

White Pudding (Scotland)

This is also called mealie pudding, but must never be confused with *boudin blanc*.

F. Marian McNeill has a good recipe for making this version in *Recipes from Scotland*:

> **Ingredients**
> **900g (2lb) oatmeal**
> **450g (1lb) beef suet**
> **2 onions**
> **salt, pepper, sugar**
> **tripeskins**

Method Lightly toast the oatmeal in the oven. Mince the suet and onions and add to the oatmeal. Mix well and season. Fill the tripeskins with the mixture, leaving room for expansion. See that the ends are securely tied. Drop into boiling water and cook for 1 hour, pricking the skins occasionally. These puddings will keep for months if hung in a dry, airy place, or buried in the meal chest. When required, warm through in hot water, dry, and brown in hot dripping.

Wiankowa (Poland)

A hard sausage, similar to *Krakowa* but formed into the shape of a horseshoe. Made of lean pork, lean beef and pork fat in a natural casing.

Wiejska (Poland)

Almost the same as *Wiankowa*.

Wienerwurst (Austria, USA, etc)

Vienna is apparently the only place where these famous sausages
are not called by this name or its derivatives. Although they are
known all over the United states as 'wienies', in the Austrian
capital they are simply *würstel*. They are often eaten there at a
second breakfast—*gebelfrühstuck*—around 10 a.m.

Some American sources say that the *Wienerwurst* was invented
in Vienna in 1852 and soon crossed the Atlantic. The Austrians
pre-date this by 47 years and give the creator as a Viennese
butcher called Hans Georg Lahner. Amongst those who manufactured the American version in the early days were William
Tamme and John Boepple, who started making sausages at
Jean-Baptiste Roy House, 2nd and Plum Street, St Louis.
Before it was demolished in 1947, this was the oldest house in
the city, having been built by a Louisiana fur trader in 1829. In
1883, so the story goes, A. L. Feuchtwanger, a sausage-pedlar,
who bought his wares from Tamme and Boepple, started selling
hot *wienerwurst* in a split bun. These buns were made by his
brother-in-law, who designed a long-shaped bun, rather than
the usual round ones, specially to accommodate a sausage.
Many people believe that this was the origin of the 'hot dog',
though the name was not given to the hot 'wienie' sandwich
until 1900—some say 1915—when Tad Morgan drew a car-
toon for his newspaper of a dachshund sausage sandwich, then
found he could not spell 'dachshund', and to meet his deadline,
hurriedly called it a 'hot dog'.

There are others who believe the *Frankfurter* is the original
hot dog. But whether they are 'franks' or 'wienies' makes no
difference to the fact that over 15,000,000,000 hot dogs are
eaten each year by the Americans.

An Austrian recipe for *Wienerwurst* gives equal parts of veal
(or sometimes beef) and pork, first cubed and lightly cured in
salt, saltpetre and sugar. After this the beef is chopped first as
it should be the finer of the two, then the pork is added. It is
seasoned with white pepper, coriander, garlic and grated shallots, then stuffed into narrow sheep casings. These are lightly
smoked, then boiled until they rise to the surface of the water,
after which they are hung up to dry. As usual, proportions vary,

and the last recipe we obtained gives 45% lean pork, 25% fat and the remaining 30% made up of beef, water and seasoning.

Wiltshire Sausage (England)
This sausage contains seven parts of lean pork to three parts of fat pork and one part of rusk. The meat should be freshly killed. The forcemeat is seasoned with mace, ginger, sage, white pepper and salt. The proportions of the ingredients in the seasoning are 66% salt, 30% pepper and about 1% each of mace, ginger and sage. Cloves too, can be added, but only half as much as the mace or ginger. When one realizes that only 15g (½oz) of this mixture is needed for each pound of sausage meat, one appreciates how necessary it is to be accurate in one's own kitchen with recipes for seasoning.

Wollwurst (Germany)
A very finely minced veal sausage, like pale paste. It comes from Bavaria and is fried in butter.

Wong Sheung Wong Fong Cheung (Hong Kong)
Wong sheung Wong means 'King of Kings', and is the speciality of the well-known firm of that name in Hong Kong. It is made of fresh, lean and fat pork, seasoned with soy and salt, sugar and Chinese wine.

Würstchen (Germany)
Small sausages usually made of two parts lean pork, one part veal and one part pork from the throat and seasoned with salt, pepper, pimento, cardamom and Rhine wine. They are tied in bunches and boiled for 3 minutes in salted water, then dried. They are grilled before serving.

Würstel (Austria/Hungary)
This word for sausage is also found in parts of northern Italy. A Hungarian recipe gives one part of beef, two parts of veal and one part of pork, minced and seasoned with lemon juice and peel, salt and pepper.

Wurst von Kalbsgekrüse (Germany)

A sausage made of finely chopped calf mesentery, with eggs and cream, seasoned with salt, pepper and nutmeg, in a hog casing.

Yorkshire Black Pudding

See under *Black Pudding*.

Yorkshire Sausage (England)

See page 74 for special seasoning.

Yugoslav Sausage (Yugoslavia)

We do not think this is the ordinary *kolbasa*, but it may be a special variety. The recipe we have gives 450g (1lb) lean beef, 450g (1lb) veal, and 50g (2oz) beef fat, which seems very little and might be better if it was bacon or pork fat.

Zampone di Modena (Italy)

This is a pork sausage, similar to a *cotechino*, but the casing is a pig's trotter from which all the bones have been removed. It is a speciality of the Emilia-Romagna province, and is served hot, having first been soaked and then simmered for 1 hour.

Zungenwurst (Germany)

A kind of *rotwurst*, in which large chunks of tongue can be seen in the forcemeat. It sometimes contains liver and is seasoned with pepper. There are different recipes, and in some of them nutmeg and paprika are used as seasoning.

Zwyczajna (Poland)

A mixture of chunky pork and beef goes to make this hard, rugged sausage in a natural casing which is knotted in long links. It is found all over Poland and is also exported.

Bibliography

ALDRICH, PAUL I., *The Packer's Encyclopaedia*, Chicago, 1922

ANON., *The Breakfast Book*, London, 1865

BABET-CHARTON, H. (revised by Lasnet de Lanty, H.), *La Charcuterie à la Campagne*, Paris, 1975

BOURNE, URSULA, *Spanish Cooking*, London, 1974

BOYD, LIZZIE (ed.) *British Cookery*, London, 1976

BURGAUD, FRANÇOISE, *Porc et Cochonailles*, Paris, 1976

CAMPBELL, ELIZABETH, *Encyclopaedia of World Cookery*, London, 1960

CARRIER, ROBERT, *Great Dishes of the World*, London, 1963

COPSEY, W. G. , *Law's Grocer's Manual*, London, 1950

CURNONSKY *Atlas de la Gastronomie Française*, Paris, 1938

CURNONSKY and SAINT GEORGES, ANDRÉ, *La Table et l'Amour*, Paris, 1950

DAVID, ELIZABETH, *Italian Food*, London, 1954

DAVID, ELIZABETH, *French Provincial Cooking*, London, 1960

Douglas' Encyclopaedia, London

DRUMMOND, SIR JACK, and WILBRAHAM, ANN, *The Englishman's Food*, London, 1957

ELLISON, J. AUDREY (ed.), *The Great Scandinavian Cookbook*, London, 1966

ESCUDIER, JEAN-NICOL, *La Veritable Cuisine Provençale et Niçoise*, Toulon, 1953

FINNEY, THOMAS B., *Handy Guide for Pork Butchers*, Manchester, 1922

FITZGIBBON, THEODORA, *The Food of the Western World*, London, 1977

FRANCATELLI, CHARLES ELMÉ, *The Cook's Guide*, London, 1888

GERRARD, FRANK *Sausage and Small Goods Production*, London, 1976

GLASSE, HANNAH, *The Art of Cooking made Plain and Easy*, London, 1747

GRIGSON, JANE, *Charcuterie and French Pork Cookery*, London, 1967

HAZELTON, NIKA S., and the EDITORS OF TIME-LIFE BOOKS, *The Cooking of Germany*, N.Y., 1974

HEATON, NELL, *The Complete Cook*, London, 1947

HUTCHINS, SHEILA, *English Recipes*, London, 1968

KRAMARZ, INGE, *The Balkan Cookbook*, 1972

MALLOS, TESS, *The Complete Middle East Cookbook*, Sydney, 1979

MANJÓN, MAITE and O'BRIEN, CATHERINE, *Spanish Cooking at Home and on Holiday*, London, 1973

MARTIN, EDITH, *Cornish Recipe Book*, Penzance, 1929

McCULLY, HELEN, *Nobody Ever Tells You These Things About Food and Drink*, London

McNEILL, F. MARIAN, *Recipes from Scotland*, Edinburgh, 1946

McNEILL, F. MARIAN, *The Scots Kitchen*, Edinburgh, 1949

McNEILL, F. MARIAN, *The Book of Breakfasts*, Edinburgh, 1975

NORWAK, MARY and HONEY, BABS, *The Complete Farmhouse Cookbook*, Compton Chamberlayne, 1973

PAYNE, A. G. (ed.), *Cassell's Dictionary of Cookery*, London

SLEIGHT, JACK and HULL, RAYMOND, *The Home Book of Smoke Cooking*, Newton Abbot, 1973

SOLOMON, CHARMAINE, *The Complete Asian Cookbook*, Sydney, 1976

ST CLAIR, LADY HARRIETT, *Dainty Dishes*, Edinburgh, 1861

SZATHMÁRY, LOUIS, *The Chef's New Secret Cookbook*, Chicago, 1975

THOMAS, KATHLEEN, *A West Country Cookery Book*, Exeter, 1961

WECHSBERG, JOSEPH, and the EDITORS OF TIME-LIFE BOOKS, *The Cooking of Vienna's Empire*, N.Y., 1968

Sausage Index

In the Geographical Index which follows, most of the names of the sausages are given in the language of their country of origin. Of the exceptions, a few are written in English because they come from an English source, such as an English book on Swedish cooking, and one or two are in French because the original reference was given to us in that language.

Africa, South
Boerewors, 114
   Lamb, 114
   Pork, 114

Algeria
Merguez, 180

America, United States of
Armadillo Sausage, 103
Block Sausage, 112
Bockwurst, 113–4
Boudin Créole, 121
Brain Sausage, 123–4
Chaurice, 131
Cotto, 138
Easternola, 142
Frankfurter, 148–9
Frizzes, 149
Holsteinerwurst, 160–1
Lebanon Bologna, 172
Summer Sausage, 226
Venison Sausage, 232
Wienerwurst, 236–7

Austria
Burgenländische Hauswürstel, 126
Dampfwürstel, 141
Dürre Rund, 142
Extrawurst, 143
Feine in Stangen *see* Extrawurst
Jausenwurst, 163
Kantwurst, 164
Käsewurst, 165

Kraine, 170
Leberstreichwurst, 172
Leberwurst, 172–3
Mährische, 178
Oderberger, 184
Pikantwurst, 188
Presskopf, 193
Reiswurstchen, 195
Sacherwürstel, 196
Salame, 201
Salzburgerwurst, 203
Schüblinge, 220
Schweinskopfwurst, 221
Selchwurst, 221
Tiroler, 227
Waldviertler, 234
Wienerwurst, 236–7
Würstel, 237

Belgium
Andouilles, 98–100
Andouillettes, 98–100
Bloedpens, 112
Boudins, 115–6
   à la Crème, 121
   à la Flamande, 122
Brussels Mosaic, 125–6
Crépinettes d'Agneau à la Liégeoise, 139
Tripes à l'Djotte, 228

Bulgaria
Domasni Nadenizi-Na Furna, 142
Karlovska Lukanka, 164

Recipe Index

Simple Sausage-making

Elaborate Sausage-making

Sausage Dishes